FOR DUMMIES™

COMPUTER
BOOK SERIES
FROM IDG

Networking For Dummies

Cheat Sheet

W9-ANQ-106

Secrets to Network Happiness

- ✔ Back up religiously.
- ✔ Document your network layout and keep your documentation up-to-date.
- ✔ Keep an adequate supply of spare parts and tools on hand.
- ✔ Automate your network login as much as possible with the STARTNET.BAT file or login script.
- ✔ Never turn off or restart the server while users are logged in.
- ✔ Don't be afraid, Luke.

Top NetWare Commands

CAPTURE	Sets up network printing.
LOGIN	Logs in to the network.
LOGOUT	Logs out of the network.
MAP	Assigns drive letters to network drives.
PCONSOLE	Controls network printing.
SEND	Sends a message to another user.

Top LANtastic Commands

NET LOGIN	Logs in to the network.
NET LOGOUT	Logs out of the network.
NET SEND	Sends a message to another user.
NET SHOW	Shows current network resources.
NET USE	Assigns drive letters to network drives or sets up network printing.
NET UNUSE	Removes network drive or printer connections.
STARTNET	Logs you in to the network and sets up your default network connections.

Help, Mr. Wizard!

Before calling the network guru, try this:

- ✔ Make sure that everything is plugged in.
- ✔ Make sure that the network cable is properly attached. For 10baseT networks, the little light on the back of your computer where the cable plugs in should be glowing.
- ✔ If your computer is frozen solid, try restarting it by pressing Ctrl+Alt+Del.
- ✔ Press Ctrl+S if error messages fly by so fast you can't read them. Press it again to resume.
- ✔ If all else fails, try restarting the entire network.

E-Mail Shorthand

BTW	By The Way
FWIW	For What It's Worth
IMO	In My Opinion
IMHO	In My Humble Opinion
IOW	In Other Words
PMJI	Pardon Me for Jumping In
ROFL	Rolling On the Floor Laughing
ROFL,PP	Rolling On the Floor Laughing, Peeing my Pants
TIA	Thanks In Advance
TTFN	Ta Ta For Now
TTYL	Talk To You Later
<g>	Grin
<bg>	Big Grin
<vbg>	Very Big Grin

COMPUTER
BOOK SERIES
FROM IDG

Networking For Dummies

Cheat Sheet

For those times when you're too lazy to read *Networking For Dummies*, here is a quick reference of a few essential items.

My Network and Welcome to It

Write down important stuff about your own network in the spaces provided below.

My user ID: _____

The command I use to log in: _____

Network drives

Drive letter   Description

_____   _____

_____   _____

_____   _____

_____   _____

_____   _____

Network Printers

Printer name   Description

_____   _____

_____   _____

_____   _____

Ethernet Cable Stuff

Thick Coax (10base5)

- ✔ Segment limited to 500 meters (1,640 feet).
- ✔ Transceivers required to connect to network card via 15-pin AUI port.
- ✔ Terminators required at both ends of segment.

Thin Coax (10base2)

- ✔ Segment limited to 185 meters (600 feet).
- ✔ Uses BNC connectors.
- ✔ T-connectors used to connect cable to computers.
- ✔ Terminators required at both ends of segment.

Twisted Pair

- ✔ Maximum cable length: 100 meters (330 feet).
- ✔ All computers cabled to central wiring hub.
- ✔ Terminators not required.
- ✔ RJ-45 connector wired as follows:

Pin 1	White/green
Pin 2	Green/white
Pin 3	White/orange
Pin 4	Orange/white

- ✔ Up to 3 hubs may be daisy chained together.
- ✔ Hubs may also be linked using thin or thick coax.

IDG
BOOKS

...For Dummies: #1 Computer Book Series for Beginners

References for the Rest of Us

COMPUTER BOOK SERIES FROM IDG

Are you intimidated and confused by computers? Do you find that traditional manuals are overloaded with technical details you'll never use? Do your friends and family always call you to fix simple problems on their PCs? Then the *". . . For Dummies"*™ computer book series from IDG is for you.

". . . For Dummies" books are written for those frustrated computer users who know they aren't really dumb but find that PC hardware, software, and indeed the unique vocabulary of computing make them feel helpless. *". . . For Dummies"* books use a lighthearted approach, a down-to-earth style, and even cartoons and humorous icons to diffuse computer novices' fears and build their confidence. Lighthearted but not lightweight, these books are a perfect survival guide to anyone forced to use a computer.

> *"I like my copy so much I told friends; now they bought copies."*
>
> **Irene C., Orwell, Ohio**

> *"Quick, concise, nontechnical, and humorous."*
>
> **Jay A., Elburn, IL**

> *"Thanks, I needed this book. Now I can sleep at night."*
>
> **Robin F., British Columbia, Canada**

Already, hundreds of thousands of satisfied readers agree. They have made *". . . For Dummies"* books the #1 introductory level computer book series and have written asking for more. So if you're looking for the most fun and easy way to learn about computers look to *". . . For Dummies"* books to give you a helping hand.

IDG BOOKS

NETWORKING
FOR
DUMMIES ™

NETWORKING
FOR
DUMMIES ™

by Doug Lowe

Foreword by Paul Merenbloom
author of *InfoWorld's* "LAN Talk" column

IDG BOOKS

IDG Books Worldwide, Inc.
An International Data Group Company

San Mateo, California ♦ Indianapolis, Indiana ♦ Boston, Massachusetts

Networking For Dummies

Published by
IDG Books Worldwide, Inc.
An International Data Group Company
155 Bovet Road, Suite 310
San Mateo, CA 94402

Library of Congress Catalog Card No.: 93-80868

ISBN: 1-56884-079-9

Printed in the United States of America

10 9 8 7 6 5 4 3 2 1

Distributed in the United States by IDG Books Worldwide, Inc.

Distributed in Canada by Macmillan of Canada, a Division of Canada Publishing Corporation; by Computer and Technical Books in Miami, Florida, for South America and the Caribbean; by Longman Singapore in Singapore, Malaysia, Thailand, and Korea; by Toppan Co. Ltd. in Japan; by Asia Computerworld in Hong Kong; by Woodslane Pty. Ltd. in Australia and New Zealand; and by Transword Publishers Ltd. in the U.K. and Europe.

For information on where to purchase IDG Books outside the U.S., contact Christina Turner at 415-312-0633.

For information on translations, contact Marc Jeffrey Mikulich, Foreign Rights Manager, at IDG Books Worldwide; FAX NUMBER 415-358-1260.

For sales inquiries and special prices for bulk quantities, write to the address above or call IDG Books Worldwide at 415-312-0650.

is a trademark of IDG Books Worldwide, Inc.

About the Author

Doug Lowe has written more than 15 computer books and knows how to present boring technostuff in a style that is both entertaining and enlightening. He is a contributing editor for the magazine *DOS Resource Guide*.

About IDG Books Worldwide

Welcome to the world of IDG Books Worldwide.

IDG Books Worldwide, Inc., is a division of International Data Group, the world's largest publisher of computer-related information and the leading global provider of information services on information technology. IDG publishes over 194 computer publications in 62 countries. Forty million people read one or more IDG publications each month.

If you use personal computers, IDG Books is committed to publishing quality books that meet your needs. We rely on our extensive network of publications, including such leading periodicals as *Macworld, InfoWorld, PC World, Computerworld, Publish, Network World*, and *SunWorld*, to help us make informed and timely decisions in creating useful computer books that meet your needs.

Every IDG book strives to bring extra value and skill-building instruction to the reader. Our books are written by experts, with the backing of IDG periodicals, and with careful thought devoted to issues such as audience, interior design, use of icons, and illustrations. Our editorial staff is a careful mix of high-tech journalists and experienced book people. Our close contact with the makers of computer products helps ensure accuracy and thorough coverage. Our heavy use of personal computers at every step in production means we can deliver books in the most timely manner.

We are delivering books of high quality at competitive prices on topics customers want. At IDG, we believe in quality, and we have been delivering quality for over 25 years. You'll find no better book on a subject than an IDG book.

John Kilcullen
President and C.E.O.
IDG Books Worldwide, Inc.

IDG Books Worldwide, Inc. is a division of International Data Group. The officers are Patrick J. McGovern, Founder and Board Chairman; Walter Boyd, President. International Data Group's publications include: **ARGENTINA's** Computerworld Argentina, InfoWorld Argentina; **ASIA's** Computerworld Hong Kong, PC World Hong Kong, Computerworld Southeast Asia, PC World Singapore, Computerworld Malaysia, PC World Malaysia; **AUSTRALIA's** Computerworld Australia, Australian PC World, Australian Macworld, Network World, Reseller, IDG Sources; **AUSTRIA's** Computerwelt Oesterreich, PC Test; **BRAZIL's** Computerworld, Mundo IBM, Mundo Unix, PC World, Publish; **BULGARIA's** Computerworld Bulgaria, Ediworld, PC & Mac World Bulgaria; **CANADA's** Direct Access, Graduate Computerworld, InfoCanada, Network World Canada; **CHILE's** Computerworld, Informatica; **COLOMBIA's** Computerworld Colombia; **CZECH REPUBLIC's** Computerworld, Elektronika, PC World; **DENMARK's** CAD/CAM WORLD, Communications World, Computerworld Danmark, LOTUS World, Macintosh Produktkatalog, Macworld Danmark, PC World Danmark, PC World Produktguide, Windows World; **EQUADOR's** PC World; **EGYPT's** Computerworld (CW) Middle East, PC World Middle East; **FINLAND's** MikroPC, Tietoviikko, Tietoverkko; **FRANCE's** Distributique, GOLDEN MAC, InfoPC, Languages & Systems, Le Guide du Monde Informatique, Le Monde Informatique, Telecoms & Reseaux; **GERMANY's** Computerwoche, Computerwoche Focus, Computerwoche Extra, Computerwoche Karriere, Information Management, Macwelt, Netzwelt, PC Welt, PC Woche, Publish, Unit; **HUNGARY's** Alaplap, Computerworld SZT, PC World, ; **INDIA's** Computers & Communications; **ISRAEL's** Computerworld Israel, PC World Israel; **ITALY's** Computerworld Italia, Lotus Magazine, Macworld Italia, Networking Italia, PC World Italia; **JAPAN's** Computerworld Japan, Macworld Japan, SunWorld Japan, Windows World; **KENYA's** East African Computer News; **KOREA's** Computerworld Korea, Macworld Korea, PC World Korea; **MEXICO's** Compu Edicion, Compu Manufactura, Computacion/Punto de Venta, Computerworld Mexico, MacWorld, Mundo Unix, PC World, Windows; **THE NETHERLAND'S** Computer! Totaal, LAN Magazine, MacWorld; **NEW ZEALAND's** Computer Listings, Computerworld New Zealand, New Zealand PC World; **NIGERIA's** PC World Africa; **NORWAY's** Computerworld Norge, C/World, Lotusworld Norge, Macworld Norge, Networld, PC World Ekspress, PC World Norge, PC World's Product Guide, Publish World, Student Data, Unix World, Windowsworld, IDG Direct Response; **PANAMA's** PC World; **PERU's** Computerworld Peru, PC World; **PEOPLES REPUBLIC OF CHINA's** China Computerworld, PC World China, Electronics International, China Network World; **IDG HIGH TECH BEIJING's** New Product World; **IDG SHENZHEN's** Computer News Digest; **PHILLIPPINES'** Computerworld, PC World; **POLAND's** Computerworld Poland, PC World/Komputer; **PORTUGAL's** Cerebro/PC World, Correio Informatico/Computerworld, MacIn; **ROMANIA's** PC World; **RUSSIA's** Computerworld-Moscow, Mir-PC, Sety; **SLOVENIA's** Monitor Magazine; **SOUTH AFRICA's** Computing S.A.; **SPAIN's** Amiga World, Computerworld Espana, Communicaciones World, Macworld Espana, NeXTWORLD, PC World Espana, Publish, Sunworld; **SWEDEN's** Attack, ComputerSweden, Corporate Computing, Lokala Natverk/LAN, Lotus World, MAC&PC, Macworld, Mikrodatorn, PC World, Publishing & Design (CAP), Datalngenjoren, Maxi Data, Windows World; **SWITZERLAND's** Computerworld Schweiz, Macworld Schweiz, PC & Workstation; **TAIWAN's** Computerworld Taiwan, Global Computer Express, PC World Taiwan; **THAILAND's** Thai Computerworld; **TURKEY's** Computerworld Monitor, Macworld Turkiye, PC World Turkiye; **UNITED KINGDOM's** Lotus Magazine, Macworld, Sunworld; **UNITED STATES'** AmigaWorld, Cable in the Classroom, CD Review, CIO, Computerworld, Desktop Video World, DOS Resource Guide, Electronic News, Federal Computer Week, Federal Integrator, GamePro, IDG Books, InfoWorld, InfoWorld Direct, Laser Event, Macworld, Multimedia World, Network World, NeXTWORLD, PC Games, PC Letter, PC World Publish, Sumeria, SunWorld, SWATPro, Video Event; **VENEZUELA's** Computerworld Venezuela, MicroComputerworld Venezuela; **VIETNAM's** PC World Vietnam

 The text in this book is printed on recycled paper.

Dedication

To Debbie, Rebecca, Sarah, and Bethany

Acknowledgments

Just when I thought I was finished with this book, Erik reminded me to write the acknowledgments.

Thanks first to John Kilcullen, David Solomon, and Janna Custer for getting this thing started, and then to Erik Dafforn, Greg Robertson, and Ray Marshall for seeing it through. And thanks to all the folks working behind the scenes doing stuff I don't even know about. Working with you guys has been a pleasure; let's do it again soon!

The publisher would like to give special thanks to Patrick J. McGovern, without whom this book would not have been possible.

Credits

Publisher
David Solomon

Managing Editor
Mary Bednarek

Acquisitions Editor
Janna Custer

Production Manager
Beth Jenkins

Senior Editors
Sandra Blackthorn

Production Coordinator
Cindy L. Phipps

Acquisitions Assistant
Megg Bonar

Editorial Assistant
Patricia R. Reynolds

Project Editor
Erik Dafforn

Editors
Greg Robertson
Barbara Potter
Kezia Endsley

Technical Reviewer
Ray Marshall

Production Staff
Tony Augsburger
Valery Bourke
Mary Breidenbach
Sherry Gomoll
Drew R. Moore
Kathie Schnorr
Gina Scott

Proofreader
Henry Lazarek

Indexer
Sharon Hilgenberg

Book Design
University Graphics

Say What You Think!

Listen up, all you readers of IDG's international bestsellers: the one — the only — absolutely world famous ...*For Dummies* books! It's time for you to take advantage of a new, direct pipeline to the authors and editors of IDG Books Worldwide. In between putting the finishing touches on the next round of ...*For Dummies* books, the authors and editors of IDG Books Worldwide like to sit around and mull over what their readers have to say. And we know that you readers always say what you think. So here's your chance. We'd really like your input for future printings and editions of this book — and ideas for future ...*For Dummies* titles as well. Tell us what you liked (and didn't like) about this book. How about the chapters you found most useful — or most funny? And since we know you're not a bit shy, what about the chapters you think can be improved? Just to show you how much we appreciate your input, we'll add you to our Dummies Database/Fan Club and keep you up to date on the latest ...*For Dummies* books, news, cartoons, calendars, and more! Please send your name, address, and phone number, as well as your comments, questions, and suggestions, to our very own ...*For Dummies* coordinator at the following address:

...*For Dummies* Coordinator
IDG Books Worldwide
3250 North Post Road, Suite 140
Indianapolis, IN 46226

(Yes, Virginia, there really is a . . . *For Dummies* coordinator: We are not making this up.)

Please mention the name of this book in your comments.

Thanks for your input!

Don't forget to fill out the Reader Response Card in the back of this book and send it in!

Contents at a Glance

Cartoons at a Glance
By Rich Tennant

page 145

page 180

page 257

page 7

page 310

page 228

page 201

page 38

page 104

page 75

Table of Contents

· ·

Foreword

・・

Computers and "computer management" used to be something of a black art reserved for people who worked behind glass walls in special rooms with air-conditioning and huge computers and stuff.

Well that was then and this is now. Today, PCs are on every desk, and terms like *LAN* (local-area network), *WAN* (wide-area network), and *MAN* (metropolitan-area network) have quickly become as common as *telephone* and *long-distance.*

The term *network,* like *PC,* is one of those strange words that has crept into our lives and just won't leave. Other technospeak, such as *bits, bytes, baud, STP, UTP, NetWare, LANtastic* — the list is endless — has invaded our vocabularies and taken over our businesses. Life may have been simpler in the days of manual typewriters, but those days are long gone. Unfortunately, much of this change has happened very quickly — and has scared many folks away from understanding the new technology.

If you think about it, networks simply speed up the rate at which we can exchange ideas and information. In a nutshell, LANs are a good thing, but they need attention and understanding.

This, then, is the premise for *Networking For Dummies.* Doug Lowe's book is a great way to break through the technobabble and really understand what networks are and what you need to know about them. If you've ever wondered what "NetWare" is, it's explained in here. So are topics like "What is a network, and why do I (or why *don't* I) need one?" And if you feel overwhelmed with "technospeak," take comfort — there is an English-to-Technoid glossary in the back of this book.

"Techie" subjects — such as *print queues* and *queuing, redirection,* and software selection and management — are all presented in easy-to-read language that, aided by examples and illustrations, breaks these seemingly complex topics into byte-size chunks that you can easily understand.

Let me take a second and tell you what this book *isn't* — it's not an advertisement for any particular network vendor or product manufacturer. It's also not a book that you'll want to read cover-to-cover in one sitting. This book will not make you an expert, nor are you a "Dummy" for reading it. Quite the contrary. *Networking For Dummies* is an excellent first step to understanding the tools that affect the daily lives of millions of people.

What you will learn are the kinds of questions to ask when you plan or implement your own LAN, as well as some things to look into as you take the role of LAN administrator. By the time you're finished reading this book, LANs may actually seem pretty neat!

Unlike other manuscripts that are written *for* techies *by* techies (meaning that the average human being will have no idea what the pages say or mean), *Networking For Dummies* takes a very straightforward approach to demystifying the magic that allows you and your neighbor to share a laser printer or to exchange documents electronically.

Basic concepts of hardware, software, and people requirements are well organized into sections that serve as handy reference material for you in the future.

Regardless of your ability, *Networking For Dummies* will prove to be one of your favorite reference books. If you're an experienced LAN administrator or architect, this book will help you explain the importance of backups or the options of wiring. If you're a novice, it is an excellent road map to the world of networks. This book is a terrific addition to your library; without a doubt, it is a valued part of mine.

> — Paul Merenbloom
> author of *InfoWorld's* "LAN Talk" column
> and Manager of Information Technology
> Otsuka America Pharmaceuticals,
> Rockville, MD

Introduction

Welcome to *Networking For Dummies*, the book that's written especially for people who have this nagging feeling in the back of their minds that they should network their computers, but haven't a clue as to how to start or where to begin.

Do you often copy a spreadsheet file to a floppy disk and give it to the fellow in the next office so that he can look at it? Are you frustrated because you can't use the fancy laser printer that's on the financial secretary's computer? Do you wait in line to use the computer that has the customer database? You need a network!

Or maybe you already have a network, but there's just one problem: They promised that the network would make your life easier, and instead it's turned your computing life upside down. Just when you had this computer thing figured out, someone popped into your office, hooked up a cable, and said, "Happy networking!" Makes you want to scream.

Either way, you've found the right book. Help is here, within these humble pages.

This book talks about networks in everyday — and often irreverent — terms. The language is friendly; you don't need a graduate education to get through it. And the occasional potshot will help unseat the hallowed and sacred traditions of networkdom, bringing just a bit of fun to an otherwise dry subject. The goal is to bring the lofty precepts of networking down to earth where you can touch them and squeeze them and say, "What's the big deal? I can do this!"

About This Book

This isn't the kind of book you pick up and read from start to finish, as if it were a cheap novel. If I ever see you reading it at the beach, I'll kick sand in your face. This book is more like a reference, the kind of book you can pick up, turn to just about any page, and start reading. There are 27 chapters, and each one covers a specific aspect of networking — like printing on the network, hooking up network cables, or setting up security so bad guys can't break in. Just turn to the chapter you're interested in and start reading.

Each chapter is divided into self-contained chunks, all related to the major theme of the chapter. For example, the chapter on hooking up the network cable contains nuggets like these:

- ✔ What Ethernet is
- ✔ The different types of network cable
- ✔ Using coax cable
- ✔ Using twisted pair cable
- ✔ Mixing coax and twisted pair on the same network
- ✔ Professional touches for your cabling

You don't have to memorize anything in this book. It's a "need-to-know" book: You pick it up when you need to know something. Need to know what 10baseT is? Pick up the book. Need to know how to create good passwords? Pick up the book. Otherwise, put it down and get on with your life.

How to Use This Book

This book works like a reference. Start with the topic you want to learn about; look for it in the table of contents or in the index to get going. The table of contents is detailed enough that you should be able to find most of the topics you'll look for. If not, turn to the index, where you'll find even more detail.

After you've found your topic in the table of contents or the index, turn to the area of interest and read as much as you need or want. Then close the book and get on with it.

Of course, the book is loaded with information, so if you want to take a brief excursion into your topic, you're more than welcome. If you want to know the big security picture, read the whole chapter on security. If you just want to know how to make a decent password, read just the section on passwords. You get the idea.

If you need to type something, you'll see the text you need to type like this:

TYPE THIS STUFF

In this example, you type **TYPE THIS STUFF** at the keyboard and press Enter. An explanation usually follows, just in case you're scratching your head and grunting "Huh?"

Whenever we describe a message or information that you'll see on the screen, we present it as follows:

```
A message from your friendly network
```

This book rarely directs you elsewhere for information — just about everything you need to know about networks is right here. For more information about DOS, try *DOS For Dummies*, published by IDG Books Worldwide. For more NetWare information, you can get a copy of *NetWare For Dummies*. And there's a *...For Dummies* book that covers just about every program known to humanity (or there will be soon).

What You Don't Need to Read

Much of this book is skippable. I've carefully placed extra-technical information in self-contained sidebars and clearly marked them so that you can steer clear of them. Don't read this stuff unless you're really into technical explanations and want to know a little of what's going on behind the scenes. Don't worry; my feelings won't be hurt if you don't read every word.

Foolish Assumptions

I'm going to make only two assumptions about who you are: (1) You are someone who works with a PC, and (2) you either have a network or you are thinking about getting one. I hope that you know and are on speaking terms with someone who knows more about computers than you do. My goal is to decrease your reliance on that person, but don't throw away his or her phone number quite yet.

How This Book Is Organized

Inside this book, you'll find chapters arranged into five parts. Each chapter is broken down into sections that cover various aspects of the chapter's main subject. There is a logical sequence to the chapters, so it makes sense to read them in order. But the book is modular enough that you can pick it up and start reading at any point.

Here's the lowdown on what's in each of the five parts:

Part I: The Absolute Basics

The chapters in this part present a layperson's introduction to what networking is all about. This is a good place to start if you're clueless about what a network is. It's also a great place to start if you're a hapless network user who doesn't give a whit about optimizing network performance, but you want to know what the network is and how to get the most out of it.

Part II: Build Your Own Network

Oh, oh. The boss just gave you an ultimatum: Get a network up and running by Friday or pack your things. The chapters in this section cover everything you need to know to build a network, from picking the network operating system to understanding a mail-order advertisement to installing the cable.

Part III: The Dummy's Guide to Network Management

I hope the job of managing the network doesn't fall on your shoulders, but in case it does, the chapters in this part will help you out. You'll learn all about backup, security, performance, dusting, mopping, and all the other stuff network managers have to do.

Part IV: The Part of Tens

It wouldn't be a ...For Dummies book without a collection of lists of interesting snippets: Ten network commandments, ten network gizmos only big networks need, ten tricks to networking Windows, and more!

Part V: References for Real People

The first three chapters in this section give an overview of the commands available with three of the most popular network operating systems: NetWare, NetWare Lite, and LANtastic. After that, there's a handy glossary to help you decipher even the ugliest of networking terms.

Icons used in this book

Hold it — technical stuff is just around the corner. Read on only if you have your pocket protector.

Pay special attention to this icon — it lets you know that some particularly useful tidbit is at hand — perhaps a shortcut or a little-used command that pays off big.

Did I tell you about the memory course I took?

Stop the presses! This icon highlights information that may help you avert disaster.

Information specific to NetWare follows. Skip this if you don't use or plan not to use NetWare.

LANtastic information on board.

Information specific to another popular networking program — Windows for Workgroups — follows.

Where to Go from Here

Yes, you can get there from here. With this book in hand, you're ready to plow right through the rugged networking terrain. Browse through the table of contents and decide where you want to start. Be bold! Be courageous! Be adventurous! And above all, have fun!

Part I

The Absolute Basics
(A Network User's Guide)

The 5th Wave   By Rich Tennant

"IT SAYS HERE IF I SUBSCRIBE TO THIS MAGAZINE, THEY'LL SEND ME A FREE DESK-TOP CALCULATOR. DESKTOP CALCULATOR?!! WHOOAA – WHERE HAVE I BEEN?!!"

In this part...

One day the Network Thugs barge into your office and shove a gun in your face. "Don't move until we've hooked you up to the network!" one of them says while the other one rips open your PC, installs a sinister-looking electronic circuit card, closes the PC back up, and plugs a cable into its back. "It's done," they say as they start to leave. "Now...don't call the cops. We know who you are!"

If this has happened to you, you'll appreciate the chapters in this part. They provide a gentle introduction to computer networks written especially for the reluctant network user.

What if you don't have a network yet and you're the one who's supposed to install one? Then the chapters in this part will clue you in to what a network is all about. That way, you'll be prepared for the unfortunately more-technical chapters that are in Part II, "Build Your Own Network."

Chapter 1

Networks Will Not Take Over the World, and Other Network Basics

Computer networks get a bad rap in the movies. In *War Games*, a kid with zits nearly starts World War III by playing games on a computer network. In *Sneakers*, the mob tries to take over the country by stealing a fancy black box that can access any computer network in existence. And in the *Terminator* movies, a computer network of the future called Skynet takes over the planet, builds deadly terminator robots, and sends them back through time to kill everyone unfortunate enough to have the name Sarah Connor.

Fear not. These bad networks exist only in the dreams of science fiction writers. Real-world networks are much more calm and predictable. They don't think for themselves, they can't evolve into something you don't want them to be, and they won't hurt you — even if your name is Sarah Connor.

Now that you're over your fear of networks, you're ready to breeze through this chapter. It's a gentle introduction to computer networks, superficial even, with a slant toward the concepts that will help you use a computer that's attached to a network. It's not very detailed; the really detailed and boring stuff comes later.

What is a Network?

A *network* is nothing more than two or more computers connected together by a cable so that they can exchange information.

There are, of course, other ways to exchange information between computers besides networks. Most of us have used what computer nerds call the *Sneakernet.* That's where you copy a file to a diskette and walk the diskette to someone else's computer. The term *sneakernet* is typical of computer nerds' attempts at humor.

The whole problem with the sneakernet is that it's slow, plus it wears a trail in your carpet. One day some penny-pinching computer geeks discovered that it was actually cheaper to connect computers together with cables than to replace the carpet every six months. Thus, the modern computer network was born.

With a computer network, you hook all the computers in your office together with cables, install a special network adapter card (an electronic circuit card that goes *inside* your computer—ouch!) in each computer so you'll have a place to plug in the cable, set up and configure special network software to make the network work, and *voilà*, you have a working network. That's all there is to it.

Figure 1-1 shows a typical network with four computers. You can see here that all four computers are connected together with a network cable. You can also see that Ward's computer has a fancy laser printer attached to it. Because of the network, June, Wally, and the Beaver can also use this laser printer. (Also, you can see that the Beaver has stuck yesterday's bubble gum to the back of his computer. Although this is not recommended, it shouldn't affect the network adversely.)

- ✔ Networks are often called LANs. *LAN* is an acronym that stands for local-area network. It's the first *TLA,* or three-letter acronym, you'll see in this book. You don't need to remember it, or any of the many TLAs that follow. In fact, the only three-letter acronym you need to remember is TLA.

- ✔ Every computer connected to the network is said to be *on the network.* The technical term (which you can forget) for a computer that is on the network is a *node.*

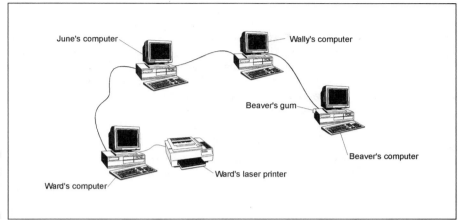

Figure 1-1:
A typical
network.

> ✔ When a computer is turned on and is able to access the network, the computer is said to be *on-line*. When the computer is unable to access the network, it is *off-line*. A computer could be off-line for several reasons. It could be turned off, it could be broken, the cable that connects it to the network could be unplugged, or there could be a wad of gum jammed into the disk drive.
>
> ✔ When a computer is turned on and working properly, it is said to be *up*. When a computer is turned off or when it's broken, it is said to be *down*. Turning off a computer is sometimes called *taking it down*. Turning it back on is sometimes called *bringing it up*.
>
> ✔ You might guess that a four-letter acronym is called an FLA, but you'd be dead wrong. A four letter acronym is called an *ETLA*, which stands for *extended three-letter acronym*.

Why Bother?

Frankly, computer networks are a bit of a pain to set up. So why bother? Because the benefits of having a network make the pain of setting one up bearable. You don't have to be a Ph.D. to understand the benefits of networking. In fact, you learned everything you need to know in kindergarten: Networks are all about *sharing*. Specifically, networks are about sharing three things: files, resources, and programs.

✔ **Sharing files.** Networks let you share information with other computers on the network. Depending on how you set your network up, you can do this in one of two ways. The most direct way is to send the file from your computer directly to your friend's computer. The second way is to send your file to an intermediate resting place, where your friend can pick it up later, kind of like dropping a bag full of ransom money at a phone booth. A third way is to permanently store the file at that intermediate place, where both of you can get at the file whenever you want. One way or the other, the data travels to your friend's computer over the network cable, not on a floppy disk like it does in a sneakernet.

✔ **Sharing resources.** This means that you can set up certain computer resources — like a disk drive or a printer — so that all of the computers on the network can access them. For example, the laser printer attached to Ward's computer in Figure 1-1 is a *shared resource*. That means that anyone on the network can use it. Without the network, June, Wally, and the Beaver would have to buy their own laser printers.

Disk drives can be shared resources, too. In fact, a disk drive must be set up as a shared resource in order to share files with other users. Suppose Wally wants to share a file with the Beaver, and a shared disk drive has been set up on June's computer. All Wally has to do is copy his file to the shared disk drive in June's computer and tell the Beaver where he put it. Then, when the Beaver gets around to it, he can copy the file from June's computer to his own. (Unless, of course, Eddie Haskel deletes it first.)

You can share other resources, too, such as CD-ROM drives (those new-fangled devices that store gigabytes of data and are most useful for large clip art libraries and encyclopedias) or modems (which let you access other computers that aren't on your network).

✔ **Sharing programs.** Sometimes, it's best to put programs that everyone uses on a shared disk, rather than keep separate copies of the programs on each person's computer. For example, if you have ten computer users who all use WordPerfect, you could store ten copies of WordPerfect — one on each computer — or you could store just one copy of WordPerfect on a shared disk.

There are advantages and disadvantages to sharing a program such as WordPerfect. On the plus side, it makes it easier to keep WordPerfect up-to-date. If you decide to upgrade to a new version of WordPerfect, you have to do the upgrade only once rather than ten times. You have to configure WordPerfect only once to work with printers that are on the network. And it's cheaper, because a network version of WordPerfect that allows up to ten users is less expensive than ten single-user copies of WordPerfect.

On the minus side, a shared version of WordPerfect can be harder to configure properly and might run just a bit slower because the WordPerfect program files have to travel over the network.

Remember that it's illegal to purchase a single-user copy of a program and put it on a shared disk so that everyone on the network can use it. If you have five people who use the program, you need to either purchase five copies of the program, or purchase a network copy that specifically allows five or more users.

Servers and Workstations

The network computer that contains the disk drives, printer, or other resources that are shared with other network computers is called a *server*. That's a term that will come up over and over again, so you have to remember it. Write it on the back of your left hand.

Any computer that is not a server is called a *workstation*. There are only two kinds of computers on a network: servers and workstations. You have to remember this, too. Write it on the back of your right hand.

The distinction between servers and workstations in a network would be kind of fun to study in a sociology class. It's kind of like the distinction between the haves and the have-nots in society.

- Usually, the most powerful and expensive computers in a network are the servers. That makes sense, because their resources are shared by every user on the network.

- The cheaper and less powerful computers are the workstations. They're the ones used by individual users for everyday work. Since workstations' resources don't have to be shared, they don't have to be as fancy.

- In most networks, there are more workstations than servers. For example, a network with ten workstations can probably get by with one server.

- In many networks, there's a clean line of segregation between servers and workstations. In other words, a computer is either a server or a workstation, not both. A server cannot become a workstation, nor can a workstation become a server. These types of networks don't offer much upward mobility.

- Other networks are more progressive, allowing any computer in the network to be a server, and allowing computers to be both server and workstation at the same time. More about this type of network in a moment.

The Three Kinds of Networks

Computer networks come in three varieties: real networks, fake networks, and networks for the rest of us.

Real networks

To a computer dweeb, a network isn't really a network unless it requires at least one and maybe two full-time specialists wearing lab coats just to keep it running. This kind of network is called a *real network*, or sometimes a *Network With an Attitude (NWA)*.

- The most popular real network is *NetWare* from a company called Novell. NetWare is so complicated that it has an intensive certification program that rivals the Bar. The lucky ones who pass the test are awarded the coveted title *Certified NetWare Engineer*, or *CNE,* and a lifetime supply of pocket protectors.

- The reason NetWare has a bad attitude is that it requires you to set up server computers that do not run DOS as their operating system. Instead, the servers use a specialized operating system called NetWare (original name, huh?). One look at the NetWare operating system's arcane commands and you'll be begging for the simplicity and clarity of DOS (tee hee).

- Well, I may have exaggerated just a little. If you've got a bit of computer savvy and you're willing to spend some time at it, you can probably manage to set up a simple NetWare network. The CNE thing is for people who want to network hundreds or even thousands of PCs together. If you want to network just a few PCs using NetWare, you can handle it.

- If you don't know what DOS is or what an operating system is, you're in way over your head. Put this book down now, run back to the bookstore, and buy a copy of *DOS For Dummies.*

Fake networks

At the opposite extreme are the fake networks. They look like networks and they work like networks, but they don't use special networking hardware. Instead, they let you connect computers together by attaching them via their serial or parallel ports. These networks are sometimes called *zero-slot networks* because they don't require a special networking card that takes up one of your computer's expansion slots.

Historical stuff that's not worth reading

Networks are nothing new. In the dinosaur era of computing, known as the Mainframerassic, the computing world was dominated by big, over-grown systems called *time-sharing* systems.

Time-sharing systems let you use a mainframe computer via a *dumb terminal,* which consisted only of a monitor and a keyboard. A dumb terminal looked superficially like a PC, but it didn't have its own computer. With dumb termi-nals, hundreds or even thousands of users could access a single mainframe computer all at the same time.

How did this work? By the magic of time-sharing, which divided the mainframe computer's time into slices, allocating time slices to the users one at a time. The slices were short, but long enough to maintain the illusion that the terminal user had the mainframe computer all to himself or herself.

In the 1970s, big time-sharing systems were re-placed by smaller minicomputer systems, which used the time-sharing concept on a smaller scale. It wasn't until the invention of the PC in the late 1970s that networks as we think of them today developed.

- ✔ Although zero-slot networks give you the same capabilities as other networks, they're slow as molasses because they use your computer's serial or parallel port instead of a real networking card.

- ✔ Zero-slot networks are useful, though, for connecting a laptop computer to a desktop computer to copy an occasional file between the two. The most popular zero-slot network used for this purpose is called *Laplink*. MS-DOS 6.0 and 6.2 come with a new program called INTERLNK that does essen-tially the same thing. The limitation of these programs is that they only work with two computers at a time; you can't use them to link three or more computers.

Networks for the rest of us

The third kind of network is in between the real networks that require certified experts to set up and the fake networks that are little more than toys. The official name for this kind of network is *peer-to-peer network*, or just *peer network*. It's called a peer network because it looks upon all of the computers on the network as peers, rather than insisting that some computers (the ones that run the special network operating system) are better than others (the ones that run lowly DOS). In this respect, these networks are much more politically correct than Novell NetWare.

With a peer network, any computer on the network can act as a server and share its resources with other computers on the network. For example, to share the printer attached to Ward's computer, you just make Ward's computer a server and tell the network to share the printer. Peer networks use special programs loaded into memory when your computer starts (usually in the AUTOEXEC.BAT file) to set it up as a server or as a workstation.

The two most popular peer networks are *LANtastic*, by Artisoft, and *Windows for Workgroups*, by your friend and mine, Microsoft. They provide similar features, and both are simple enough for even novices to set up.

- ✔ The beauty of peer networks is that they provide most of the advanced features found in real networks like NetWare, but they're much easier to set up and use because you don't have to waste your time learning how to use a different operating system.

- ✔ Another great thing about peer networks is that you don't have to dedicate computers to be strictly servers if you don't want to. With a peer network, any computer on the network can be a server if it has resources like disks or printers that other users want to share. And while that computer is working as a server, you can still use that same computer for other functions like word processing.

- ✔ Even with a peer network, though, it's still best to use a *dedicated server,* a computer that's used only as a server and not as a workstation. That's because when you use a server for word processing or some other application, everything slows to a snail's pace. If you can afford it, set aside at least one computer to be a server and nothing else.

- ✔ Artisoft has recently come out with an even simpler version of LANtastic called—hold your breath—*Simply LANtastic*. It's a scaled-back version of LANtastic that's ideal for networks of just three or four computers, where there is no need for security features or other fancy stuff. If you just want to dip your feet into the networking pool to see how the water is, Simply LANtastic is a great place to start.

- ✔ Besides being dedicated, it's helpful if your servers are sincere.

What Makes It Tick? (You Should Probably Skip This)

To use a network, you don't really have to know much about how it works. Still, you'll feel a little better about using the network if you realize that it doesn't work by voodoo. It may seem like magic, but it isn't. Following is a list of the inner workings of a typical network.

- **Network interface cards.** Inside any networked computer is a special electronic circuit card called a *network interface card*. The TLA (Come on! *Three-letter acronym!*) for network interface card is NIC. Important note: Using your network late into the evening is not the same as watching NIC at night.

- **Network cable.** The network cable is what actually connects the computers together. It plugs into the network interface card at the back of your computer. The most common type of cable, *coaxial* (sometimes called *coax*), is similar to the cable used to bring Nick at Night to your TV. The cable used for cable TV is not the same as the cable used for computer networks, though. So don't try to replace a length of broken network cable with TV cable. It won't work.

  A second kind of cable that's often used in networks looks like phone cable. In fact, in some offices the computer network and the phone system can share the same cable. Beware, though, that ordinary phone cable won't work for a computer network. For a computer network, each pair of wires in the cable must be twisted in just a certain way. That's why this type of cable is called *twisted pair*. Standard phone cable doesn't have the right twists.

- **Network hub.** If your network is set up using twisted pair cable, your network probably also has a *network hub*. The hub is a small box with a bunch of cable connectors on it. Each computer on the network is connected by cable to the hub. The hub, in turn, connects all the computers to each other. If your network uses coax cable, the cable goes directly from computer to computer, so a network hub isn't used.

Bogus buzzword dribble you should skip

An introductory chapter on networking concepts wouldn't be complete if it didn't include a definition for the computer industry's most popular networking buzzword, *client/server*. Unfortunately, nobody really knows what client/server means, not even the experts who made up the term. The lowest-common-denominator definition is: "A computer network in which a workstation or PC (the client) can request information from a computer that can share resources (the server)." In other words, a network.

A more technically precise definition is: "A computer application in which a significant portion of the application's processing is performed on the server computer rather than on the client computer." This is a bit much to swallow at this stage of your network education, so don't worry too much about it.

Very few networks fit this technical definition of client/server, but client/server is such a trendy buzzword, most computer vendors want to be able to claim they do client/server. Hence the third definition, one more suitable for the real world: "Any computer product, hardware or software, that the manufacturer's marketing department feels will sell more if this trendy buzzword appears in its advertising."

> ✔ **Network software.** Of course, it's the software that really makes the network work. To make any network work, a whole bunch of software has to be set up just right. Fortunately, the commands needed to get this software going are almost always put in special batch files. And better yet, someone else puts them there for you. (Unless, of course, setting up the network software happens to be your job. Bummer.)

Here's what a typical batch file looks like for a LANtastic network. Close your eyes when you look at it, because you really don't have to worry about it.

```
@ECHO OFF
AEX /IRQ=15 /IOBASE=300 /VERBOSE
AILANBIO
REDIR WALLY /LOGINS=3
NET LPT TIMEOUT 10
NET USE M: \\WARD\C-DRIVE
NET USE LPT2: \\WARD\@PRINTER
```

If you're going to set up a network yourself, open your eyes, because you *will* have to worry about these batch files. Sorry.

It's Not a Personal Computer Anymore!

If there's one thing I want you to remember from this chapter more than anything else, it's that once your PC is hooked up to a network, it's not a *personal* computer anymore. You are now a part of a network of computers, and in a way, you've given up one of the key things that made PCs so successful in the first place: independence.

I got my start in computers back in the days when mainframe computers ruled the roost. Mainframe computers are big, complex machines that used to fill whole rooms and had to be cooled with chilled water. My first computer was a water-cooled Binford Power-Proc Model 2000. Argh argh argh. (I'm not making up the part about the water. A plumber was frequently required to install a mainframe computer. I am making up the part about the Binford 2000.)

Mainframe computers required staffs of programmers and operators just to keep them going. They had to be carefully *managed*. A whole bureaucracy grew up around managing mainframes.

Mainframe computers looked so impressive that they were often housed in rooms behind big glass windows to show them off. One of the trendiest computer buzzwords is *glass house,* which refers to the room where the mainframe was kept and, by extension, to the mainframe itself and the bureaucracy that surrounded it. (Use this term at a cocktail party sometime to impress your friends.)

Mainframe computers used to be the dominant computer in the workplace. Personal computers changed all that. Personal computers took the computing power out of the glass house and put it on the user's desktop, where it belongs. It severed the tie to the centralized control of the mainframe computer. With a PC, a user could look at his or her computer and say, "This is mine...all mine." Mainframes still exist, but they're nowhere near as popular as they once were.

The network changes everything all over again. In a way, it's a change back to the mainframe computer way of thinking. True, the network isn't kept in a glass house and doesn't have to be installed by a plumber. But you can no longer think of your PC as your own. You're part of a network, and like the mainframe, the network has to be carefully managed.

- ✔ You can't just indiscriminately delete files from the network. They may not be yours.

- ✔ Just because Wally sends something to Ward's printer doesn't mean it will immediately start printing. The Beave may have sent a two-hour print job before that. Wally will just have to wait.

- ✔ You might try to retrieve a Lotus 1-2-3 spreadsheet file from a network disk, only to discover that someone else is using it. Like Wally, you'll just have to wait.

- ✔ If you copy that 15MB database file to a server's disk, you may get a call later from an angry coworker complaining that there's no room left on the server's disk for his or her important file.

- ✔ If you want to access a file on Ward's computer but Ward hasn't come in and turned his computer on yet, you'll have to go into his office and turn it on yourself.

- ✔ If your computer is a server, you can't just turn it off when you're through using it. Someone else might be accessing a file on your hard disk or printing on your printer.

- ✔ Why does Ward always get the best printer? If *Leave It to Beaver* were made today, I bet the good printer would be on June's computer.

The Network Administrator

Because there's so much that can go wrong even with a simple network, it's important that one person be designated as the *network administrator*. That way, someone will be responsible for making sure that the network doesn't fall apart or get out of control.

The network administrator doesn't have to be a technical genius. In fact, some of the best network administrators are complete idiots when it comes to technical stuff. What's important is that the administrator be *organized*. The administrator's job is to make sure that there's plenty of space available on the file server, the file server is backed up regularly, new employees are able to access the network, and so on.

It's also the network administrator's job to solve basic problems that the users themselves can't solve, and to know when to call in an expert when something really bad happens.

- ✔ An entire section of this book is devoted to the hapless network administrator. So if you're nominated, you should read that section. If you're lucky enough that someone else is nominated, celebrate by buying him or her a copy of this book so that they can read about their new job.

- ✔ In small companies, it's common to pick the network administrator by drawing straws. The shortest straw loses.

- ✔ Of course the network administrator can't really be a complete technical idiot. I was using a bit of exaggeration (for those of you in Congress, that means I was appropriating necessary hyperbole) to make the point that organizational skills are more important than technical skills. As I said earlier, the network administrator needs to know how to do various maintenance tasks. This requires at least a little technical know-how, but the organizational skills are more important.

What Have They Got That You Don't Got?

With all of this stuff to worry about, you may begin to wonder if you're smart enough to use your computer once it's attached to the network. Let me assure you that you are. If you're smart enough to buy this book because you know you need a network, you're more than smart enough to use the network once it's put in. You're also smart enough to install and manage it yourself. This isn't rocket science.

I know people who use networks all the time. And they are no smarter than you are. But they do have one thing that you don't have: certification. And so, by the powers vested in me by the International Society for the Computer Impaired, I present you with the certificate in Figure 1-2, confirming that you have earned the coveted title, *Certified Network Dummy*, better known as *CND*. This title is considered much more prestigious in certain circles than the more stodgy CNE badge worn by real network experts.

Congratulations.

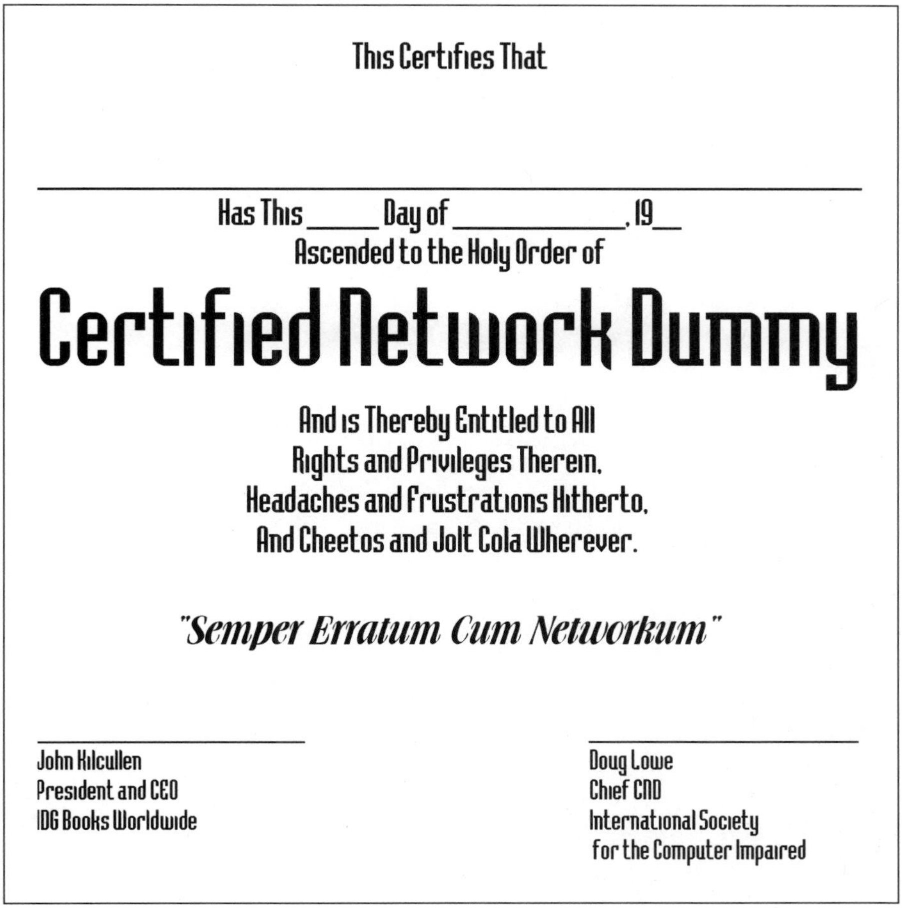

This Certifies That

_____

Has This _____ Day of _____, 19__
Ascended to the Holy Order of

Certified Network Dummy

And is Thereby Entitled to All
Rights and Privileges Therein,
Headaches and Frustrations Hitherto,
And Cheetos and Jolt Cola Wherever.

"Semper Erratum Cum Networkum"

_____   _____
John Kilcullen   Doug Lowe
President and CEO   Chief CND
IDG Books Worldwide   International Society
                                 for the Computer Impaired

Figure 1-2:
Your official
CND
certificate.

Chapter 2
Life on the Network

● ●

In This Chapter

▶ Using local resources and network resources

▶ Logging in to the network

▶ Accessing a network drive

▶ Using a network printer

▶ Logging off the network

● ●

*W*hen your PC is hooked up to a network, it's not an island anymore, separated from the rest of the world like some kind of isolationist fanatic waving a "Don't tread on me" flag. The network connection changes your PC forever. Now your computer is a part of a "system," connected to "other computers" on the "network." "You" have to worry about annoying network details like local and shared resources and logging in and accessing network drives and using network printers and logging off and who knows what else.

Bother.

This chapter brings you up to speed on what it's like to live with a computer network. Unfortunately, it gets a little technical at times, so you'll need your pocket protector.

Local Resources and Network Resources

In case you didn't catch this in the last chapter, one of the most important differences between using an isolated computer and using a network computer is the distinction between *local resources* and *network resources*. Local resources are things such as disk drives and printers that are connected directly to your computer. You can use local resources whether you're connected to the network or not. Network resources are the disk drives, printers, and other goodies such as modems or CD-ROM drives that are connected to the network's server computers. You can use network resources only when you're connected to the network.

The whole trick to using a computer network is knowing which resources are local resources (they belong to you) and which are network resources (they belong to the network). In most networks, your C: drive is a local drive. And if there's a printer sitting next to your PC, it's probably a local printer. You can do anything you want with these resources without affecting the network or other users on the network.

- You can't tell whether a resource is a local resource or a network resource just by looking at it. The printer that sits right next to your computer is probably your local printer, but then again it might be a network printer. The same holds for disk drives: The hard disk in your PC is probably your own, but it might be a network disk, which can be used by others on the network.

- Because dedicated network servers are full of resources, you might say they are not only dedicated (and sincere) but also resourceful. (Groan. Sorry, this is but another in a tireless series of bad computer-nerd puns.)

What's in a Name

Just about everything on a computer network has a name: The computers themselves have names, the people that use the computers have names, and the disk drives and printers that can be shared on the network have names. It's not essential that you know all of the names that are used on your network, but you do need to know some of them.

- Every person who can use the network should have a *user identification* (*user ID* for short). You need to know your user ID in order to log in to the network. You also need to know the user IDs of your buddies, especially if you want to steal their files or send them nasty notes. More about user IDs and logging in later.

- ✔ It's tempting to let everyone use his or her first name for their user IDs, but that's not a good idea. Even in a small office, you'll eventually run into a conflict. (And what about that Mrs. McCave, made famous by Dr. Seuss when she had 23 children and named them all Dave?) I suggest you use your first name plus the first two letters of your last name. Then, Wally's user ID would be Wallycl, Beaver's would be Beavercl.

- ✔ Every computer that's on the network must have a unique *computer name*. You don't have to know the names of all the computers on the network, but it helps if you know your own computer's name and the names of any server computers you need to access. The computer name is often the same as the user ID of the person who uses the computer most often. Sometimes the names indicate the physical location of the computer, like OFFICE-12 or BACK-ROOM, for example. Server computers often have names that reflect the group that uses the server most, like ACCTNG-SERVER or CAD-SERVER.

- ✔ Then again, some network nerds like to assign techie-sounding names like BL3K5-87A.

- ✔ Network resources like disk drives and printers have names too. For example, a network server may have two printers, named LASER and MATRIX (to indicate the type of printer), and two disk drives, named C-DRIVE and D-DRIVE.

- ✔ When NetWare is used, disk drives names are called *volume names*. Often, names like SYS1, SYS2, and so on are used. NetWare administrators often lack sufficient creativity to come up with more interesting volume names.

- ✔ Most people think Juliet said, "A rose by any other name would smell as sweet." Hah! The actual quote, in full, is "What's in a name? That which we call a rose by any other *word* would smell as sweet." (*Romeo and Juliet*, Act II, Scene ii, 43-44.)

- ✔ Every network has a user ID for the network supervisor. If you log in using the supervisor's id, you can do anything you want: add new users, define new network resources, change Wally's password, anything. The supervisor's user ID is usually something very clever, like SUPERVISOR.

Logging In to the Network

To use network resources, your computer must be connected to the network, and you must go through a super-secret process called *logging in*. The purpose of logging in is to let the network know who you are so it can decide if you're one of the good guys.

Logging in is the computer network equivalent of the exchange from *The Andromeda Strain* in which Leavitt completed a ritual exchange of code words, and was allowed to enter the top-secret underground laboratory. Gaining access to a computer network usually requires a similar exchange:

"User ID," the computer said.

The human replied tersely, "Beave."

The computer nodded. "Password?"

"Gumwad," the human replied.

"Verified."

Logging in is also a little like cashing a check: It requires two forms of identification. The first is your *user ID*, the name by which the network knows you. Your user ID is sort of like a nickname, and is usually some variation of your real name, like "Beave" for "The Beaver." Everyone who uses the network must have a user-id.

Your *password* is a secret word that only you and the network know. If you type the right password, the network believes you are who you say you are. Every user has a different password, and the password should remain a secret.

✔ *Login* is pronounced as if it were two words, like *log in*. *Logon* (also pronounced as two words, *log on*) means the same thing.

✔ The terms *user name* and *login name* are sometimes used instead of *user ID*. They mean the same thing.

✔ As far as the network is concerned, you and your computer are *not* the same thing. Your user ID refers to you, not to your computer. That's why you have a user-id and your computer has a computer-name. You can log in to the network using your user ID from any computer that's attached to the network. And other users can log at your computer in using their own user IDs.

✔ Your computer may be set up so that it logs you in automatically whenever you turn it on. In that case, you don't have to type your user ID and password. This is convenient, but takes the sport out of it. And it's a terrible idea if you're the least bit worried about bad guys getting into your network.

✔ Guard your password with your life. I'd tell you mine, but then I'd have to shoot you.

Logging in with NetWare

If your network is Novell NetWare, you login by using the LOGIN command. Most NetWare networks are set up so that each computer's AUTOEXEC.BAT file has a LOGIN command in it. Then, you have to enter your user ID and password every time you start your computer:

```
Enter your login name:
BEAVER
Enter your password:
```

When you type your password, it's not displayed on the screen. That way, no one can see your password (unless they watch your fingers while you type!).

If you want, you can type the user ID on the LOGIN command line like this:

```
C:\>LOGIN BEAVER
```

Then, LOGIN will ask you for just your password.

- ✔ After NetWare decides that your user ID and password are acceptable, it runs a *login script,* the network equivalent of the AUTOEXEC.BAT batch file that runs every time you start your computer. The login script sets up your computer so you can access network drives and printers.

- ✔ If your AUTOEXEC.BAT file doesn't contain a LOGIN command, you log in by first changing to the network server drive (usually drive F:) and typing LOGIN. Then, you enter your user ID and password.

Don't let me tell you about the LOGIN directory

In a Novell NetWare network, one of the directories on the file server is available to you even when you haven't logged on to the network. It's called the LOGIN directory, and it's usually accessed as drive F:. The LOGIN directory contains the program file for the LOGIN command as well as any files and programs the network administrator decides can be made available to

anyone on the network — even folks who haven't logged in.

Before you can use the LOGIN command, you must make the network drive that accesses the LOGIN directory the current drive. That's why your AUTOEXEC.BAT file probably contains the line F: immediately before the LOGIN line.

Logging in with LANtastic

If your network is LANtastic, you log in by typing the command **STARTNET**. This actually runs a batch file named STARTNET.BAT, which is created when LANtastic is installed on your computer. It contains the commands necessary to load the LANtastic software, to log you in to one or more file servers, and to access network drives and printers. When you run STARTNET.BAT, you'll be asked to enter your password if you have one.

Unlike NetWare, LANtastic does not automatically run a login procedure when you log in. The commands that would be placed in a NetWare login procedure are placed instead in the STARTNET.BAT batch file.

In case you're interested, the command in STARTNET.BAT that actually logs you in to the network is NET LOGIN. A NET LOGIN command includes the name of the server you want to log in to, preceded by two backslashes, and your user ID:

```
NET LOGIN \\WARD BEAVE
```

NET LOGIN prompts you to type your password.

- ✔ In most LANtastic networks, each computer's AUTOEXEC.BAT file is modi-fied so that it automatically runs the STARTNET batch file. That way, you're logged in to the network automatically when you start your computer.

- ✔ You can put your password directly on the NET LOGIN command in STARTNET.BAT, but you shouldn't. The whole point of a password is that you have to remember it because it's not written down anywhere. If you add it to your STARTNET.BAT file, anyone can log in to the network using your user ID.

- ✔ I didn't make up the rule that says you have to precede the server name with two backslashes. Blame someone else if you want, but get used to it. This goofy notation for referring to network servers is pretty common in the networking world.

Logging in with Windows for Workgroups

If your network uses Windows for Workgroups, you are automatically asked to enter your Logon name (same as user ID) and password when you start Windows for Workgroups.

✔ Windows for Workgroups doesn't have login scripts that are run automatically whenever you log in. However, Windows for Workgroups does let you set up network connections that specify "Reconnect at startup," which means that you are automatically connected to these network disk drives and printers whenever you log in. (Connections to network drives are made using File Manager, and printer connections are established using Print Manager.)

✔ You can log off and log back on to the network at any time by using the Control Panel.

Network Disk Drives

Before Network (B.N.), your computer probably had just one disk drive, known as drive C:. Maybe two, C: and D:. Either way, these drives are physically located inside your PC. They are *local drives*.

Now that you're on a network, you probably have access to one or more *network drives*, drives that are not physically located inside your PC, but are located instead in one of the other PCs on the network.

Just like local drives, network drives are accessed using drive letters. However, the drive letters used for network drives aren't necessarily assigned in alphabetical order (C, D, E, ...). For example, your computer might have a local C: drive and access to two network drives: F and M. Or Q and W. Or whatever.

Network drives have directories and files just like any other drive. Depending on how your network is set up, you might have complete freedom to use the drive in any way you want, so you can copy files to or from it, delete files on it, create or remove directories on it, and so on. Or your access to the drive might be limited to certain directories, or maybe you can copy files to or from the drive, but you can't create or remove directories.

Every network is set up differently, so I can't tell you what your network drive letters are or what restrictions are in place for accessing your network drives. But your network guru can tell you, and you can write it down here so you won't have to ask him or her again when you forget:

Drive letter for first network drive:

What I'm supposed to use it for:

What I can or can't do with it:

Drive letter for second network drive:

What I'm supposed to use it for:

What I can or can't do with it:

Drive letter for third network drive:

What I'm supposed to use it for:

What I can or can't do with it:

(If you have more than three network drives, you'll have to make your own chart. Sorry. We had to cut costs somewhere. Write your senator.)

✔ Assigning a drive letter to a network drive is called *mapping the drive* or *linking the drive* by network nerds. "Drive H is mapped to a network drive," they'll say. The commands required to map your network drives had darn well better be placed in your login script (Novell), STARTNET.BAT (LANtastic), or equivalent start-up file. They don't pay you enough to make you fuss with these commands yourself.

✔ The drive letter you use to map a drive on a network server doesn't have to be the same drive letter that the server uses to access the file. For example, suppose you use drive H to link to the server's C drive. This is confusing, so have another cup of coffee. In this scenario, drive H on your computer is the same drive as drive C on the server computer. This shell game is necessary for one simple reason: You can't access the server's C drive as drive C because your computer has it's own drive C! You have to pick an unused drive letter and *map* or *link* it to the server's C drive.

✔ If you're not sure what network drives are available to you, an easy way to find out is to run the DOS Shell. Just type **DOSSHELL** at the DOS prompt and look at the row of drive icons it displays. Network drives have a special icon that says "Net" in the middle of the drive.

✔ If you use Novell NetWare, you can find out what network drives are available by typing **MAP** at a DOS prompt. With LANtastic, type **NET SHOW**.

✔ Network drive letters don't have to be assigned the same way for every computer on the network. For example, a network drive that is assigned drive letter H on your computer might be assigned drive letter Q on someone else's computer. In that case, your drive H and the other computer's drive Q are really the same drive. This can be very confusing. If your network is set up this way, put pepper in your network administrator's coffee.

✔ Most networks can use a trick whereby a single directory on a network drive can be made to look like an entire drive on your computer. This trick is often used to give each network user a little "private" space on a network drive. For example, June, Wally, and Beave might each have access to private space on Ward's computer as network drive P. June, Wally, and the Beave think of the P drive as an entire drive, but in reality, June's P drive is really a directory named \JUNE; Wally's P drive is a directory named \WALLY; and Beaver's P drive is a directory named \BEAVE. June, Wally, and the Beave cannot access files created in one another's P drive.

Four Good Uses for a Network Drive

Now that you know what network drives are available to you, you might be wondering what you're supposed to do with them. Here are four good uses for a network drive.

1. Use it to store files everybody needs

A network drive is a good place to store files that more than one user need to access. Without a network, you have to store a copy of the file on everyone's computer, and you have to worry about keeping the copies synchronized (which can't be done, no matter how hard you try). Or you can keep the file on a diskette and pass it around. Or you can keep the file on one computer and play musical chairs — whenever someone needs to use the file, he or she goes to the computer that contains it.

With a network, you can keep one copy of the file on a network drive and everyone can access it.

There is an inherent problem with storing a shared file on a network drive, and that's that you have to make sure two people don't try to update the file at the same time. For example, suppose you retrieve a spreadsheet file and start to work on it, when another user retrieves the same file a few minutes later. That user won't see the changes you've made so far because you haven't saved the file back to disk yet. Now, suppose you finish making your changes and you save the file while the other user is still staring at the screen. Guess what happens when the other user saves his or her changes a few minutes later? All of the changes you made are gone, lost forever in the Black Hole of Unprotected Concurrent Access.

The root cause of this problem is that these programs do not "reserve" the file while they are working on it. As a result, other programs are not prevented from working on the file at the same time. The result is a jumbled mess. Fortunately, most newer application programs tend to be more tolerant of networks, so they *do* reserve files when you open them. These programs are much safer for network use.

2. Use it to store your own files

You can also use a network drive as an extension of your own disk storage. For example, if you have a puny 30MB drive with almost no free space, but there's 600MB of free space on a network drive, you have plenty of disk space. Just store your files on the network drive!

- Using the network drive for your own files works best if the network drive is set up for private storage that other users can't access. That way, you don't have to worry about the nosy guy down in Accounting who likes to poke around in other people's files.

- Don't overuse the network drive. 600MB might seem like a lot of disk storage, but if your network has 20 users, that's only 30MB each.

- Before you store personal files on a network drive, make sure you have permission. A note from your mom will do.

3. Use it as a pit stop for files on their way to other users

"Hey, Wally, could you send me a copy of last month's baseball stats?"

"Sure, Beave." But how? If the baseball stats file resides on your local drive, how does Wally send a copy of the file to Beaver's computer? The easiest way is for Wally to copy the file to a network drive. Then, Beaver can copy the file to his local drive.

- ✔ Don't forget to delete files you've saved to the network drive after they've been picked up! Otherwise, the network drive will quickly fill up with unnecessary files!

- ✔ If you use Windows File Manager to copy a file to a network, don't forget that dragging a file from one spot to another *moves* the file. That means that the file is copied, then your original is deleted. If you want to copy the file rather than move it, hold down the Ctrl key while you drag the file's icon.

- ✔ It's a good idea to create a directory on the network drive just for holding files enroute to other users. Call this directory PITSTOP or something similar to suggest its function.

- ✔ Some electronic mail packages also let you deliver files to other users. The advantage of sending a file via e-mail is that you don't have to worry about details like where to leave the file on the server and who's responsibility it is to delete the file.

4. Use it to back up your local disk

If there's enough disk space on the file server, you can use it to store backup copies of the files on your hard disk. Suppose that all of your data files are stored on your C: drive in subdirectories under a directory named \DATA, and that F is a network drive that contains a directory named WALLY, your user ID. To back up all of your data files to the network, you would issue this command at a DOS prompt:

```
C:\XCOPY \DATA\*.* F:\WALLY /S
```

The /S switch tells the XCOPY command to include all of the files in subdirectories under the \DATA directory in the copy.

Obviously, copying all of your data files to the network drive can quickly fill up the network drive. You'd better check with the network administrator before you do it.

Accessing a Network Drive

Suppose you have one or more network drives available — for the sake of argument, let's say you have two, and they're assigned drive letters F and G. How can you access them to create or retrieve files?

The following sections look briefly at the techniques you can use to access network data from the DOS prompt and from three popular application programs: WordPerfect, Lotus 1-2-3, and dBASE IV. These three programs are typical of how other word processing, spreadsheet, and database programs handle network data.

Accessing a network drive from DOS

You can access a network drive from the DOS command prompt by using its drive letter just as you use drive letters for local drives. Here's an example of a command that copies some files from a directory on network drive F to a directory on a local C: drive:

```
C:\>COPY F:\WALLY\BSTAT59.DBF C:\TEMP\*.*
```

Here's an example of a command that deletes a file on network drive G:

```
C:\>DEL G:\JUNE\MEAT.LOF
```

To switch to a network drive, just type the drive letter followed by a colon.

You can also run a program that resides on a network drive. For example, these commands show how you might run WordPerfect 5.1 from a network drive:

```
C:\>F:
F:\>CD \WP51
F:\WP51\>WP
```

(I assume here that WordPerfect 5.1 is installed in the directory named \WP51. If you installed WordPerfect into a different directory, or if you're using a different version of WordPerfect, you'll have to adjust.)

Remember, of course, that you must have a network license for a program to legally run it from a network drive.

✔ Be careful whenever you use commands that delete files, such as DEL or the DOS 6 DELTREE command. Make sure that you don't accidentally delete files that don't belong to you!

✔ There are a few DOS commands that you can't use with network drives, most notably CHKDSK and the new DOS 6.2 ScanDisk command.

Accessing a network drive from WordPerfect

There are several ways to retrieve WordPerfect document files that reside on a network drive. WordPerfect looks for document files in whatever directory was current when you started the program. So the easiest way to access files in a directory on a network drive is to make that directory current before starting WordPerfect:

```
C:\>F:
F:\>cd \LETTERS
F:\LETTERS\>C:\WP51\WP
```

Here, I first switch to network drive F, then make the \LETTERS directory current. Then, I start WordPerfect, specifying the drive and directory that contains the WP program file in the command.

✔ You can temporarily direct Retrieve (Shift+F8) or List Files (F5) to a network drive just by specifying the network drive letter after you press the function key.

✔ If you retrieve a file that someone else is currently editing, WordPerfect will retrieve the file in read-only mode. The filename at the bottom of the screen will be displayed in brackets to let you know this. For example:

```
[JUNREC.WP]
```

When a document is retrieved in read-only mode, you can edit it but you cannot overwrite the existing file with your changes. When you press the Save key, WordPerfect requires you to enter a file name so your changes are saved to a new file. (If you type the name of the file that you retrieved, you'll get the dreaded Access denied message.)

Accessing a network drive from Lotus 1-2-3

Accessing network drives from Lotus 1-2-3 is easy; all you do is use the network drive letter whenever you use one of the File commands to save or retrieve files.

1-2-3 uses a feature called *File reservations* to make sure that several users don't modify the same spreadsheet file at the same time. When you retrieve a file from a network drive, 1-2-3 reserves the file. Then, any other users who retrieve the file before you release the reservation will see the message Retrieve without reservation?, meaning that they can retrieve the file but they won't be able to save changes to it. The reservation is released when you save the file or retrieve another file.

If you get the Retrieve without reservation? message when you open a file, you should have some reservations of your own about proceeding. If you agree to open the file without a reservation, you won't be able to save any changes you make to the file using the same filename; you'll have to specify a new filename when you save the file. I suggest you retrieve the file without a reservation only if you don't plan on changing the file.

Accessing a network drive from dBASE IV

The popular database program *dBASE IV* lets you access database files that reside on network drives without worrying about other users accessing the same files at the same time. Unlike *WordPerfect* and *Lotus 1-2-3*, which lock an entire file when you retrieve it from a network drive, dBASE IV protects the individual records in a database file from simultaneous updates. So although several users can access the same file at the same time, they cannot access the same individual records within a shared file.

For example, suppose both Wally and the Beaver want to update their baseball card database file at the same time. dBASE IV will let them do that, provided they don't try to update the same data record at the same time. Wally could update the data record for Babe Ruth while the Beaver updates the record for Joe DiMaggio, but Wally would have to wait until the Beaver is finished before he could update Joe DiMaggio's record.

Using a Network Printer

Using a network printer is much like using a network disk drive. The network uses smoke and mirrors to trick your application programs into believing that the network printer is actually attached to your own computer as a local printer. Once the smoke and mirrors are in place, you use your progam's regular printing functions to print to the network printer.

Printing on a network printer is not exactly the same as printing on a local printer, though. When you print on a local printer, you are the only one who is using that printer. But when you print to a network printer, you are sharing that printer with other network users. This complicates things in several ways:

- If several users print to the network printer at the same time, the network has to keep the print jobs separate from one another. If it didn't, the result would be a jumbled mess, with your 35-page report being mixed up with the payroll checks. That would be bad. Fortunately, the network takes care of this, using a fancy feature called *print spooling*.

- It never fails that when I get in line at the hardware store, the person in front of me is trying to buy something that doesn't have a product code on it. I end up standing there for hours waiting for someone in Plumbing to pick up the phone for a price check. Network printing can be like that. If someone sends a two-hour print job to the printer before you send your half-page memo, you'll have to wait. Network printing works on a first-come, first-served basis.

- Before you were forced at gunpoint to use the network, your computer probably had just one printer attached to it. Now, you may have access to a local printer and several network printers. You may want to print some documents on your cheap (oops, I mean local) dot-matrix printer, but use the network laser printer for really important stuff. To do that, you'll have to learn how to use your application programs' functions for switching printers.

- Network printing is really too important a subject to squeeze into this chapter. So the next chapter goes into it in more detail.

Logging Off the Network

When you are finished using the network, you should *log off*. Logging off the network makes the network drives and printers unavailable. Your computer is still physically connected to the network (unless you cut the network cable with pruning sheers — Bad idea! Don't do it!), but the network and its resources are unavailable to you.

- When you turn off your computer, you are automatically logged off of the network. When you start your computer, you'll have to log in again. (If your login command is included in your AUTOEXEC.BAT file, this is automatic.)

- It's a good idea to log off the network if you're going to leave your computer unattended for a while. As long as your computer is logged in to the network, anyone can use it to access the network. And since they'll do it under your user-id, you'll get the blame for any damage they do.

- If you use Novell NetWare, log off by typing the command **LOGOUT**.

✔ If you use LANtastic, use the NET LOGOUT command. To log completely off the network, use this command:

```
NET LOGOUT *
```

This logs you off of all servers. To log off of a particular server, but remain logged in to other servers, type the name of the server:

```
NET LOGOUT \\WARD
```

The preceding command logs you off the server named WARD. (Don't forget the two backslashes before the server name.)

✔ If you use Windows for Workgroups, you can log off by double-clicking the Network icon in the Control Panel, selecting the Network Settings dialog box, clicking the Logon button to pop up the Logon Settings dialog box, then clicking the Log Off button. Click. Click. Click. Click. Isn't Windows great?

✔ You can also log off by exiting Windows.

The 5th Wave
By Rich Tennant

"SOMEONE KEEPS GOING INTO MY PERSONAL FILE. I'D SURE AS HECK LIKE TO FIND OUT WHO USES THE PASSWORD 'PEANUT-BREATH'."

Chapter 3

Using a Network Printer

● ●

In This Chapter

▶ Why network printing is such a big deal

▶ Setting up your computer to use a network printer

▶ Printing on a network printer

▶ Playing with the print queue

▶ Stupid printer tricks

● ●

*I*f there's one thing you'll come to hate about using a network, it's using a network printer. Oh, for the good ol' days when your slow but simple dot-matrix printer sat on your desk right next to your computer for you and nobody else but you to use. Now you have to share the printer down the hall. It may be a neat printer, but now you can't watch it all the time to make sure that it's working.

Now you send an 80-page report to the printer, and when you go check on it 20 minutes later, you discover that it hasn't printed yet because someone else sent an 800-page report before you. Or the printer's been sitting there for 20 minutes because it ran out of paper. Or your report just disappeared into Network-Network Land.

What a pain. This chapter can help you out. It'll clue you in to the secrets of network printing and give you some Network Pixie Dust (NPD) to help you find those lost print jobs.

What's So Special about Network Printing?

Why is network printing such a big deal? In the last chapter, we talked about sharing network disk drives and saw that it's really pretty simple. After everything is set up right, there's not much more to using a network drive than knowing which drive letter is assigned to it.

It would be great if sharing a printer were just as easy. But it isn't.

Ports and printer configuration

Let's start with some printing basics. A *port* is a connection on the back of your computer. You use ports to connect devices to the computer. You plug one end of a cable into the port and plug the other end of the cable into a connector on the back of the device you want to connect. Most computers have only one device connected via a port: a printer. Some also have a mouse, and some have a modem.

Ports come in two varieties: parallel and serial. *Parallel* ports are the type most often used for printers. Certain types of older printers used serial port connections, but most of these printers have long since been used to make beehives. The *serial* port is used nowadays mostly to connect a mouse or a modem to the computer.

- ✔ Most computers have one parallel port and two serial ports. The maximum limit is three parallel ports and four serial ports.

- ✔ DOS assigns the names LPT1, LPT2, and LPT3 to the parallel ports (*LPT* stands for "Line Printer"). The first parallel port (and the only parallel port on most computers) is LPT1. LPT2 and LPT3 are the second and third parallel ports.

- ✔ LPT1 has a pseudonym: PRN. The names LPT1 and PRN both refer to the first parallel port and can be used interchangeably.

- ✔ COM1, COM2, COM3, and COM4 are the names DOS uses for the four serial ports. (*COM* stands for "communications," a subject the people who came up with names like LPT1 and COM1 should have studied more closely.)

- ✔ For a program to be able to print, it must be *configured* for your printer. Basically, that means it has to know what type of printer you're using and what port the printer is connected to. For example, a configuration like "Binford LaserBlaster 450P on LPT1" means that you have a Binford LaserBlaster model 450P printer attached to your computer via the first parallel port (LPT1).

- ✔ If your computer has more than one printer, each is attached to a separate port. Then you have to configure your application programs for each printer and select the printer you want to use whenever you print something.

Please skip this explanation of parallel and serial ports

Parallel and serial ports use different methods to send individual bytes of data from one end of the cable to the other. A parallel port has eight wires, one for each of the bits that make up a byte (well, it really has more than eight wires, but we'll be good citizens and not ask too many questions). Parallel ports use all eight wires to send data one byte at a time.

A serial port is like a funnel that's only wide enough to let one bit through at a time. Instead of sending all eight bits through at once, a serial port forces the bits to go through the cable single file.

Redirecting Printer Output

When you use an application program's Print command to send output to a network printer, the application program assumes it is sending output to a local printer connected to one of the computer's printer ports. Ha! Sucker! Without your program even realizing it, the network software jumps in, intercepts the print output, and redirects it to a network printer.

Figure 3-1 shows how John Madden might explain network printer redirection by using his famous electronic chalkboard. The application program (WordPerfect, Lotus 1-2-3, or whatever) sends output to a printer port. Before it gets there, the network software comes out of nowhere and — bam! — intercepts the output and hands it off to the network print queue.

- Because DOS supports three printer ports (LPT1, LPT2, and LPT3), you can create up to two or three printer redirections at once. For example, you can redirect LPT1 to a network laser printer and LPT2 to a network dot-matrix printer. To switch between these printers, you must use your application program's printer configuration commands. For example, to print a Lotus 1-2-3 spreadsheet on the network dot-matrix printer, you configure Lotus 1-2-3 so that it prints to LPT2.

- If your computer has a local printer attached to it, the local printer is probably set up as LPT1. The network printers will be LPT2 and LPT3.

- The command used to set up the network printer you use most of the time should be placed in your AUTOEXEC.BAT file. That way, your primary network printer will be set up for you automatically. I'll show you how to use those commands later in this chapter.

✔ A common way to handle network printing is to always print to LPT1. Then you set up batch files that redirect LPT1 to the appropriate network printer or to the local printer. Before you start an application program, you run the batch file to choose the printer you want to use. For example, if you have a local printer, a network laser printer named LASER, and a network dot-matrix printer named DOTTY, you can create three batch files, named LOCAL.BAT, LASER.BAT, and DOTTY.BAT. Then you run one of these batch files to select the printer you want to use. You'll see examples of these batch files for Novell NetWare and LANtastic later in this chapter.

✔ *The Last Action Hero* is an example of a movie that should have been redirected.

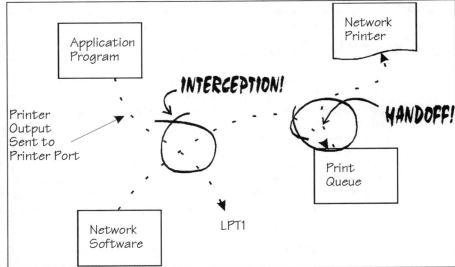

Figure 3-1:
How John
Madden
might
explain
printer
redirection.

Spooling and the print queue

Printers are far and away the slowest part of any computer. As far as your computer's CPU is concerned, it takes the printer an eternity to print a single line of information. To keep the CPU from twiddling its microscopic thumbs, computer geeks invented *spooling*.

Spooling is really pretty simple. Suppose that you use an application program like WordPerfect to print a 20-page report. Without spooling, WordPerfect sends the report directly to the printer. You have to sit there and daydream until the printer finishes printing the report, which takes maybe ten minutes.

With spooling, WordPerfect doesn't send the report directly to the printer. Instead, WordPerfect sends it to a disk file that lives on a network server computer. Because the network server's disk drive is so much faster than the printer, you have to wait only a few seconds for the print job to finish.

Well, that's not the whole story. After the report has been sent to the network server, you can continue to use WordPerfect for other work. But your print job hasn't actually printed yet. The print job isn't really finished until the network server has copied it from the temporary disk file to an actual printer. The network server does that automatically. That's what spooling is all about.

Don't forget that you have to share the network printer with other users. If someone else sends a print job to the printer before you send yours, your print job has to wait in line before the server can print it. That's where the *print queue* comes in. Print queue is the network nerd term for the line your print job has to wait in while other print jobs that got in line before it are printed. Your print job won't actually be printed until it gets to the front of the line; that is, until it gets to the front of the queue.

- ✔ The people who invented network printing way back in the 60s thought it would be uncool to call the line that print jobs wait in a "line." The Beatles and anything British were popular back then, so they picked the British-sounding word "queue" instead.

- ✔ Although it's rude, it's possible to cut to the front of the queue. You'll learn how later in this chapter. This is a good thing to know, especially if you're the *only one* who knows.

- ✔ Brits always use too many letters. They like to throw extra ones into words like "colour." The word "queue" is pronounced like "cue," not "cue-you." "Cue-you" is spelled queueue and is often used by Certified Network Dummies as an insult.

What spool stands for, as if you care

Believe it or not, the word *spool* is actually an acronym — a five-letter acronym, or EETLA ("*Ex*panded *E*xtended *T*hree-*L*etter *A*cronym") to be precise. Brace yourself, because this acronym is really nerdy: Spool stands for "*S*imultaneous *P*eripheral *O*utput *O*n-*L*ine."

Remember, you read it here first.

What is a print job?

I've used the term *print job* several times without explaining what it means, so you're probably already mad at me. I'd better explain before it's too late. A *print job* is a collection of printed pages that should be kept together, treated as a set. If you print a 20-page document from WordPerfect, the entire 20-page printout is a single print job. Every time you use WordPerfect's Print command or 1-2-3's Print command or any other application program's print command, you create a print job.

How does the network know when one print job ends and the next one begins? Because application programs that know about networks send a special code at the end of each Print command that says, "This is the end of the print job. Everything up to this point belongs together, and anything I print after this point belongs to my next print job."

Metaphor alert! You can think of this code as kind of like the little stick you use at the grocery-store checkout stand to separate your groceries from the groceries that belong to the person in line behind you. The stick tells the clerk that all the groceries in front of the stick belong together, and the groceries behind the stick belong to the next customer.

✔ Not all application programs know enough about network printing to put the stick down behind their print jobs. These programs just stop when they finish printing; they don't send the special code. When you print to the network with one of these programs, the network waits for a certain amount of time — usually ten seconds — before deciding that a print job has been completed. This isn't a perfect solution, but it works most of the time. I'll show you how to change this *time-out* setting later in this chapter.

✔ When you print to a network, you can do lots of neat stuff with print jobs. You can tell the print server to print more than one copy of your job, to print a full page *banner* at the beginning of the job to make it easy to find in a stack of print jobs, or to stop printing when your job gets to the front of the line so that you can change from plain paper to preprinted invoices or checks. You'll learn how to do these tricks later in this chapter.

Setting Up Printer Redirection

The commands you use to set up redirection for a network printer vary, depending on the network you use.

Redirecting printer output with Novell Netware

If your network is Novell NetWare, you set up redirection for a network printer by using the CAPTURE command. This command tells the NetWare software to capture everything sent to a particular printer port and redirect it to a network print queue.

Here's a typical CAPTURE command:

```
CAPTURE Q=LJET TI=10
```

This command redirects any printer output you send to LPT1 to a print queue named LJET. TI=10 sets the time-out value to ten seconds. If your program stops sending output to the printer for ten seconds, NetWare assumes the print job is finished.

If you have a local printer attached to your LPT1 port, you should set up LPT2 as a network printer. Here's a CAPTURE command that does that:

```
CAPTURE L=2 Q=LJET TI=10
```

The L=2 tells CAPTURE to redirect LPT2.

- ✔ A CAPTURE command should be set up in your AUTOEXEC.BAT file, after the LOGIN command. That way, your network printer is set up for you automatically when you start your computer.

- ✔ Sometimes, five seconds isn't long enough for the time-out value. If your reports are being broken apart into several print jobs, try a higher time-out value. If you omit TI altogether, time-out checking is turned off. Then your programs can take as long as they want to create the output.

- ✔ To cancel printer redirection, use the ENDCAP command. Good news! ENDCAP doesn't have any parameters, switches, or other adornments! Just say **ENDCAP**.

- ✔ CAPTURE has an AUTOENDCAP option that automatically releases output to the network printer whenever you exit an application. Don't confuse this option with the ENDCAP command, which not only releases any pending printer output to the network, but cancels printer redirection as well.

- ✔ Suppose that you have a local printer and two network printers: a laser printer named LASER and a dot-matrix printer named DOTTY. To easily switch between these printers, create three batch files, named LOCAL.BAT, LASER.BAT, and DOTTY.BAT. The LOCAL.BAT file should contain this command:

```
ENDCAP
```

LASER.BAT should contain this command:

```
CAPTURE Q=LASER TI=10
```

And DOTTY.BAT should contain this command:

```
CAPTURE Q=DOTTY TI=10
```

To switch to the local printer, just type **LOCAL** at the DOS prompt. To switch to a network printer, type **LASER** or **DOTTY**.

Redirecting printer output with LANtastic

If your network is LANtastic, you set up printer redirection by using the NET USE command. This command tells LANtastic to use a particular network printer whenever you send output to a printer.

Here's a typical NET USE command to set up a network printer:

```
NET USE LPT1 \\WARD\LASER
```

This command redirects any printer output you send to LPT1 to a printer named LASER on the server named WARD.

LANtastic uses a separate commmand, NET LPT, to set network printing options such as the time-out value. For example, the command,

```
NET LPT TIMEOUT=10
```

sets the printer time-out to 10 seconds. If your application program stops sending data to the printer for 10 seconds, LANtastic assumes the print job has finished. If you set the time-out value to 0, time-out testing is disabled altogether. (For programs that automatically signal the end of a print job, the printer time-out doesn't matter.)

- ✔ A NET USE command should be set up in your STARTNET.BAT file. That way, your network printer is set up for you automatically when you access the network.

- ✔ Sometimes five seconds isn't long enough for the time-out value. If your reports are being broken apart into several print jobs, try a higher time-out value.

✔ To cancel printer redirection, use the NET UNUSE command, like this:

```
NET UNUSE LPT1
```

✔ Suppose that you have a local printer and two network printers: a laser printer named LASER and a dot-matrix printer named DOTTY. To easily switch between these printers, create three batch files, named LOCAL.BAT, LASER.BAT, and DOTTY.BAT. The LOCAL.BAT file should contain this command:

```
NET UNUSE LPT1
```

LASER.BAT should contain this command:

```
NET USE LPT1 \\WARD\LASER
```

And DOTTY.BAT should contain this command:

```
NET USE LPT1 \\WARD\DOTTY
```

To switch to the local printer, just type **LOCAL** at the DOS prompt. To switch to a network printer, type **LASER** or **DOTTY**.

Setting up a Windows for Workgroups printer

Network printing for Windows for Workgroups is pretty slick. When you configure a network printer at your workstation, you tell Windows for Workgroups that the printer is a network printer, and you supply the name of the server the printer is attached to.

✔ You configure Windows for Workgroups for network printing by clicking the Printers icon in the Control Panel or by choosing Printer Setup from the Print Manager's Options menu.

✔ You can speed up network printing by bypassing the Print Manager on your workstation. That way, your programs send output directly to the Print Manager spooler on the computer to which the network printer is attached. If you don't bypass Print Manager on your computer, your print output is spooled twice: first by Print Manager on your computer, and then by Print Manager on the printer's computer.

To bypass Print Manager, choose Background Printing from the Print Manager's Options menu and check the Send Documents Directly to Network box.

Sending Output to a Network Printer

After your computer's printer port has been redirected to a network printer, printing to the network printer is easy: All you do is use your application program's normal commands for printing. The only difference is that you have to make sure that the print output is sent to the printer port you've redirected to the network. If you've redirected port LPT1 to a network printer, this isn't a problem because most application programs are set up to print to LPT1 by default.

If you have a local printer attached to LPT1 and you've redirected LPT2 or LPT3 to a network printer, you must use whatever commands your application program provides for sending output to LPT2 or LPT3 rather than to LPT1. Each application program does this differently. I'll show you how it works with WordPerfect, Lotus 1-2-3, and dBASE IV. For other programs, you're on your own.

Switching to the network printer with WordPerfect

WordPerfect lets you manage printers from the print menu. To access it, start WordPerfect and then press Shift+F7. Press S to select the printer to use. WordPerfect displays a list of the printers that have been configured previously. If you're lucky, the network printer you want to use is already on this list. Move the cursor to it and press S to select it. Then press F7 to return to the document.

If you're down on your luck, you have to add the network printer to WordPerfect's printer list. Press A for Additional Printers, and then press L to list the available printer drivers. If the correct printer driver for the network printer appears in the list, select it and then set its Port option to the printer port you redirected to the network. If the printer driver for the network printer isn't displayed, you have to find the WordPerfect installation disks (they're probably tossed in the back of a drawer somewhere; good luck finding them) to install the driver.

- ✔ As a lowly network user, configuring WordPerfect for a network printer isn't really your job. If your network geek hasn't done it already, offer him or her a large bag of Cheetos. But make sure that he washes his hands before touching your keyboard.

- ✔ If you're crazy enough to have learned how to create and use WordPerfect macros, switching to the network printer and back is a good candidate for macro-ization. For example, you can make a macro named NETPRT, which selects the network printer, and another macro named LOCALPRT, which selects the local printer. Then assign these macros to key combinations you think you'll remember (like Shift+F12 for the NETPRT and Ctrl+F12 for LOCALPRT).

  If you don't already know how to do this, this isn't the place to find out. Sorry.

✔ The term for that orange gunk that gets on your fingers when you eat Cheetos is *Cheetum*.

Switching to the network printer with Lotus 1-2-3

With Lotus 1-2-3, switching from a local printer to a network printer can get you all tied up in knots. Assuming that 1-2-3 has been configured with the printer drivers required for your local printer and your network printer, you must change both the printer name and the printer port to switch from the local printer to the network printer and back again. Both settings are changed from the /Worksheet Global Default Printers menu. Type **/WGDP** to get there.

To change the printer name, press N. A list of defined printers appears; pick the one that represents the network printer you want to use.

To change the port, press I (for Interface) and then pick option 5, 6, or 7 for DOS Device LPT1, LPT2, or LPT3, depending on which device you've redirected to the network printer.

To switch from the network printer back to your local printer, you again must access the /Worksheet Global Default Printer menu. Use the Name command to select the printer name and the Interface command to select the local printer port (usually option 1, Parallel 1).

✔ Lotus 1-2-3 provides two ways to access the printer ports. Options 1 and 3 access Parallel 1 and Parallel 2, and options 5-8 access DOS Device LPT1 through DOS Device LPT2. Options 1 and 5 both send output to LPT1, and 3 and 6 both send output to LPT2. There is a significant technical difference between how options 1 and 3 versus options 5-8 work. You don't want to know what the difference is, but you *do* want to know that options 5-8 are best for network printers, and 1 and 3 are best for local printers.

✔ If the network printer you want to use doesn't show up on the list when you pick the Names command from the /Worksheet Global Default Printer menu, get help. Unless you're a Lotus wiz, you don't want to contend with installing a printer device driver for 1-2-3 if you can possibly avoid it.

Switching to the network printer with dBASE IV

With dBASE IV, you use the SET PRINTER command to change the destination for printed output. You issue this command from the infamous dot prompt.

Suppose that a local printer is attached to LPT1 and that LPT2 is redirected to a network printer. dBASE IV print output is sent to LPT1 by default, so no action is required to print to the local printer. To send output to the network printer, you use a SET PRINTER command, like this:

```
SET PRINTER TO LPT2
```

If you later want to revert to the local printer, you use this command:

```
SET PRINTER TO LPT1
```

Then output is sent to LPT1.

Database reports can take forever and a day to prepare, especially if more than one file is accessed. You may have to increase the time-out value or disable the time-out feature altogether.

Playing with the Print Queue

After you've sent your output to a network printer, you usually don't have to worry about it. You just go to the network printer and *voilà!*, your output is there waiting for you.

That's what happens in the ideal world. In the real world where you and I live, all sorts of things can happen to your print job between the time you send it to the network printer and the time it actually is printed:

- ✔ You discover that someone else already sent a 50-trillion page report ahead of you that isn't expected to finish printing until the national debt is completely paid off.

- ✔ The price of framis valves goes up $2 each, rendering foolish the recommendations you made in the report.

- ✔ Your boss calls and tells you that his brother-in-law will be attending the meeting, and won't you please print an extra copy of the proposal for him. Oh, and a photocopy won't do. Originals only, please.

- ✔ You decide to take lunch, so you don't want the output to be printed until you get back.

Fortunately, your print job isn't totally beyond your control just because you've already sent it to the network printer. By using your network software's features for managing the print queue, you can change the status of jobs you've already sent. You can change the number of copies to be printed, hold a job so that it won't be printed until you say so, or cancel a job altogether.

You can probably make your network print jobs do other tricks, too — like shake hands, roll over, and play dead. But the basic tricks — hold, cancel, and print multiple copies — are enough to get you started.

NetWare print queue tricks: the PCONSOLE command

If your network is Novell NetWare, you use the PCONSOLE command to perform print queue tricks. You don't have to go to the file server to use the PCONSOLE command; just type **PCONSOLE** at the DOS prompt on your own computer and press Enter. PCONSOLE displays the menu shown in Figure 3-2.

Figure 3-2:
The
NetWare
Available
Options
menu.

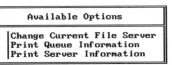

Choose Print Queue Information, and the menu shown in Figure 3-3 appears.

Figure 3-3:
The Print
Queue
Information
menu.

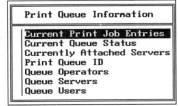

Choose Current Print Job Entries, and PCONSOLE displays a list of print queues. Choose the one you redirected print output to, and you see a list of all the jobs waiting in the queue.

To change the status of a print job, highlight the job you want to change and press Enter. PCONSOLE displays a screen like the one in Figure 3-4.

From this display, you can:

- Place a User Hold on the job, which holds the job in the queue until you or someone with operator or supervisor rights releases it.

- Place an Operator Hold on the job, which holds the job in the queue until an operator releases it.

🖙 Change the number of copies to be printed.

🖙 Change the job's position in the queue by typing a new value for the Service Sequence field.

🖙 Specify a special form for the print job, like invoices or checks. If you do that, NetWare prompts the operator to mount the correct forms in the printer before it prints the job.

🖙 Tell NetWare to print a banner page at the start of the print job. This makes it easier to separate print jobs from one another.

🖙 Do lots of other stuff, which you probably won't ever worry about.

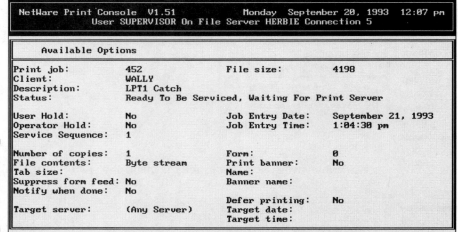

Figure 3-4:
PCONSOLE
displays the
status of a
print job.

LANtastic print queue tricks

To perform printer tricks with LANtastic, you use the NET command. Type **NET** and then select Printer and Queue Management from the menu. You see a list of servers currently active; select the one you sent the print job to, and you see a list of the files currently in that server's print queue. For each print job, NET displays the sequence number, the name of the printer the job was sent to, the status of the job, and the name of the user who sent the job.

To change a job in the queue, highlight it and press Enter. The menu shown in Figure 3-5 appears.

Figure 3-5:
The
LANtastic
Queue
Control
Menu.

```
Queue Control

Show     More information about selected entry
Delete   Remove selected entry from queue
Hold     Suspend despooling of selected entry
Release  Allow selected entry to be despooled
View     View contents of selected entry
Copy     Copy selected entry to file
Rush     Gives queue entry top priority
```

This menu lets you control the queue entry in the following ways:

- ✔ **Show** displays more information about the queue entry, including the time the print job was created, the size of the print file, and the number of copies to be printed.

- ✔ **Delete** removes the print job from the queue.

- ✔ **Hold** places a hold on the print job. It won't be printed until you release it.

- ✔ **Release** releases a previously held print job.

- ✔ **View** displays the contents of the print job. This is handy if you're not sure that you've selected the right job.

- ✔ **Copy** copies the print job to a file. This is useful if you think you may want to print the job again later.

- ✔ **Rush** lets the print job cut to the front of the line. The other print jobs in the queue may whine a bit, but who said life is fair?

Printer tricks with Windows for Workgroups

With Windows for Workgroups, you control network printing by using a beefed-up version of the familiar Print Manager. Controlling a print job in the Print Manager queue is easy. You can find the commands for manipulating print jobs in the Print Manager's Document menu.

As expected, Windows Print Manager uses slightly different terminology to describe network printing functions. A print job isn't a "print job," it's a *document*. You don't "hold" a print job, you *pause* it. Get used to it. It's the Windows Way.

- ✔ To hold a print job so that it won't be printed until it's released, highlight the job and use the Document menu's Pause Printing command.

- ✔ To release a held print job, use the Document menu's Resume Printing command.

> ✔ To cut to the front of the line, use the Document menu's Move Document Up command. Use the Move Document Down command to move toward the end of the queue.
>
> ✔ In keeping with the Windows Way, you also can activate these commands by clicking buttons that have pictures, which resemble the intended functions about as much as a Picasso represents real life.

What to Do When the Printer Jams

The only three sure bets in life are (1) *Rocky* will always be Sylvester Stallone's best movie, (2) the 49ers will never be the same without Joe Montana, and (3) the printer will always jam shortly after your job reaches the front of the queue.

What do you do when you walk in on your network printer while it's printing all 133 pages of your report on the same line?

1. **Start by yelling "Fire!" No one will save you if you yell "Printer!"**

2. **Find the printer's on-line button and press it.**

   This should take the printer off-line so that the server will stop sending information to it and the printer will stop. This doesn't cure anything, but it stops the noise. If you must, turn the printer off.

3. **Pull out the jammed paper and reinsert it into the printer. Nicely.**

4. **Restart the job that was printing, from the beginning.**

   For NetWare, run PCONSOLE to "rewind" the printer. Select Print Server Information and then Print Server Status/Control. Then select Printer Control and Rewind Printer. Rewind the printer to the beginning of the file by specifying "Rewind to byte 0." This resets the print job so that it will be reprinted.

   For LANtastic, type this command at the DOS prompt:

   ```
   NET QUEUE RESTART \\WARD
   ```

   (Instead of **\\WARD**, type the name of your network server.)

5. **Press the on-line button so that the printer resumes printing.**

Chapter 4

Mr. McFeeley's Guide to E-Mail

- -

- -

Do you often return to your office after a long lunch to find your desk covered with those little pink "While You Were Out" notes and your computer screen plastered with Post-It™ Notes?

If so, maybe it's time you bite the bullet and learn how to use your computer network's *electronic mail*, or *e-mail*, program. Most computer networks have one. If yours doesn't, bug the network geek until he or she gets one.

This chapter introduces you to what's possible with a good e-mail program. So many e-mail programs are available that I can't possibly show you how to use all of them, so I'll focus on the e-mail programs that come with LANtastic and Windows for Workgroups. Neither Novell's NetWare or NetWare Lite network programs come with e-mail, so if you use either one of these networks, you have to use a separate e-mail program like cc:Mail from Lotus or Microsoft Mail from you-know-who.

What E-Mail Is, and Why It's So Cool

e-mail is nothing more than the computer-age equivalent of Mr. McFeeley, one of your neighbors and mine from Mr. Rogers' Neighborhood. e-mail lets you send messages to and receive messages from other users on the network. Instead of writing the messages on paper, sealing them in an envelope, and giving them to Mr. McFeeley to deliver, e-mail messages are stored on disk and electronically delivered to the appropriate user.

Sending and Receiving Mail

To send an e-mail message to another network user, you must activate the e-mail program, compose the message by using a text editor, and provide an *address* — the *user ID* of the user you want the message sent to. Most e-mail programs also require that you create a short comment that identifies the subject of the message.

After you receive a message from another user, the e-mail program copies the message to your computer and displays it on-screen so that you can read it. You then can delete the message, print it, save it to a disk file, or forward it to another user. You also can reply to the message by composing a new message to be sent back to the user who sent the original message.

- ✔ When someone sends a message to you, most e-mail programs immediately display a message on your computer screen to tell you to check your mail. If your computer isn't on the network when the message is sent, you're notified the next time you log in to the network.

- ✔ Most e-mail packages require that you add a command to your login script or STARTNET.BAT file so that mail is automatically checked when you log in to the network.

- ✔ Besides sending text messages, most e-mail packages let you attach a file to your message. You can use this feature to send a word processing document, a spreadsheet, or a program file to another network user.

- ✔ Most e-mail programs let you keep a list of users you commonly send mail to in an *address book*. That way you don't have to retype the user ID every time.

- ✔ Most programs also let you address a message to more than one user — the electronic equivalent of a carbon copy. Some programs also enable you to create a list of users and assign a name to the list. Then you can send a message to each user in the list by addressing the message to the list name. For example, June might create a list including WARD, WALLY, and BEAVER, and call the list BOYS. To send e-mail to all the boys on her family network, she then addresses the message to BOYS.

The Post Office

Most e-mail programs use a network server as an electronic post office where messages are stored until they can be delivered to the recipient. This post office is sometimes called a *mail server*. A network server used as a mail server doesn't have to be dedicated to that purpose, although in larger networks it sometimes is. In smaller networks, the network file server doubles as the mail server.

✔ Depending on the e-mail program, it's possible to set up more than one mail server on a network. In that case, you must check mail on all the servers. If you check just one of the mail servers, you won't be notified of any mail that's waiting for you on the other mail servers.

✔ Disk space on a mail server is often at a premium. Be sure to delete unneeded messages as you read them.

Using LANtastic's E-Mail

Unlike most other network systems, LANtastic comes with a built-in e-mail program. LANtastic's e-mail program is limited in function, but it gets the job done. Here's how to use it.

Sending mail

To send an e-mail message to another LANtastic user, start the NET program and pick the Mail Services option. A list of available server computers appears; choose the one that your office uses for e-mail. You then see a screen like the one in Figure 4-1.

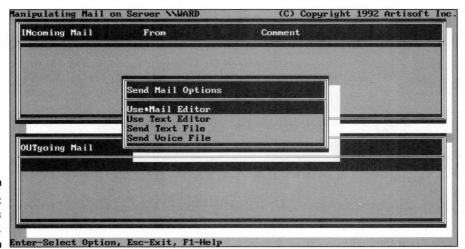

Figure 4-1:
LANtastic's
mail screen.

This screen has two windows: one for incoming mail (mail sent to you by another user), the other for outgoing mail (mail you have sent to other users). You move from the Incoming window to the Outgoing window by pressing the Tab key.

To send mail to another user, press Tab to move to the Outgoing window and press the Ins key to create a new mail item. The Send Mail Options menu pops up, as Figure 4-1 shows. The following options are available:

- ✔ **Use Mail Editor.** Use this option to type your message by using LANtastic's built-in editor. It's not a very powerful editor, but it's OK for short messages.

- ✔ **Use Text Editor.** Use this option if you can't stand LANtastic's mail editor. It lets you use your favorite text editor instead. Real computer geeks use this option so that they can specify EDLIN as the text editor.

- ✔ **Send Text File.** If you've already created the message as a separate file, use this option to send it; LANtastic asks you for the name of the file.

- ✔ **Send Voice File.** Pay no attention to this option. It applies only if you use Sounding Board, a voice-mail product offered by Artisoft.

Figure 4-2 shows how you use LANtastic's mail editor to create an e-mail message.

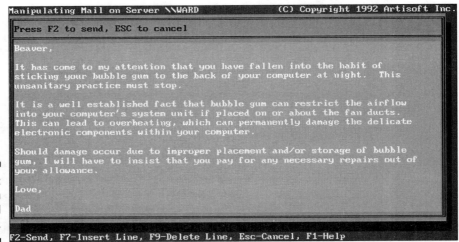

Figure 4-2:
Creating an
e-mail
message.

When you've finished typing your message, press F2 to send the message. LANtastic asks you for the user ID of the user you want to send the message to; you can type the user ID directly or press F10 to display a list of all user IDs.

LANtastic also lets you type a comment for the message. This comment appears in the recipient's Incoming mail window. Try to think of something that accurately describes the content of your message.

✔ If the recipient's computer is on the network, a pop-up message appears, informing him or her that your message has been sent. Otherwise, the user must check for mail by running the NET POSTBOX command.

✔ LANtastic's e-mail doesn't let you keep a personalized address list, but F10 displays all the users on the network. (If you have a huge network, pressing F10 could be a mistake!)

✔ To send a message to all users, type * for the user ID.

Reading your mail

To read mail sent to you by other users, run the NET command and select the Mail Services option. A description of any messages sent to you appears in the Incoming Mail window. Move the highlight to the message you want to read and press Enter. The menu shown in Figure 4-3 appears.

Figure 4-3:
LANtastic's
Mail Options
menu.

```
Mail Options

Read Mail
Forward Copy of Mail
Copy Mail to File
Print Mail
Delete Mail
```

Here's what these options do:

✔ **Read Mail.** Pick this option to display the message.

✔ **Forward Copy of Mail.** Use this option to send a copy of the message to another user.

✔ **Copy Mail to File.** This option copies the message to a file. Use this option if you want to keep a permanent copy of the message or if you want to incorporate the message into a word processing document.

✔ **Print Mail.** Use this option to print a copy of the message.

✔ **Delete Mail.** Delete the message with this option. Don't neglect this command; if you don't delete your mail, the mail server eventually will run out of disk space.

Windows for Workgroups Has Mail, Too!

Like LANtastic, Windows for Workgroups also comes with a built-in e-mail program called *Mail*. It's the little brother of Microsoft's full-blown e-mail program called *Microsoft Mail*. Windows for Workgroups Mail provides all the e-mail features you're likely to need for a small network.

✔ Windows for Workgroups Mail requires that you designate one of your server computers to act as a post office. Make sure that the post office computer has plenty of free disk space, because mail tends to accumulate.

✔ Mail lets you set up a personalized address list that contains just the users you frequently send mail to. On a small network, this isn't such a big deal. On a large network, though, keeping a personal address list can save you from having to wade through dozens of user names to find the ones you frequently use.

✔ Mail is, of course, a Windows application. So it makes extensive use of windows, buttons, and cute icons. For example, incoming mail that you haven't yet read is represented by an unopened envelope. After you read the message, the icon changes to an open envelope. What will they think of next?

✔ Mail has several options for sending and receiving messages that aren't found in LANtastic's mail program. For example, you can send copies of a message to other users, you can request confirmation that a user has received a message you have sent, and you can forward a message you've received to another user.

✔ Mail also lets you attach files to e-mail messages. This is a convenient way to exchange files with other users. In keeping with Windows tradition, the file can be copied into the message, attached to the message, or embedded in the message as an object.

Other E-Mail Goodies

Most e-mail packages include features beyond simply reading and writing messages.

Chatting on-line

Some e-mail systems let you chat with another network user. This feature is similar to vanilla e-mail, but it's not the same thing. With e-mail, you compose a message that is delivered to another user, who may read the message immediately, a few minutes later, or a few days later. Chatting on-line is more like using the phone: You "call" a network user; if the user is available, he or she answers and you talk electronically.

✔ Chatting is a two-way form of communication. You type something, the other party types something, you type again, he types again. You can even both type at the same time.

✔ When you call someone to chat, you may not get an answer. The other user may not be there. Or he may be chatting with another user. Or he may know it's you and just not answer— especially if you reminded him about the $20 he owes you from the last time you chatted.

✔ Avoid the chat feature if you're embarrased about your typing skills. Chat sends characters across the network one at a time as you type them, so the other person sees all your typing mistakes as you make them!

✔ Network chat is a great feature, especially for offices that don't have phones yet. If you've already arrived in the twentieth century and your office has a phone system, you should probably use it instead.

Electronic scheduling

Scheduling software takes advantage of the communication features of e-mail to let you schedule meetings with other network users. You tell the scheduling program the people you want at the meeting as well as when and where you'd like the meeting to occur, and the program checks the people's schedule to see whether they can make the meeting. If so, the scheduling program notifies everyone of the meeting by sending an e-mail note. If not, the scheduling program suggests an alternate meeting time.

✔ Most scheduling programs also keep track of room usage so that they don't schedule two meetings at the same place and time.

✔ For scheduling software to work, everyone must use it religiously. If Bob forgets to tell the scheduling program about his Friday golf match, the program may well schedule him for a meeting Friday morning.

✔ Scheduling software is most appropriate for large offices. It's not worth the money to purchase the software and maintain it for an office of three.

E-Mail Etiquette

Communicating with someone via e-mail is different from talking with that person face-to-face or over the phone. You need to be aware of these differences, or you'll end up insulting someone without meaning to. Of course, if you *do* mean to insult someone, pay no attention to this section.

✔ Always remember that e-mail isn't as private as you'd like it to be. It's not that difficult for someone to electronically steam open your e-mail and read it. Be careful what you say, to whom you say it, and about who you say it about.

✔ Don't forget that all the rules of social etiquette and office decorum apply to e-mail, too. If you wouldn't pick up the phone and call the CEO of the company, don't send her e-mail, either.

✔ When you reply to someone else's e-mail, keep in mind that the person you're replying to may not remember the details of the message he or she sent to you. It's polite to provide some context for your reply. Some e-mail systems do this for you by automatically tacking on the original message at the end of the reply. If yours doesn't, be sure to provide some context — such as including a relevant snippet of the original message in quotation marks — so that the recipient knows what you're talking about.

✔ e-mail doesn't have the advantage of voice inflections. This can lead to all kinds of misunderstandings, so you have to be careful that people know when you're joking and when you mean it. e-mail nerds have developed a peculiar way to convey tone of voice: they string together symbols on the computer keyboard to create *smileys*. Table 4-1 shows some of the more commonly used (or abused) smileys.

Table 4-1   Commonly Used and Abused Smileys

Smiley	What It Means
: -)	Just kidding
; -)	Wink
: - (	Bummer
: - 0	Well, I Never!
: - x	My lips are sealed

✔ If you don't get it, tilt your head to the left and look at the smiley sideways.

✔ The smileys in Table 4-1 are old news. If a bunch of Certified Network Dummies are going to get in on the e-mail game, we're going to need some Certified Dummy Smileys. Table 4-2 shows a few to get us started. (These are truly advanced smileys because they require four lines each. Use them only for special occasions.)

Table 4-2   Certified Dummy Smileys

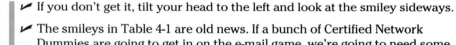

Dummy Smiley	Description
{ { '0 - ; [{ ,0 [{	The Official Dummy Smiley
{ { '0 - ; [{ ,0 [{	Little Orphan Annie Variant
} } '0 - ; [} ,0 [}	Bad Hair Day Variant
{ { '0 - \ [{ ,0 / [{	"It Worked!" Variant

✔ e-mail nerds also like to use short hand abbreviations for common words and phrases, like FYI for "For Your Information" and ASAP for "As Soon As Possible." Table 4-3 lists the more common ones.

Table 4-3	Common E-Mail Abbreviations
Abbreviation	*What It Stands For*
BTW	By The Way
FWIW	For What It's Worth
IMO	In My Opinion.
IMHO	In My Humble Opinion.
IOW	In Other Words
PMJI	Pardon Me for Jumping In
ROFL	Rolling On the Floor, Laughing
ROFL,PP	Rolling On the Floor Laughing, Peeing my Pants
TIA	Thanks In Advance
TTFN	Ta Ta For Now (quoting Tigger)
TTYL	Talk To You Later
<g>	Grin
<bg>	Big Grin
<vbg>	Very Big Grin

Note that the abbreviations that refer to gestures or facial expressions are typed between a less-than sign and a greater-than sign: <g>. Other gestures are spelled out, like <snif>, <groan>, or <sigh>.

✔ Most e-mail programs don't let you italicize or underline text. Type an asterisk before and after a word you *wish* you could italicize. Type an underscore _ before _ and _ after _ a word you'd like to underline.

✔ Capital letters are the electronic equivalent of SHOUTING. TYPING AN ENTIRE MESSAGE IN CAPITAL LETTERS CAN BE VERY ANNOYING AND CAN CAUSE YOU TO GET THE ELECTRONIC EQUIVALENT OF LARYNGITIS.

Chapter 5

Help! The Network's Down!

*F*ace it: Networks are prone to break.

They have too many "C" parts. Cables. Connectors. Concentrators. Cards. All these parts must be held together in a delicate balance; the network equilibrium is all too easy to disturb. Even the best-designed computer networks sometimes act as if they were held together with baling wire and chewing gum.

To make matters worse, networks breed suspicion. After your computer is attached to a network, you'll be tempted to blame the network every time something goes wrong, regardless of whether the problem has anything to do with the network. Can't get WordPerfect's columns to line up? Must be the network. Your spreadsheet doesn't add up? The @#$% network's acting up again.

This chapter doesn't begin to cover everything that can go wrong with a computer network. If it did, you'd take this book back and demand a refund after we got about 40 pages into "Things that can go wrong with IPX.COM."

Instead, this chapter focuses on the most common things that go wrong with a network *that an ordinary network user (that's you) can fix*. And best of all, it points you in the right direction when you come up against a problem you can't fix yourself.

When Bad Things Happen to Good Computers

What do you do when your computer goes on the blink? Here are some general ideas for finding out what the problem really is and deciding whether you can fix it yourself:

1. **Make sure that your computer and everything attached to it is plugged in.**

   Computer geeks love it when a user calls for help and he gets to tell the user that the computer isn't plugged in. They write it down in their geek logs so they can tell their geek friends about it later. They may even want to take your picture so that they can show it to their geek friends. (Most "accidents" involving computer geeks are a direct result if this kind of behavior.)

2. **Make sure that your computer is properly connected to the network.**

   More on how to do that later.

3. **Note any error messages that appear on the screen.**

4. **Do a little experimenting to find out whether the problem is indeed a network problem or a problem with just your computer.**

5. **Try restarting your computer.**

   First, get out of whatever program is running, if you can. Save your work if possible. Then, take a deep breath and press the Reset button, or turn the computer off, leave it off for 15 seconds or so, and turn it back on again.

6. **Try restarting the entire network.**

   You can find instructions for doing that later in this chapter.

7. **If none of these steps corrects the problem, scream for help.**

   Have a suitable bribe prepared to encourage your network guru to work quickly. (You'll find a handy list of suitable bribes at the end of this chapter.)

My Computer's Dead!

If your computer seems totally dead, here are some things to check:

- Is it plugged in?
- If your computer is plugged into a surge protector or a power strip, make sure that the surge protector or power strip is plugged in and turned on. If the surge protector or power strip has a light, it should be glowing.

✔ Make sure that the computer's On/Off switch is turned on. This sounds too basic to include even here, but many computers are set up so that the computer's actual power switch is always left in the "On" position and the computer is turned on or off by means of the switch on the surge suppressor or power strip. Many computer users are surprised to learn that their computers have an on/off switch on the back of the cases.

✔ If you think your computer isn't plugged in but it looks like it is, listen for the fan. If the fan is turning, the computer is getting power and the problem is more serious than an unplugged power cord. (If the fan isn't running but the computer is plugged in and power is on, it could be that the fan is out to lunch.)

✔ If the computer is plugged in, turned on, and still not running, plug a light into the outlet to make sure that power is getting to the outlet. It could be that you need to reset a tripped circuit breaker.

✔ The monitor has a separate power cord and switch. Make sure that the monitor is plugged in and turned on.

✔ Your keyboard, monitor, mouse, and printer are all connected to the back of the computer by cables. Make sure that these cables are all plugged in securely.

✔ Make sure that the other ends of the monitor and printer cables are plugged in properly, too.

✔ Most monitors have knobs that let you adjust the contrast and brightness of the monitor's display. If the computer is running but your display is dark, try adjusting these knobs. They may have been turned all the way down.

Checking Your Network Connection

There's a saying among network gurus that 95 percent of all network problems are cable problems. The cable that connects your computer to the rest of the network is a finicky beast. It can break at a moment's notice, and by "break," I don't necessarily mean "physically break in two." Sure, sometimes the problem with the cable is that Eddie Haskel got to it with pruning sheers. But cable problems are not usually visible to the naked eye.

✔ If your network uses twisted-pair cable (the cable that looks something like phone wire and is sometimes called "10baseT" cable), you can quickly tell whether the cable connection to the network is good by looking at the back of your computer. There should be a small light near the place where the cable plugs in. If this light is glowing steadily, the cable is good. If it is dark or if it is flashing intermittently, you have a cable problem.

If the light is not glowing steadily, try removing the cable from your computer and reinserting it. This may cure the weak connection.

✔ It's more difficult to detect a cable problem in a network that's wired with coax cable, the kind that looks like cable-TV cable. The connector on the back of the computer forms a T. The base end of the T plugs into your computer. One or two coax cables plug into the outer ends of the T. If only one coax cable is used, a special plug called a terminator must be used in place of a cable at the other end of the T. If you can't find a terminator, try conjuring one up from the 23rd century. Warning: DO NOT do this if your name happens to be Sarah Connor.

Do not unplug a coax cable from the network while the network is running. Data travels around a coax network the way the baton travels around the track in a relay race. If one person drops it, the race is over. The baton never gets to the next person. Likewise, if you unplug the network cable from your computer, the network data will never get to the computers that are "down the line" from your computer. (Well, actually, Ethernet isn't dumb enough to throw in the towel at the first sign of a cable breakage. You can disconnect the cable for a few seconds without permanently scattering network messages across the galaxy, but don't do it unless you have a good reason and a really good bribe for the network manager, who is sure to find out.)

✔ Some networks are wired so that your computer is connected to the network with a short (six feet or so) *patch cable*. One end of the patch cable plugs into your computer, and the other end plugs into a cable connector mounted on the wall. Try quickly disconnecting and reconnecting the patch cable. If that doesn't do the trick, see whether there's a spare patch cable you can use.

If you can't find a spare patch cable, try borrowing a fellow network user's patch cable. If the problem goes away when you use your neighbor's patch cable, you can assume that yours has gone south and needs to be replaced.

✔ If you come in late at night while no one is around, you can swap your bad patch cable with someone else's good cable, and they'll never know. The next day, they'll want to borrow this book from you so that they can find out what's wrong with the network. The day after that, someone else will need the book. You may never get your book back. You'd better buy a copy for everyone now.

Notice: Neither the author nor the publisher endorses such selfish behavior. We mention it here only so that you'll know what happened when one day someone down the hall has a network problem, and **you** *suddenly have a network problem the next day.*

✔ In some networks, computers are connected to one another via a small box called a *concentrator*, or *hub*. The concentrator is prone to cable problems, too — especially those concentrators that are wired in a "professional manner" involving a rat's nest of patch cables. Don't touch the rat's nest. Leave problems with the rat's nest to the rat — er, that is, the network guru.

A Bunch of Error Messages Flew By!

Did you notice any error messages on your computer screen when you started your computer? If so, write them down. They are invaluable clues that can help the network guru solve the problem.

- Don't panic if you see lots of error messages fly by. Sometimes a simple problem that's easy to correct can cause every command in your STARTNET.BAT or login script to fail, generating tons of error messages. It looks like your computer is falling all to pieces, but the fix may be very simple.

- If the messages fly by so fast that you can't see them, press your computer's Pause key. Your computer will come to a screeching halt, giving you a chance to catch up on your error-message reading. When you've read enough, press the Pause key again to get things moving. (On some computers, the Pause key is labeled "Hold." On computers that don't have a pause key, pressing Ctrl+Num Lock or Ctrl+S does the same thing.)

- If you missed the error messages the first time, restart you computer and watch them again.

Time to Experiment

If you can't find some obvious explanation for your troubles — like the computer's unplugged — you need to do a little experimenting to narrow down the possibilities. Your experiments should be designed to answer one basic question: Is this a *network* problem, or is the problem local to your computer?

- Try performing the same operation on someone else's computer. If no one on the network can access a network drive or printer, there's something wrong with the network. On the other hand, if you're the only one having trouble, the problem is with your computer alone. It could be that your computer isn't reliably talking to the network or isn't configured properly for the network, or the problem may have nothing to do with the network at all.

- If you're able to perform the operation on someone else's computer without problems, try logging on to the network with someone else's computer but using your own user ID. Then see whether you can perform the operation without error. If you can, your network guru will want to know.

- Try the operation without using the network. Log off the network completely by typing **LOGOUT** or **NET LOGOUT** or whatever command your network uses to log you out. Then try the operation again.

If the symptoms of the problem remain the same whether your computer is logged on to the network or not, the problem is probably not with the network.

✔ What if the operation simply can't be done without the network? For example, what if the data files are on a network drive? Try copying the files to your local drive. Then log off the network and try the operation again, this time using the files on your local drive.

How to Restart Your Computer

Sometimes trouble gets your computer so tied up in knots that it can't even move. Your computer just sits there unresponsively, no matter how hard you press the Esc key or the Enter key. That's when it's time to restart your computer by pressing the Ctrl, Alt, and Del keys at the same time.

✔ Pressing Ctrl+Alt+Del is a drastic action that you should take only when your computer has become completely unresponsive. Any work you haven't yet saved to disk will be lost. (Sniff.)

✔ Pressing Ctrl+Alt+Del is called *rebooting* your computer, or, to use more technically precise language, *giving your computer the three-finger salute.* It's appropriate to say "Queueue" as you do it.

✔ Sometimes your computer gets tied up so badly it can't even hear you when you give it the three-finger salute. When that happens, press the computer's reset button, if it has one. If it doesn't, turn off the computer, count to 15 to let you and your computer cool off, then turn it back on.

✔ If at all possible, save your work before restarting your computer. Any work you haven't saved will be lost. Unfortunately, if your computer is totally tied up in knots, you probably can't save your work. In that case, you have to choice but to jump off the cliff.

How to Restart the Network

If you think the network is causing your trouble, you can restart the network to see whether the problem goes away. Follow this procedure:

1. **Get everyone to log off the network and turn off their computers.**

2. **When you are sure the users have logged off the network and shut down their computers, shut down the network server (assuming you have a dedicated server).**

You want to do this like a good Presbyterian if possible, decently and in order. If you use Novell NetWare, type **DOWN** at the server's keyboard and then reboot the server. For LANtastic, press Ctrl+Alt+Del. LANtastic pops up a message that asks whether you want to reboot the computer or just shut down the server; press <u>S</u> to shut down the server.

3. **Reboot the server computer, or turn it off and then on again. Watch the server start up to make sure that no error messages appear.**

4. **Turn on each computer one at a time, making sure that each computer starts up without error.**

- ✔ Restarting the network is even more drastic than pressing Ctrl+Alt+Del to restart your individual computer. *Make sure that everyone saves his or her work and logs off the network before you do it!* You can cause major problems if you blindly turn off the server computer while users are logged on.

- ✔ Obviously, restarting the network is a major inconvenience to every network user. Better offer treats.

- ✔ Restarting the network is a job for the network guru. Don't do it yourself unless the network guru isn't around, and even then, do it only after asking his or her permission in writing, preferably in triplicate.

The Care and Feeding of Your Network Guru

Your most valuable asset when something goes wrong with the network is your network guru. If you've been careful to stay on good terms with your guru, you'll be way ahead of the game when you need his or her help.

Make an effort to solve the problem yourself before calling in the cavalry. Check the network connection. Try rebooting. Try using someone else's computer. The more information you can provide the guru, the more appreciative he or she will be.

Be polite, but assertively tell your guru what the problem is, what you've tried to do to fix it, and what you think may be causing the problem (if you have a clue). Say something like this:

"Hi, Joe. I've got a problem with the network: I can't log in from my computer. I tried a few things to try to figure out the problem. I was able to log in from Wally's computer using my user ID, so I think the problem may be just with my computer.

"To be sure, I checked some other things. The green light on the back my computer where the network cable plugs in is glowing, so I don't think it's a cable problem. I also rebooted my computer, but I still couldn't log on. Then I had everyone log off, and I restarted the server, but still no luck. My guess is that something may be wrong with my computer's STARTNET.BAT file."

Blow into your guru's ear like that, and he'll follow you anywhere. (Of course, that may be an undesirable result.)

✔ Always remember your manners. No one likes to be yelled at, and even computer geeks have feelings. (Believe it or not.) Be polite to your network guru even if you're mad or you think it's his fault. This may sound obvious, but you want your guru to *like* you.

✔ Don't call your guru every time the slightest little thing goes wrong. Computer experts hate explaining that the reason the computer will only print in capital letters is that you've pressed the Caps Lock key.

✔ Read the manual. It probably won't help, but at least your guru will think you tried. Gurus like that.

✔ Humor your network guru when he tries to explain what's going on. Nod attentively when he describes what the bindery is or when he says something is wrong with the File Allocation Table. Smile appreciatively when he tries to simplify the explanation by using a colorful metaphor. Wink when he thinks you understand.

✔ Mimick your guru's own sense of humor, if you can. Say something like, "It's Joe, fixin' the network. Crimpin' the cable. Jumpin' Joe, the Net-o-Rama, rentin' an apartment at 802.3 Ethernet Lane. Captain Joe of the Good Ship NetWare, goin' down with the server." Don't worry if it's not funny. *He* will think it is.

Computer Bribes for Serious Network Trouble

A *For Dummies* book wouldn't be complete without a bribe list. You probably know already about the common foodstuffs most computer gurus respond to: Cheetos, Doritos, Jolt Cola, Diet Coke (I wish they made Diet Jolt — twice the caffeine, twice the NutraSweet), Twinkies, and so on.

Bribes of this sort are suitable for small favors. But if you're having a serious problem with your network, you may need to lay it on a bit thicker. More serious bribes include the following:

- Computer games, especially flight simulator programs. Wing Commander is the best.

- Videotapes of any Pink Panther, Monty Python, or Mel Brooks movie.

- T-shirts with strange stuff written on them or T-shirts from computer companies.

- Star Trek paraphernalia. A high percentage of computer gurus are also Trekkies.

Be sure to find out in advance whether your guru prefers Star Trek classic (the original cast), The Next Generation, or Deep Space Nine. Most are very opinionated about this, and now is not the time to offend.

- Digitized sounds, if your guru has a sound card. You can never have enough digitized sounds. Anything from a Pink Panther movie ("Does your dog bite?"), Saturday Night Live ("All right, have a beer, make some copies, havin' a party!"), or Home Improvement ("Say, Al, do you suppose they call these *coping saws* because they're good at handling stress?") will do. Clips from his favorite Star Trek show are good bribes, too.

Do *not* give him a digitized recording of the famous "I've fallen and I can't get up" line. He already has five of those.

You can find an ample supply of digitized sounds on CompuServe. If you don't have access to CompuServe, it may be worth the cost just for the constant supply of bribes these files can provide.

Part II

Build Your
Own Network

In this part...

You learn how to build a network yourself, which includes planning it and installing it. You'll learn what choices are available for cable types, network operating systems, and all the other bits and pieces you have to contend with.

Yes, there is some technical information in these chapters. But fear not! I bring you tidings of great joy! Lo, a working network is at hand, and you, yea even you, can design it and install it yourself.

Chapter 6

The Bad News: You Have to Plan Ahead

O K, so you're convinced you need to network your computers. What now? Do you stop by Computers-R-Us on the way to work, install the network before morning coffee, and expect the network to be fully operational by noon?

I don't think so.

Networking your computers is just like any other worthwhile endeavor: To do it right requires a bit of planning. This chapter is designed to help you think your network through *before* you start spending money. It shows you how to come up with a networking plan that's every bit as good as the plan a network consultant would charge you $1,000 for. See? This book is already saving you money!

Making a Network Plan

If you were to pay a consultant to study your business and prepare a networking plan, the result would be a 500-page proposal whose sole purpose, aside from impressing you with bulk, is to prevent you from understanding just exactly *what* the consultant is proposing.

Truth is, you don't have to be a computer science major to make a good network plan. Despite what computer consultants want you to think, designing a small computer network isn't rocket science. You can do it yourself.

 ✔ Don't rush through the planning phase. The most costly networking mistakes are the ones you make *before* you put the network in. Think things through and consider alternatives.

 ✔ Write down the network plan. It doesn't have to be a fancy, 500-page document. (If you want to make it look good, pick up a ½" 3-ring binder. It will be big enough to hold your network plan with room to spare.)

 ✔ Let someone else read your network plan before you buy anything, preferably someone who knows more about computers than you do.

Taking Stock

One of the most challenging parts of planning a network is figuring out how to work with the computers you already have. In other words, how to you get there from here? Before you can plan how to get "there," you have to know what "here" is. In other words, you have to take a thorough inventory of your current computers.

What you need to know

You need to know the following information about each of your computers:

 ✔ The processor type and, if possible, its clock speed. Is it an 8088 (heaven forbid!) or a 286, 386, or 486? Is it 25MHz, 33MHz, or faster?

 Sometimes, you can't tell what kind of processor you have just by looking at the box. Most computers, however, display the processor type when you turn them on or reboot them by pressing Ctrl+Alt+Del. For example, my computer displays the screen shown in Figure 6-1 when I start it. From this screen, you can tell that I have a 486 processor and the speed is 33MHz. (Aren't you impressed?)

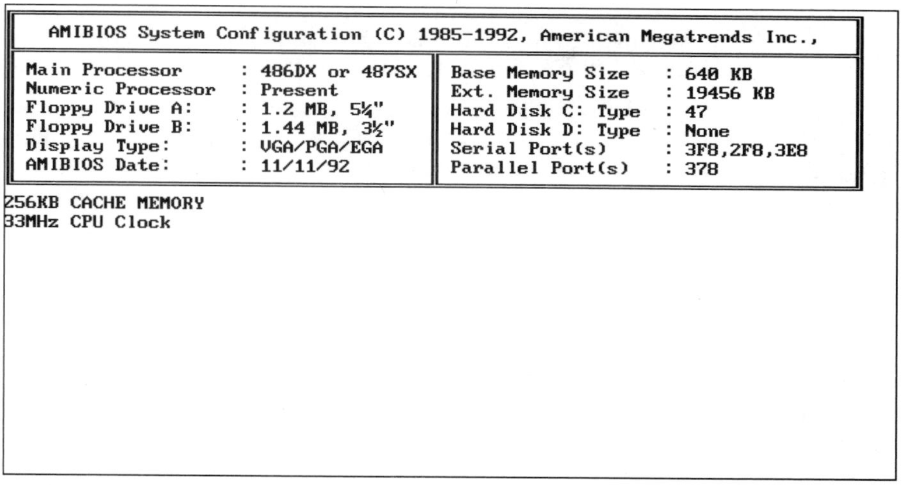

```
AMIBIOS System Configuration (C) 1985-1992, American Megatrends Inc.,

Main Processor      : 486DX or 487SX  | Base Memory Size  : 640 KB
Numeric Processor   : Present          | Ext. Memory Size   : 19456 KB
Floppy Drive A:     : 1.2 MB, 5¼"      | Hard Disk C: Type  : 47
Floppy Drive B:     : 1.44 MB, 3½"     | Hard Disk D: Type  : None
Display Type:       : VGA/PGA/EGA      | Serial Port(s)     : 3F8,2F8,3E8
AMIBIOS Date:       : 11/11/92         | Parallel Port(s)   : 378

256KB CACHE MEMORY
33MHz CPU Clock
```

Figure 6-1: A typical start-up screen showing useful information about the computer.

✔ The size of the hard disk and the arrangement of its partitions. Many older computers have a 40MB hard disk divided into two partitions, so that the partitions appear to be two separate hard disks. That's OK, so long as you know how the partitions are set up.

To find out the size of your hard disks, run the CHKDSK command on each one. When you run the CHKDSK command, it displays a whole bunch of numbers:

```
Volume DOS    created on 09-15-1992 2:04p
Volume Serial Number is 16EA-0958
     44363776      bytes total disk space
        79872      bytes in 2 hidden files
        40960      bytes in 15 directories
     19443712      bytes in 569 user files
        20480      bytes in bad sectors
     24778752      bytes available on disk
         2048      bytes in each allocation unit
        21662      total allocation units on disk
        12099      available allocation units on disk
       655360      total bytes memory
       584512      bytes free
```

The two numbers you're interested in here are the bytes of total disk space (44363776, about 44 million, or 44MB) and the bytes available on disk (24778752, about 24 million, or 24MB).

With DOS 6.2, Microsoft finally realized that most mortals cannot quickly tell whether the number 44363776 is 443 thousand or 44 million, so they added commas to the numbers. Now, 44363776 appears as 44,363,776. Who says DOS isn't user friendly?

✔ The amount of memory. Memory comes in three flavors: conventional, expanded, and extended. Use the CHKDSK command to find out how much conventional memory a computer has. If you have DOS 4.0 or a later version of DOS, you can type **MEM** to find out how much extended memory you have.

Expanded memory is found most often on older 8088 or 286 computers and doesn't affect the network much. Don't worry about it.

✔ The version of DOS you're using. Type **VER** to find out. To use a network, you should be running at least version 3.3. Network life is simpler if all your computers use the same DOS version.

✔ What kind of monitor the computer has — monochrome, CGA, EGA, or VGA. Often you can find out by reading the messages that appear when you turn on your computer.

✔ What kind of printer, if any, is attached to the computer.

✔ What software is used on the computer. WordPerfect? Lotus 1-2-3? Windows? Make a complete list.

MSD to the rescue!

If you're lucky enough to have DOS Version 6.0 or 6.2, or if you have Microsoft Windows Version 3.1, you can use the handy program called MSD, which stands for "Microsoft Diagnostics," to gather information about your computers. Just run MSD, and it will display the information you need automatically.

✔ If you just type **MSD** at the DOS prompt, MSD displays a screen like the one in Figure 6-2. You can find out more information about the various components of your computer by pressing the letter that's highlighted in each button. For example, to find out more about your computer's processor, press P. To find out more about its disk drives, press D.

✔ MSD creates a text file that describes your computer's configuration in detail if you use the /F switch and provide a filename, like this:

```
MSD /F WALLY.MSD
```

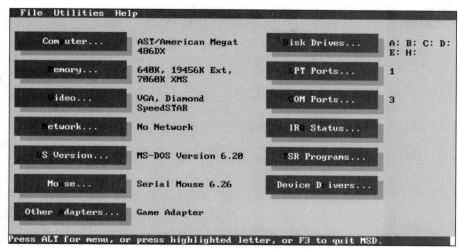

Figure 6-2:
The MSD
program
tells you
more about
your
computer
than you
want to
know.

In this case, the configuration report is stored in a file named WALLY.MSD. MSD asks you for some information like your name, company, address, and a comment. This information is included in the report, so be sure to provide enough info so that you can tell which of your computers the report belongs to.

✔ After you create the MSD report using MSD /F, you can print it by using the PRINT command:

```
PRINT WALLY.MSD
```

Press Enter if PRINT asks you for the name of the list device.

✔ MSD /F generates much more information about your computer than you need to know. Its report can run 15 or 20 pages. Most of these pages are filled with stuff only your computer guru cares about. Unfortunately, it doesn't tell you what software is being used on the computer. You have to gather that information yourself.

✔ Don't run MSD from a DOS prompt while Windows is running; Windows hampers MSD's ability to collect information. Quit Windows first, then run MSD.

Why Do You Need a Network, Anyway?

An important step in planning your network is making sure that you understand why you want the network in the first place. Here are some of the more common reasons for needing a network, all of them quite valid:

- ✔ My coworker and I exchange files using a floppy disk just about every day. With a network, we could trade files without using the floppies.

- ✔ I don't want to buy everyone a laser printer when I know the one we have now just sits there taking up space most of the day. Wouldn't it be cheaper to buy a network than to buy a laser printer for every computer?

- ✔ Someone figured out that we're destroying seven trees a day by printing interoffice memos on real paper, so we'd like to set up an e-mail system.

- ✔ Business is so good that one person typing in orders eight hours each day can't keep up. With a network, I could have two people entering orders, and I wouldn't have to pay either one overtime.

- ✔ My brother-in-law just put in a network at his office, and I don't want him to think I'm behind the times.

Make sure that you identify all the reasons you think you need a network, and write them down. Don't worry about winning the Pulitzer Prize for your stunning prose. Just make sure that you've written down what you expect a network will do for you.

- ✔ If you were making a 500-page networking proposal, you would place the description of why a network is needed in a tabbed section labeled "Justification." In your ½" network binder, file it under "Why."

- ✔ As you consider the reasons you need a network, you may come to the conclusion that you don't need a network after all. That's OK. You can always use the binder for your stamp collection.

Three Basic Network Decisions You Can't Avoid

When you plan a computer network, you are confronted with three inescapable network decisions. You can't install the network until you've made these decisions. The decisions are weighty enough that I've devoted a separate chapter in this section to each one.

It's been a long time since I've introduced a new TLA (Three-Letter Acronym), so let's call these basic network decisions *BNDs*, which stands for — you guessed it — "Basic Network Decisions."

Stupid stuff about printer switches

If your only reason for networking is to share a printer, there may be a cheaper way: Buy a switch box instead of a network. Switch boxes let two or more computers share a single printer. Instead of running a cable directly from computer to printer, you run cables from each computer to the switch box, then run one cable from the switch box to the printer. Only one of the computers has access to the printer at a time; the switch decides which one.

There are two kinds of printer switches:

Manual printer switches have a knob on the front that lets you select which computer is con-nected to the printer. When you use a manual switch, you first must make sure that the knob is set to your computer before you try to print. Turning the knob while someone else is printing probably will cost you a bag of doughnuts.

Automatic printer switches have a built-in electronic ear that listens to each computer. When it hears one of the computers trying to talk to the printer, it automatically connects that computer to the printer. The switch also has a electronic holding pen called a *buffer* that can hold printer output from one computer if another computer is using the printer. Automatic switches aren't fool-proof, but they work most of the time.

BND #1: What network operating system will you use?

There are many network operating systems to chose from, but from a practical point of view, your choices are limited to:

Novell's NetWare, the most popular network operating system for large networks. NetWare requires that you dedicate at least one computer to act as a network server, and it can be a challenge for a novice user to install.

Artisoft's LANtastic is the most popular network operating system for DOS-based, peer-to-peer networks, where a dedicated server computer isn't required.

Novell's NetWare Lite, a peer-to-peer network operating system, is similar to LANtastic.

Microsoft's Windows for Workgroups is an ideal choice if all your computers run Windows.

> 🖝 Other network operating systems exist. I've limited the choices here to the ones that you easily can purchase through the mail or at a discount software store. You're more likely to use one of the others if you hire a consultant to install the network for you.

- ✔ LANtastic, NetWare Lite, and Windows for Workgroups are available in *starter kits* that include everything you need to connect two computers, as well as add-on kits that contain everything you need to add one computer to the network. These kits make it easy to set up your network, but they're not always the way to go. More on starter kits later in this chapter.

- ✔ LANtastic comes in a baby version called *Simply LANtastic*. It's kind of the Happy Meal of networks, except that you don't get a toy. Still, it's a great way to dabble in networking if you have just a few computers, you don't want to spend much money, and you don't care about security. You can get Simply LANtastic bundled with special network cards that are simpler to hook up than regular cards.

- ✔ It's possible to start with a simple peer-to-peer network now and upgrade to NetWare later. All four of the networks listed at the beginning of this section can use the same cable, network interface cards, hubs, and so on. Changing from one to another is a matter of reconfiguring the software. (Of course, to change from a peer-to-peer network to NetWare, you must have a dedicated server computer.)

- ✔ Chapter 7 describes the advantages and disadvantages of each of these systems so that you can decide which is the best choice for your network.

BND #2: What arrangement of server computers will you use?

Just because peer-to-peer networks like LANtastic, NetWare Lite, and Windows for Workgroups don't require you to use dedicated server computers doesn't mean dedicated server computers can and should be used only with NetWare. On the contrary, if you can possibly afford it, a dedicated server computer is almost always the way to go, no matter what network operating system you use.

- ✔ Using a dedicated server computer even on a peer-to-peer network makes the network faster, easier to work with, and more reliable. Consider what happens when the user of a server computer doubling as a workstation decides to turn the computer off, not realizing that someone else is accessing files on his or her disk drive.

- ✔ You don't necessarily have to use your biggest and fastest computer as your server computer. I've seen networks where the slowest computer on the network is the server. This is especially true when the server is used mostly to share a printer.

- ✔ When you plan your server configuration, you must also plan how your data and program files will be dispersed on the network. For example, will all users have copies of WordPerfect on their local drives, or will one copy of WordPerfect be stored on the server drive? (Within the limits of your software license, of course.)

✔ Planning your server configuration also means assigning drive letters to network drives. You should be consistent about this, so that a particular network drive is accessed by using the same drive letter from every computer.

✔ Server configuration is heady enough to merit its own chapter: Chapter 8.

BND #3: How will you cable the network?

The third basic networking decision is how to connect your computers.

✔ You must choose between twisted-pair cable (called *UTP or 10baseT*) and standard coax cable (called *thinnet*). There are advantages and disadvantages to each, and it's possible and sometimes desirable to use a mixture of both.

✔ You must also pick the network interface cards to install in each computer. It's best to use the same card in each computer, although it's also possible to mix and match. The card you select must be compatible with the cable you select.

✔ If you use twisted-pair cable, you also need a network hub.

✔ As you plan your network cabling, you need to draw a floor plan showing the location of each computer and the route the cables will follow.

✔ The details of network cabling are covered in Chapter 9.

Networks to Go: Using a Network Starter Kit

All three of the peer-to-peer network operating systems described in this chapter can be purchased in bundles that include everything you need to set up a small network. These kits contain the network software, interface card, cable, and any other doodads that you need to get going. Kits are the ideal way to purchase the components you need for a small network.

You begin by purchasing a starter kit, which contains two network interface cards, two copies of the network operating system, and a cable to connect the computers. Figure 6-3 shows a starter kit for Artisoft's LANtastic.

Figure 6-3: A starter kit for LANtastic.

The starter kit accommodates the first two computers in your network. For each additional computer you want to connect, you purchase an add-on kit that contains one network interface card, one copy of the software, and usually a cable.

- ✔ The prices of these kits vary but average around $500 for the starter kit and $250 for each one-computer add-on kit. Shop around to get the best price.

- ✔ Network starter kits use thinnet coax cable, and the interface cards that they include may be limited to coax only. If you want to wire your network using twisted-pair wiring, or if you think you may want to convert to twisted-pair later, you'd better buy the components separately, or make sure that the cards that come with the starter kit can accommodate both cable types.

- ✔ The coax cable in the starter kit is generally 25 feet long. If your computers are farther apart than that, you have to buy a separate cable. You can buy another 25-foot length of cable and a special barrel connector to splice the two cables together, or you can purchase a longer length of cable.

- ✔ One-computer add-on kits don't always include a cable. Check to make sure; if not, you have to purchase the cable separately.

- ✔ Network kits typically come with moderately priced network interface cards. You often can save money by purchasing the components separately so that you can buy a less-expensive interface card.

A Sample Network Plan

Let's consider a typical family business — Cleaver's Baseball Card Emporium, which buys and sells valuable as well as worthless baseball cards and other baseball memorabilia.

The Cleaver's Computer Inventory

The Cleavers have four computers:

Ward's computer is a brand-new 33MHz 486 with 4MB of RAM and a 170MB disk drive. Ward runs Microsoft Windows for spreadsheet analysis (Excel) and occasional word processing (Word for Windows). He also has a laser printer.

June's computer is a 25MHz 386 with 2MB of RAM and an 80MB hard disk. June does not run Windows but does most of the company's word processing work with WordPerfect. She has a near-letter-quality dot-matrix printer but would like to use Ward's laser printer to print letters.

Wally's computer is a 286 with 1MB of RAM and a 20MB hard drive. Wally keeps the company's inventory records on his computer by using a database program called Q&A.

The Beave's computer is a genuine IBM AT computer, with a 286 processor, 512K of RAM, and a 20MB hard disk. Beaver's computer also includes a modem. Beaver uses the computer mostly to communicate with an on-line service for market research and to play Pong.

Why the Cleavers need a network

The Cleavers want to network their computers for two simple reasons:

1. So that everyone can access the laser printer.
2. So that everyone can access the inventory database.

If it weren't for reason 2, a network wouldn't be necessary. They could share the laser printer by purchasing a simple printer sharing switch that would enable all four computers to access the printer. But to give everyone access to the inventory database, a network is required.

Network operating system

None of the Cleavers is a computer whiz, so they've opted for a simple peer-to-peer network operating system: LANtastic. It will allow them to share the printer and the disk drive containing the inventory database — so it adequately meets their needs.

Ward wanted to use Windows for Workgroups because he heard it has a great Hearts game. But he backed off when he remembered that his computer is the only one capable of running Windows. They ruled out NetWare because the family can't afford a separate server computer (see the following section).

Server configuration

Because the Cleavers can't afford a separate computer to use as a server, two of the computers will do double duty as both workstations and servers. Ward's computer will be set up as a workstation/server so that everyone can access his printer, and Wally's computer will be set up as a workstation/server so that everyone can access the inventory database.

After the network is up and running, Wally is considering moving the inventory database to Ward's computer. That way, only one server computer will have to be managed. Because Ward doesn't use his computer often, he probably won't mind the small reduction in performance as other users access his disk.

Network cabling

For simplicity, the Cleavers have opted to wire their network with thinnet coax cable. All four computers are located in the spacious den, so the floor plan presents no unusual wiring problems. To simplify shopping, the Cleavers decided to purchase a LANtastic starter kit for two of the computers and two one-computer add-on kits for the other two.

Figure 6-4 shows the floor plan for the Cleaver's network setup. You can see how they plan to run the cable.

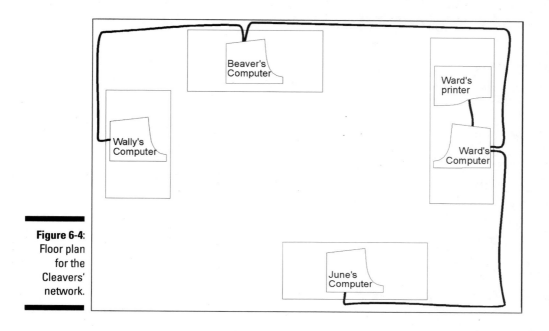

Figure 6-4:
Floor plan
for the
Cleavers'
network.

Next, Chapter 7 gives you an informal tour of several networking packages, giving you the information to decide which network is the right one for you.

Chapter 7

Choose Your Weapon (or, Which Network Should I Use?)

*O*ne of the basic choices you must make before you go too far is which network operating system you will use as the foundation for your network. This chapter provides an overview of the advantages and disadvantages of the most popular network operating systems. It starts with Novell's NetWare, the most popular network operating system. Then it describes three peer-to-peer networks: Novell's NetWare Lite, Artisoft's LANtastic, and Microsoft's Windows for Workgroups. Finally, it briefly describes other network systems that are less popular.

Novell's NetWare

NetWare is far and away the most popular network operating system, especially for larger networks. You can use NetWare to build networks consisting of hundreds of computers. But you also can use it for smaller networks.

Novell has released many updated versions of NetWare over the years and currently sells three versions of NetWare: 2.2, 3.11, and 4.0. Yes, it *would* be nice if the version numbers made sense, like 1, 2, and 3. Hey, don't shoot me, I'm just the messenger.

What's so great about NetWare?

I've pounded NetWare a bit for being overly complicated. However, there's a lot to be said in favor of NetWare. NetWare can be complicated to set up and administer, but it is far and away the most popular network operating system in use. There must be something good to say about it!

- ✔ When Novell set out to design NetWare, it recognized that DOS just doesn't cut it when it comes to networking. Rather than work around DOS like peer-to-peer networks such as LANtastic, NetWare bypasses DOS altogether. NetWare file servers don't run DOS; instead, NetWare itself is the operating system for the file server. This frees NetWare from the many built-in limitations of DOS.

- ✔ With NetWare, file servers must be dedicated as file servers; you can't have a file server double as a user's workstation. Although this costs more because you must purchase a separate server computer, it's more efficient because the server computer can concentrate on servicing the network.

- ✔ Workstations on a NetWare network can be DOS-based computers, computers running OS/2, or Macintoshes. If you have a mix of PCs and Macintoshes, NetWare may be your best choice.

Technical Stuff

Mumbo jumbo about why NetWare is slicker than DOS

Because NetWare doesn't rely on the primitive file management of DOS, it's free to use more efficient file-handling techniques. A survey of NetWare's standard efficiency techniques reads like a syllabus for a graduate-level computer science class:

Caching means keeping a copy of recently read disk data in memory with the hope that the same data will be needed again. If it is, disk access can be avoided. Caching used to be one of NetWare's slickest features, but even DOS does caching nowadays (that's what the DOS SMARTDRV command does).

Directory hashing is an efficient way to locate directory files on disk. Because of directory hashing, NetWare can find a file much faster than DOS can.

Elevator seeking is a way to improve disk access for a busy file server. Picture the way an elevator works, and you'll get the idea. Suppose that three people get on an elevator. The first presses the button for the 10th floor, the second for the 4th floor, and the third for the 7th floor. The elevator doesn't go to floor 10, then come back to floor 4, then go up to floor 7. Instead, it stops at the floors in order: 4, then 7, then 10. If three people request disk access at nearly the same time, DOS services the requests in the order in which they were received. NetWare, on the other hand, rearranges the requests so that they can be serviced as efficiently as possible.

✔ The NetWare file server uses a more efficient structure for organizing files and directories than DOS. With NetWare, you can divide each disk drive into one or more *volumes*, which are similar to DOS logical drives. Novell volumes have names rather than single drive letters. To access a NetWare volume from a DOS workstation, however, a drive letter is assigned to the volume.

✔ NetWare provides a special filing system called *Btrieve*. Btrieve is used mostly by specialized application programs that you can buy for your business. For example, if your business is a video store, you can buy specialized video-store software that uses Btrieve. If you run a farming operation, you can buy specialized agricultural software that uses Btrieve. But general-purpose software such as word processing and spreadsheet programs doesn't use Btrieve.

If you use specialized software that uses Btrieve, that software will run more efficiently on NetWare than it will on a peer-to-peer network.

✔ All versions of NetWare provide features for *System Fault Tolerance* (*SFT*), which are designed to keep the network running even if a hardware failure occurs. Each successive version has better SFT features: 3.11 has better SFT features than 2.2, and the SFT features of 4.0 are better yet.

The disadvantages of NetWare

NetWare is the best networking system available, but that doesn't mean it's the best choice for your network. There are a number of disadvantages to using NetWare for small networks.

✔ NetWare is definitely more complicated than peer-to-peer networks. The learning curve is steep. Figure 7-1 shows three versions of NetWare: NetWare 2.2 on the left, 3.11 on the right, and NetWare Lite in the middle. Take a look at the stack of manuals for 2.2 and 3.11. Now do you see why I suggest you consider a peer-to-peer network instead?

If you learn computer stuff pretty quickly, you can probably handle NetWare. Otherwise, using NetWare probably means you'll have to hire a consultant to install it for you. That's not necessarily a bad thing; just remember that installing NetWare is not a do-it-yourself project unless you're pretty good with DOS.

Figure 7-1:
If you choose NetWare, hire a consultant to read these manuals for you.

- ✔ The hardware for a NetWare system costs more than for a peer-to-peer network because you must dedicate at least one computer as a file server. (However, the networking components — adapter cards, cable, and so on — do not cost any more. And if you use a dedicated file server for your peer-to-peer network, the hardware costs are the same.)

- ✔ The NetWare operating system costs more per computer than a peer-to-peer system. Plus, you don't buy the NetWare software one computer at a time. Instead, you purchase the NetWare software along with a licensing option that allows you to use it for 5, 10, 20, 50, 100, 250, 500, or 1000 users. If your network has 6 users, you must pay for the 10-user version. If you have 11 users, you must buy the 20-user version.

  This pricing scheme isn't so bad for larger networks. But because peer-to-peer networks are usually sold one copy per user, they're often cheaper for small networks.

Do you have the savvy to install NetWare?

How do you know whether you have what it takes to contend with NetWare? Try this little self test. If you know all (or most) of the answers to these questions, you probably have enough computer savvy to figure out NetWare. If not, don't feel bad. As it says (sort of) in the Good Book, "some are prophets, some are evangelists, some are teachers, some are NetWare administrators, some are Computer Dummies..."

1. What command do you use to copy all the files, including files in subdirectories, from drive A to the current directory?

   A. COPY A:*.* C:*.*

   B. DELETE A:*.*

   C. FORMAT C:

   D. XCOPY A:*.* /S

2. Which of these files is processed every time you start your computer?

   A. STARTUP.BAT

   B. BOOTIT.COM

   C. TURNON.BAT

   D. AUTOEXEC.BAT

3. Which of the following bribes are appropriate when enlisting the help of a computer guru?

   A. Cheetos

   B. Doritos

   C. Doughnuts

   D. All the above

4. Who is the most dangerous man in all of France?

   A. Jacques Cousteau

   B. Marcel Marceau

   C. Big Bird

   D. Chief Inspector Jacques Clouseau

If you answered D to three or more of these questions, you probably have the savvy to install NetWare yourself, unless the one you missed was #3, in which case you don't have a prayer.

NetWare 2.2

NetWare version 2.2 is the simplest and least expensive version of NetWare that's available. It is also the oldest. It's designed to run on 286-based computers, which were hot stuff when this version of NetWare was written. It's still appropriate for smaller networks.

- ✔ NetWare 2.2 comes in versions that support 5, 10, 50, or 100 users. For more than 100 users, you have to use NetWare 3.11.

- ✔ NetWare 2.2 imposes the following limits on the server:

    Number of volumes: 32

    Max size of a volume: 256MB

    Max disk space for server: 2GB

    Largest file: 256MB

    Max amount of RAM in server: 12MB

    Max number of open files: 1000

    Note: MB stands for megabyte, or roughly one million bytes. *GB* stands for gigabyte, or roughly one billion bytes.

    These limits are well above what most smaller networks require, although the 256MB limit on volume size feels a bit tight these days.

- ✔ With NetWare 2.2, you must bring down the server whenever you want to make a change to it. This is a minor inconvenience, but it can be annoying. The larger the network, the more annoying it is.

- ✔ NetWare 2.2 supports a feature called *Value Added Processes* (*VAP*s), which lets specialized programs run on the server. The most common VAP is Btrieve.

- ✔ Upgrading from NetWare 2.2 to 3.11 is not an easy process. If you think you'll outgrow 2.2, you'd better just start with 3.11.

Get thee to a bindery!

NetWare versions 2.11 and 3.2 store information about network users, passwords, access rights, and so on in a database called the *bindery*. Each server has its own bindery, so if you have two servers, you have to maintain two separate lists of users, passwords, and so on. That's why you must log in to each server you want to use. Most peer-to-peer networks follow this model, even though they don't use the term *bindery* to refer to the database.

Sometimes, the bindery gets messed up. When that happens, it's appropriate to refer to it as the *bakery* or the *brewery*. NetWare provides a utility called BINDFIX that's designed to repair broken binderies.

NetWare 3.11

NetWare Version 3.11 is the NetWare version designed to take advantage of the advanced features of the 386 processor chip. It provides all the features of NetWare 2.2, plus some.

- ✔ NetWare 3.11 requires that the server computer have a 386 processor (a 486 or Pentium will work, too). The workstations don't have to be 386s, though. Any workstation computer that can work with NetWare 2.2 also can work with 3.11.

- ✔ NetWare 3.11 is more expensive than 2.2. It comes in versions for 5, 10, 20, 50, 100, or 250 users. If you have more than 250 users, you need NetWare 4.0. But you probably don't need this book.

- ✔ NetWare 3.11 relaxes the server limits imposed by 2.2 just a bit:

    Number of volumes: 1,024

    Max size of a volume: 32GB

    Max disk space for server: 32,768GB

    Largest file: 4GB

    Max amount of RAM in server: 4GB

    Max number of open files: 100,000

Obviously these limits are miles ahead of anything a small network will approach. You won't outgrow NetWare 3.11.

✔ With NetWare 3.11, Novell replaced the VAP feature with an improved feature called *NetWare Loadable Modules*, or *NLMs*. Unlike a VAP, an NLM can be activated or deactivated while the server is running. That means that you have to bring down the server less often.

NetWare 4.0

The latest and greatest version of NetWare is version 4.0. Although you can purchase it for as few as five computers, it's unlikely that you'll use it for small networks. Its main benefits are for larger networks with hundreds of computers.

✔ NetWare 4.0 is expensive. The list price for a 10-user system is $3,195. Because it is so new, it is not readily available through mail-order houses at steep discounts.

✔ NetWare 4.0 has the same file and disk limits as NetWare 3.11. However, it allows for 1,000 users rather than 250.

✔ The most significant change introduced with Version 4.0 is that information about the resources of each server is no longer stored in a bindery. Instead, a feature called *NetWare Directory Services* (*NDS*) treats the entire network as a whole. With 2.2 or 3.11, you must log in to a server to use that server's resources. With 4.0, you log in to the network and then have access to resources on any of the network's servers.

NDS isn't particularly important for small networks with only one server. For large networks with dozens of servers, though, it's a major improvement, because it dramatically simplifies management of the servers.

I don't get a penny for promoting *NetWare for Dummies*

If you think NetWare is the networking system for you, be sure to get a copy of IDG's *NetWare for Dummies*, by Ed Tittel. Ed is the director of communications at Novell, so he really knows his stuff. This is a great book that will show you how to install, use, and manage your network and keep your sanity.

I thought I should get like a 2 percent commission or something for promoting *NetWare for Dummies* here, but no such luck. Bummer. Get the book anyway.

Peer-to-Peer Networks

If you're not up to the complexity of NetWare, you may want to opt for a simpler, DOS-based, peer-to-peer network such as NetWare Lite, LANtastic, or Windows for Workgroups.

Why peer-to-peer networks are easier to use

Peer-to-peer networks are easier to set up and use than NetWare mainly because they're based on DOS. You can think of NetWare as a replacement for DOS, at least on the file server. In contrast, peer-to-peer networks don't replace DOS; they work within the limited framework of DOS to provide network capabilities.

Although DOS limits the capabilities of these networks, it makes them easier to use because you don't have to learn the ins and outs of a foreign operating system. Everything you already know about DOS — even if that's not very much — will help you when you set up a peer-to-peer network.

✔ Peer-to-peer networks do not require that you use a dedicated server computer. Any computer on the network can function both as a network server and as a user's workstation. (However, you can configure a computer as a dedicated server if you want to. This results in better performance.)

✔ One reason peer-to-peer networks are easier than NetWare to set up and use is that they don't provide as many advanced features as NetWare. Peer-to-peer networks don't provide the same fault tolerance features that NetWare does, their security systems aren't as advanced, and they don't provide as many options for tweaking performance. With fewer variables to worry about, it's easier to master the equation.

✔ You can purchase most peer-to-peer networks in kits that include software, adapter cards, and cable: a network in a box. A two-station starter kit includes everything you need to network two computers: two adapter cards, two copies of the software, and a cable with appropriate connectors. A one-station add-on kit lets you add a computer to your network: It includes an adapter card, one copy of the software, and a cable with connectors.

Drawbacks of peer-to-peer networks

Yes peer-to-peer networks are easier to install and manage than NetWare, but they are not without their drawbacks.

- ✔ Because peer-to-peer networks are DOS-based, they are subject to the inherent limitations of DOS. DOS just isn't designed with a network server in mind, so it can never manage a file server as efficiently as NetWare.

- ✔ Although peer-to-peer networks provide most of the basic features of NetWare, one important feature they do not provide is the capability to run the equivalent of a VAP or NLM module. As a result, programs that use Btrieve won't run as efficiently on a peer-to-peer network as they would on a NetWare network.

- ✔ Although a peer-to-peer network may have a lower cost per computer for smaller networks, the cost difference between peer-to-peer networks and NetWare is less significant in larger networks (say, 20 or more workstations).

Artisoft's LANtastic

Artisoft's LANtastic is the most popular peer-to-peer network operating system. It's ideal for networks of 2 to 25 computers but can be used on larger networks of 100 or more computers.

- ✔ LANtastic is easy to install. The entire program comes on one disk and can be installed in just a few minutes.

- ✔ With LANtastic, you can set up a dedicated server computer, or your computers can do double duty as both servers and user workstations. The network operates more efficiently if you use a dedicated server.

- ✔ Artisoft also manufactures top-quality network interface cards, and you can purchase the LANtastic software in kits bundled with Artisoft's cards.

- ✔ Artisoft makes proprietary (that is, nonstandard) adapter cards called *2Mbps adapters*. Avoid using these cards if you can; Artisoft's standard Ethernet cards (designated AE, for "Artisoft Ethernet") or its newer NodeRunner cards aren't much more expensive, are compatible with other networks including NetWare, and are five times as fast as the 2Mbps cards. See Chapter 8 for more information.

- ✔ You can use LANtastic with network interface cards made by other vendors, as long as the cards are NE2000 compatible (I'll explain what that means in the next chapter). To use another vendor's network card with LANtastic, you must purchase a copy of the Adapter Independent version of the LANtastic software (known as LANtastic AI) for each computer. You often can save $25-$50 per computer by purchasing a less-expensive network adapter card and LANtastic AI rather than purchasing an Artisoft adapter card.

✔ LANtastic includes a built-in electronic mail program. Although primitive, it gets the job done.

✔ A version of LANtastic known as LANtastic for Windows provides all the features of the standard LANtastic system plus Windows utilities that let you control the network while Windows is running. The standard LANtastic software is compatible with Windows, but requires that you exit Windows before changing the network configuration.

✔ A scaled-back version of LANtastic called *Simply LANtastic* is ideal for small outfits that want to get a start in networking. It doesn't have all the bells and whistles of full-blown LANtastic, but if you want bells and whistles, you have to have experienced bell-ringers and whistle-blowers. Simply LANtastic is easy to install: you just plug in the special network cards, hook up the cables, install the software from the disks, and *voil`a!* Instant network!

Novell's NetWare Lite

NetWare Lite is a peer-to-peer network operating system that is superficially similar to NetWare but is in reality a completely different product. It's designed for small networks of 2 to 25 computers. Novell introduced it primarily to compete with Artisoft's LANtastic, which is more popular.

✔ NetWare Lite doesn't include many of the sophisticated features of NetWare 2.2, 3.3, or 4.0. Contrary to what you may expect, it is *not* a "subset" of the full NetWare system. Instead, it's a completely different product. However, the hardware you use to set up a NetWare Lite network — that is, the network adapter cards and the cable — are compatible with the full NetWare system. So if you decide to upgrade to NetWare 2.2 or 3.11 later, the money you spent on hardware won't go to waste.

✔ Unlike LANtastic, NetWare Lite does not include an e-mail program.

✔ Novell also sells a separate Windows utility for NetWare Lite called WNET, which enables you to perform NetWare Lite functions such as logging in to a server from within Windows. WNET isn't required to use NetWare Lite with Windows, but WNET can make life easier.

✔ NetWare Lite is limited to 25 users. Novell assumes that by the time your network reaches that size, you'll have upgraded to the full NetWare system.

Windows for Workgroups

Windows for Workgroups is Microsoft's recent entry into the peer-to-peer networking scene. Its advantage over LANtastic and NetWare Lite is that it's designed for Windows from the ground up. In fact, Windows for Workgroups is basically a networked version of Windows. It completely replaces the existing version of Windows on your computer.

- Windows for Workgroups includes an enhanced version of File Manager that provides menu functions for managing network disk drives and an enhanced version of Print Manager for managing network printers.

- One of the most interesting features of Windows for Workgroups is the network clipboard, which lets you cut or copy data from an application on one computer and paste it into an application on another.

- Windows for Workgroups also comes with Microsoft Mail, a sophisticated electronic mail program, and a scheduling program that lets you schedule meetings with other network users.

- Microsoft sells starter kits that include two network interface cards, two copies of Windows for Workgroups, and a cable; and one-user add-on kits that include the software and a card. You also can run Windows for Workgroups on standard Ethernet adapter cards.

- Windows for Workgroups works best on networks where all the computers run Windows. To use a non-Windows computer with a Windows for Workgroups network, you must purchase a separate program called Workgroup Connection. A DOS computer running Workgroup Connection can access resources on a Windows for Workgroups server but can't act as a server itself.

- Windows for Workgroups can be integrated with a NetWare network or a Microsoft LAN Manager network. That task, however, is best left to a professional.

- The best feature of Windows for Workgroups is its Hearts game, which lets you play Hearts with other network users. If you can't round up three other players, the game can play the missing hands for you, but its play borders on pathetic. It's a great ego booster.

Other Network Operating Systems

The four network operating systems I've described so far in this chapter aren't the only choices that are available. The ones I've already described are readily available from discount software stores and mail-order outlets; pick up a recent copy of *Computer Shopper* and you'll find plenty of sources for these systems. But other good networking systems are available as well.

- ✔ Microsoft's LAN Manager is a sophisticated server-based system, which uses dedicated server computers that run the OS/2 operating system.

- ✔ IBM sells a network system called LAN Server, which is almost identical to LAN Manager. Microsoft and IBM jointly developed LAN Manager and LAN Server back in the days when Microsoft and IBM were best buddies. Now that the two aren't on speaking terms, these two network systems will probably go their separate ways.

- ✔ Banyan Systems' Vines is a server-based network system in which the servers use the UNIX operating system.

- ✔ The winner of the coveted Most Creative Network System Name is PromiseLAN from Moses Computers. PromiseLAN is a peer-to-peer system that runs on proprietary network adapter cards. A faster version called ChosenLAN is also available.

Chapter 8
Planning Your Servers

● ●

In This Chapter

▶ Deciding whether to use dedicated servers

▶ Making sure that you provide enough disk space

▶ Storing programs and data files on a server

▶ Using a separate print server

▶ Buying a reliable server computer

● ●

*O*ne of the key decisions you must make when you network your computers is how you will make use of server computers. Even if you use a peer-to-peer network system like LANtastic, you must still deal with the question of servers.

This chapter helps you make the best use of your network server, first by convincing you to use a dedicated server if possible, and then by suggesting ways to use the server efficiently.

To Dedicate or Not to Dedicate

If you've been asleep up to this chapter, you may not have caught on that I'm a big believer in dedicated server computers, even if you use a peer-to-peer network. Yes, one of the strengths of LANtastic and other peer-to-peer networks is that they let any computer on the network operate both as a server and as a user's workstation. Does that mean it's a good idea to make every computer a server? No way.

You give up a lot when your desktop computer doubles as a network server:

▶ The network software required to make your computer work as a server takes up valuable RAM, leaving less RAM for your own work.

▶ Every time someone accesses data on your hard disk, your own work is temporarily suspended. If your hard disk is popular, you'll become annoyed with the frequent delays.

✔ You lose the sense of privacy that comes with having your own computer. Remember that nasty memo about your boss? You'd better not leave it lying around on your disk...someone else may lift it off the network. (You can set up your disk so that you have some private space where other users can't snoop about, but you have to make sure you set it up right, and you have to remember to store confidential files in private space.)

✔ You lose the independence of having your own computer. You have to leave your computer on all day even when you're not using it, because someone else may be. Want to reboot your computer to test a change to your CONFIG.SYS or AUTOEXEC.BAT file? You can't. Want to delete some unnecessary files to free up some hard disk space? You can't if the files don't belong to you.

✔ Your computer isn't immune to damage caused by other network users. What if someone accidentally deletes an important file on your disk? What if someone copies a 10MB file onto your hard disk while you aren't looking, so that there's no free space available when you try to save the spreadsheet you've been working on all afternoon?

I hope you're convinced. If you can at all afford it, set aside a computer for use as a dedicated server. Beg, borrow, or steal a computer if you must.

✔ Most peer-to-peer networks let you adjust certain configuration options for network servers. If you use a computer as both a server and a workstation, you must balance these options so that they provide reasonable performance for both server and workstation functions. But if you dedicate the computer as a server, you can skew these options in favor of the server functions. In other words, you're free to tweak the server's configuration for peak network performance. Details on doing this are found in Chapter 13.

✔ As a general rule, try to limit the number of servers on your network. It's better to have one server that shares a 200MB drive than two servers that each share a 100MB drive. That's because you must maintain a separate list of user IDs and network resources for each server. The more servers you have, the bigger the maintenance chore.

✔ In a larger network, you may want to use two dedicated server computers: one as a file server, the other as a print server. This improves the performance for file operations and network printing.

✔ If you're the greedy type, offer to donate your computer as the network server if the company will purchase a new computer for your desktop.

Actually, this idea has merit: The file server doesn't have to be the fastest computer on the block, especially if it's used mostly to store and retrieve word processing, spreadsheet, and other types of document files rather than for intensive database processing.

How Much Disk Space?

The general rule of thumb for a network is that you never have enough disk space. No matter how much you have, you'll eventually run out. Do not delude yourself into thinking that 200MB is twice as much space as you'll ever need. Make that space available to the network, and it fills up in no time.

What then? Should you just keep adding a new disk drive to your file server every time you run out of space? Certainly not. The key to managing network disk space is just that — managing it. Someone has to sign on the dotted line that he or she will keep tabs on the network disk and let everyone know when it's about to burst its seams. And every network user must realize that disk storage on the server is a precious resource, to be used judiciously and not squandered.

- ✔ If you use a peer-to-peer network, install DOS 6.2 on the file server and activate its DoubleSpace feature. To set up DoubleSpace properly, you first must quote from *Wayne's World:* Say "Ex-squeeze me," and DoubleSpace will politely compress the data on your hard disk so that the disk's capacity is effectively doubled. And it really, really works.

  I wrote an entire book about DoubleSpace, published by another publisher, but I'm afraid that if I mention it here my IDG editor will lay a curse upon me, and my family will never hear from me again. So I won't mention it here at all.

- ✔ Make sure that all network users are encouraged to remember that their computers have local disk drives in addition to the network drives. Just because you have a network, that doesn't mean that everything has to be stored on a network drive!

- ✔ Do not try to cut costs by using diskless workstations. Some networks are set up so that the workstations have no local drives at all. For this to work, a special chip is required in the network interface card so that the computer can boot without a disk drive. Diskless workstations are cheaper, but they force the user to store everything on the network. In addition, they bog down the network because routine disk accesses, such as locating DOS program files, have to travel across the network cable.

What to Put on a File Server

Of course, the only way to really predict how much network disk space you'll need is to plan what files you're going to store on the server. You need enough space to accommodate the network itself, shared data files, private data files, and shared application programs.

The network itself

Not all the space on the network server's disk can be made available to network users; some of it is required for the network operating system itself. It's not unreasonable to set aside 50MB of disk space for the network operating system, print spool files, sealing wax, and other fancy stuff.

- ✔ For NetWare or a similar server-based NOS, allow 20MB of disk space for the network operating system itself. For a peer-to-peer network such as LANtastic, allow 10MB for the NOS and MS-DOS. Windows for Workgroups weighs in at about 15MB.

- ✔ If the server will support a printer, allow an additional 10MB for spool files. If you routinely print large graphics files on the network printer, you may have to allow even more spool space.

- ✔ Allow space for any additional programs you may want to have available on the server, such as a utility program like PC Tools. The latest version of PC Tools requires about 15MB.

Shared data files

Allow sufficient space on the file server for data files that network users will share. Most of this space may be taken up by one large database file, or it could consist of hundreds or even thousands of small word processing or spread-sheet files. Either way, don't skimp on space here.

Estimate the amount of space you'll need for shared files. The only way you can do this is to add up the size of the files that will be shared. Double the result. If you can afford to, double it again.

Private data files

Every user will want access to network disk space for private file storage — perhaps because their own disks are getting full, or they want the security of knowing that their files will be backed up regularly, or they just want to try out the network. There are two approaches to providing this private space:

- ✔ Create a subdirectory for each network user on a shared network drive. For example, the Cleavers set up the following private directories:

  Ward   \WARD

  June   \JUNE

  Wally   \WALLY

  Beaver \BEAVER

Now, just tell each network user to store private files in his or her own subdirectory. The problem with this setup is that these directories aren't really private; there's nothing to keep Beaver from looking at files in Wally's directory.

✔ Create a separate network drive mapping for each private directory. For example, you can map drive P to each network user's private directory. Then you can tell each user to store private files on his or her P drive. For Wally, the P drive refers to the \WALLY directory, but for Beaver, P refers to \BEAVER. This keeps Beaver out of Wally's files.

The net effect (groan....sorry) of this setup is that each user seems to have a separate P drive on the server. In reality, these drives are merely subdirectories on the server drive.

✔ Estimating the disk space required for private file storage is more difficult than estimating shared file storage. After your users figure out that they have seemingly unlimited private storage on the network server, they'll start filling it up.

Shared programs

If several users use the same application program, you should consider purchasing a network version of the program and storing the program file on the network server. The advantage of doing this rather than storing a separate copy of the program on each user's local disk is that you have to manage only one copy of the software. For example, if a new version of the software comes out, you have to update just the copy on the server rather than separate copies on each workstation.

✔ The network version of most programs lets each network user set the program's options according to his or her preferences. Thus, one user might run the program using the default setup with boring colors, while another user prefers to change the screen colors so the program displays magenta text on a cyan background. Stalin probably would have outlawed network versions.

✔ Many application programs create temporary files that you're not aware of and don't normally need to worry about. When you use these programs on a network, you should be sure to configure them so that the temporary files are created on a local drive rather than on a network drive. That not only gives you better performance, but it ensures that one user's temporary files don't interfere with another's.

Planning Your Network Drive Mapping

When you've decided what files will be stored on your server's drive, you should scope out the drive letters you'll use to access those files from network workstations. Here are some general rules to follow:

- ✔ Be consistent. If a network drive is accessed as drive Q from one workstation, it should be mapped as drive Q from all workstations that access the same drive. Don't have one user referring to a network drive as drive Q and another using the same drive but with a different letter.

- ✔ Use drive letters that are high enough to avoid conflicts with drive letters that are used by local drives. For example, suppose that one of your computers has three disk partitions, a CD-ROM drive, and a RAM drive. This computer would already have drive letters C through G assigned. I usually start network drive assignments with drive M and continue with N, O, P, and so on.

- ✔ Novell NetWare usually begins drive assignments at drive F.

- ✔ If you use MS-DOS 6.0 or 6.2 and DoubleSpace, be aware that DoubleSpace will cause drive letter crashes if you're not careful. To protect yourself, start your network before you install DoubleSpace so that DoubleSpace can find its way around your network drive assignments. And always wear a helmet and safety goggles when using DoubleSpace.

If you read this, your dog will die

NetWare decides which drive letter to assign to the first network drive by peeking inside that scariest-of-all DOS files, CONFIG.SYS. NetWare looks in CONFIG.SYS to see whether it contains a line that looks like this:

```
LASTDRIVE=E
```

This CONFIG.SYS line tells DOS how many drive letters to set aside for local use. NetWare knows its ABCs, so it picks the next letter in the alphabet after the LASTDRIVE letter to use for the first network drive letter. If LASTDRIVE is set to E, NetWare uses F for the first network drive. If LASTDRIVE is set to G, NetWare uses H. You get the idea.

Not all CONFIG.SYS files have a LASTDRIVE line. If LASTDRIVE is missing, DOS assumes that E is the highest drive letter in use. That's why NetWare usually picks F for the network drive.

You can change LASTDRIVE if you want, but that's heady DOS stuff that requires a pocket protector.

Using a Separate Print Server

If you have a larger network (say, eight or more computers) and shared printing is one of the main reasons you're networking, you may want to consider using two dedicated server computers: one as a file server, the other as a print server.

✔ Most network operating systems have configuration options that enable you to balance disk performance against printer performance. By using separate computers for your file server and print server, you can set these options accordingly. If the same computer works as both a file server and a print server, you must set these options somewhere in the middle, compromising performance one way or the other.

✔ If the printer is a dot-matrix printer or a laser printer used exclusively for text output, the print server can be the slowest computer on the network and you still won't notice any performance delay. If you do a lot of graphics printing on a high-quality laser printer, however, don't use a dog computer for the print server. I once saw 10-minute print jobs slowed to an hour or more by a cheap print server.

Buying a Server Computer

If you have a spare computer lying around that you can use as a server, great. Most of us don't have spare computers in the closet, though. If you plan to buy a new computer to use as a network server, here are some tips for configuring it properly:

✔ A network server computer need not have the latest in high-resolution color monitors. Monochrome is fine. After all, the server just sits there all day with the same boring display. No need to spend $600 on a VGA monitor and card when a $200 monochrome monitor and card will do just as well. (Unless, of course, you're running Windows for Workgroups, which requires the server to run Windows.)

✔ On the other hand, do not scrimp when it comes to the processor and memory. If you can afford it, buy a 486 processor and at least 8MB of RAM. Sixteen megabytes is better. Every last byte of extra memory can be put to good use on a server.

✔ Buy the biggest disk drive you can afford. If you're gutsy, double its capacity with DoubleSpace or another disk-compression program (if you're using a peer-to-peer network).

✔ Don't pay for Windows and a mouse. You don't need either for a dedicated server computer. (Unless, of course, you use Windows for Workgroups.)

✔ Have the computer built in a tower-style case that has plenty of room for expansion: several free bays for additional disk drives and a more-than-adequate power supply. You want to make sure that you can expand the server when you realize you didn't buy enough disk space.

Keeping the Power On

One feature people often overlook when setting up a network server is the power. You can simply plug the server computer into the wall, or you can plug it into a surge protector to smoothe out power spikes before they damage your computer. Using a surge protector is good, but even better is connecting your server computer to a device called an *uninterruptible power supply*, or *UPS*.

Inside the UPS box is a battery that is constantly charged and some electronics that monitor the condition of the power coming from the wall outlet. If a power failure occurs, the battery keeps the computer running. The battery can't run the computer forever, but it can keep it running long enough — anywhere from 10 minutes to more than an hour, depending on how much you paid for the UPS — to shut things down in familiar Presbyterian fashion (decently and in order). For most small networks, a UPS that keeps you going for 10 minutes is enough. You just want to make sure that any disk I/O in progress has time to finish. A decent UPS can be had for about $150.

  ✔ Using a UPS can prevent you from losing data when a power outage occurs. Without a UPS, your server computer can be shut down at the worst of times, such as while it is updating the directory information that tracks the location of your files. With a UPS, the computer can stay on long enough for such meticulous operations to be completed safely.

  ✔ In a true UPS, power is always supplied to the computer from the battery; the current from the wall outlet is used only to keep the battery charged. Most inexpensive UPS devices are actually *stand-by power supplies* (*SPSs*). An SPS runs the computer from the wall-outlet current but switches to battery within a few gazillionths of a second if a power failure occurs. With a true UPS, there is no delay between the power failure and the battery takeover. SPSs are less expensive than UPSs, though, so they're more commonly used.

  ✔ The ultimate power-failure protection is to attach a UPS to every computer on the network. That gets a bit expensive, though. But at least protect the server.

  ✔ If a power outage occurs and your server is protected by a UPS, get to the server as quickly as you can, log everyone off, and shut down the server. It's also a good idea to go to each computer and turn off the power switch. Then, when power is restored, you can restart the server, then restart each workstation, and assess the damage.

Location, Location, and Location

The final network server consideration to address in this chapter is where to put the server. In the old days, you put the network server in a room with glass windows all around, had a full-time lab technician in a white coat tending to its every need, and gave it a name like "ARDVARC" or "SHADRAC."

Nowadays, the most likely location for a file server is in the closet. There's no reason the server has to be in a central location; it can be in the closet down at the end of the hall, atop the filing cabinets in the storage room, or in the corner office. It can be almost anywhere, as long as it's near an electrical outlet and network cable can be routed to it.

Of course, a print server is different. It should be near the printer, which should be in an accessible location with storage space for paper, toner (for laser printers), a place to leave printouts that belong to other users, and a box to drop wasted paper so that it can be recycled.

Some bad locations for the server:

- ✔ In the attic. Too dusty.
- ✔ In the bathroom. Too much moisture.
- ✔ In the kitchen. Your computer gurus will raid your refrigerator every time you call them. They'll start showing up spontaneously "just to check."
- ✔ In your boss's office. You don't want him or her to think of you every time the server beeps.

The good news is that you still get to name your server computer. You can call it something boring like SERVER1, or you can give it an interesting name like BERTHA or HERBIE.

Chapter 9

Oh, What a Tangled Web We Weave (Cables, Adapters, and Other Stuff)

* *

In This Chapter

▶ What Ethernet is

▶ The different types of network cable

▶ Using coax cable

▶ Using twisted-pair cable

▶ Mixing coax and twisted pair on the same network

▶ Selecting your network interface cards

▶ Professional touches for your cabling

▶ Reading a network mail-order advertisement

* *

*I*f you've ever installed an underground sprinkler system, you'll have no trouble cabling your network. Working with network cable is a lot like working with sprinkler pipe: You have to use the right size pipe (cable), the right valves and headers (hubs and repeaters), and the right sprinkler heads (network interface cards).

Network cables have one compelling advantage over sprinkler pipes: You don't get wet when they leak.

This chapter tells you far more about network cables than you probably need to know. It introduces you to Ethernet, the most common system of network cabling for small networks. Then it shows you how to work with the cables used to wire an Ethernet network. It also shows you how to select the right network interface cards that let you connect the cables to your computers.

What Is Ethernet?

Ethernet is a standardized way of connecting computers together to create a network. You can think of Ethernet as kind of like a municipal building code for networks: It specifies what kind of cables should be used, how the cables should be connected together, how long the cables can be, how computers transmit data to one another using the cables, and more.

There are two other popular network building codes you may have heard of: Token Ring and ARCnet. Ethernet is more commonly used than Token Ring because it is less expensive. Ethernet is used more than ARCnet because ARCnet is slower.

Some people treat Ethernet, Token Ring, and ARCnet like religions they are willing to die for. To a Token Ring zealot, Ethernet represents the Antichrist. Ethernet fanatics often claim you can hear satanic messages if you send data backwards through a Token Ring network. Both treat ARCnet as if it were a cult, possibly because there have been reports of ARCnet disciples giving away flowers at airports. Do *not* engage an Ethernet, Token Ring, or ARCnet Pharisee in a discussion about the merits of his or her network beliefs over opponents' beliefs. It is futile.

Without regard to the technical merits of Ethernet, Token Ring, or ARCnet, the fact is that the vast majority of small networks use Ethernet. 'Nough said.

- ✔ Ethernet is a set of standards for the infrastructure a network is built on. All the network operating systems I've discussed in this book — NetWare, NetWare Lite, LANtastic, and Windows for Workgroups — can operate on an Ethernet network. If you build your network on a solid Ethernet base, you can easily change network operating systems later.

- ✔ Ethernet is often referred to by network gurus as 802.3 (pronounced *eight-oh-two-dot-three*) because that's the official designation used by the IEEE (pronounced *Eye-triple-ee*), a group of electrical engineers who wear bow ties and have nothing better to do than argue about inductance all day long. It's a good thing, though, because if it weren't for them, you wouldn't be able to mix and match Ethernet components made by different companies.

- ✔ Ethernet transmits data at a rate of 10 million bits per second, or 10Mbps. Because there are 8 bits in a byte, that translates into roughly 1.2 million bytes per second. In practice, Ethernet can't move information that fast because data must be transmitted in packages of no more than 1,500 bytes, called *packets*. So, a 150K file would have to be split into 100 packets.

This speed has nothing to do with how fast electrical signals move on the cable. The electrical signals themselves travel at about 70 percent the speed of light, or, as Picard would say, "Warp factor point-seven-oh. Engage."

Who cares what CSMA/CD stands for?

Besides specifying the mechanical and electrical characteristics of network cables, Ethernet specifies the techniques used to control the flow of information over the network cables. The technique Ethernet uses is called CSMA/CD, which stands for "carrier sense multiple access with collision detection." This is a mouthful, but if we take it apart piece by piece, you'll get an idea of how Ethernet works (as if you want to know).

Carrier sense means that whenever a computer wants to send a message on the network cable, it first listens to the cable to see whether anyone else is already sending a message. If it doesn't hear any other messages on the cable, the computer assumes it is free to send one.

Multiple access means that there is nothing to prevent two or more computers from trying to send a message at the same time. Sure, each computer listens before sending. But suppose

that two computers listen, hear nothing, and then proceed to send their messages? Picture what happens when you and someone else arrive at a four-way stop sign at the same time. You wave the other driver on, he or she waves you on, you wave, he or she waves, you all wave, and then you both end up going at the same time.

Collision detection means that after a computer sends a message on the network, it listens carefully to see whether it crashed into another message. Kind of like listening for the screeching of brakes at the four-way stop. If the computer hears the screeching of breaks, it waits for a random period of time and tries to send the message again. Because the delay is random, two messages that collide will be sent again after different delay periods, so a second collision is unlikely.

Wasn't that a waste of time?

Stop me before I tell you about Token Ring!

Just in case you do get into an argument about Ethernet with a Token Ring fanatic, here's where he or she's coming from. Ethernet can get bogged down if the network gets really busy and messages start colliding like crazy. Token Ring uses a more orderly approach to sending packets through the network. Instead of sending a message whenever it wants to, a computer on a Token Ring network must wait its turn. In a Token Ring network, a special packet called the *token* is constantly passed through the network from computer to computer. A computer can send a packet of data only when it has the token. In this way, Token Ring ensures that collisions won't

happen.

Sometimes, a computer with a defective network interface card will accidentally swallow the token. If the token disappears for too long, the network assumes it's been swallowed, so the network generates a new token.

Two versions of Token Ring are in use. The older version runs at 4Mbps. The newer version runs at 16Mbps, plus it allows two tokens to exist at once, which makes the network even faster.

Oh, in case you're wondering, ARCnet uses a similar token-passing scheme.

Three Types of Ethernet Cable

An Ethernet network can be constructed using three different types of cable: thick coax (called *yellow cable* because it's usually yellow), thin coax (called *thinnet* because it's thinner than the yellow stuff, or *cheapernet* because it's cheaper than the yellow stuff), or twisted pair, which looks like phone cable. Twisted-pair cable is sometimes called UTP or 10baseT cable, for reasons I'll try hard not to explain later.

The yellow stuff isn't used much for small networks, but I'll describe it anyway. The real choice you must make is between thinnet cable and twisted pair.

Worthless filler about network topology

A networking book wouldn't be complete without the usual textbook description of the three basic "network topologies." The first type of network topology is called a *bus*, in which network nodes (that is, computers) are strung together in a line, like this:

This is the simplest type of topology, but it has its drawbacks. If the cable breaks somewhere in the middle, it splits the network into two.

The second type of topology is called a *ring*:

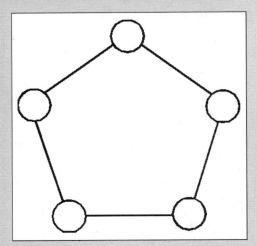

A ring is very much like a bus, except there's no end to the line: The last node on the line is connected to the first node, forming an endless loop.

The third type of topology is called a *star*.

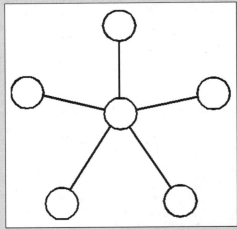

In a star network, all the nodes are connected to a central *hub*. In effect, each node has an independent connection to the network, so a break in one cable doesn't affect the others.

Ethernet networks are based on a bus design.

The yellow stuff

The original Ethernet networks were wired with thick, heavy cable called thick coax, or yellow cable, because of its color. Thick coax isn't used much anymore, especially for small networks, because it is expensive, heavy, and not very flexible (I mean that literally: It's difficult to make yellow cable bend around tight corners).

- ✔ The yellow stuff is less susceptible to interference from mongo-magnets and motors and what not, so it's still used sometimes in factories, warehouses, nuclear test sites, Frankenstein laboratories, and so on.

- ✔ Yellow cable can be strung for greater distances than other types of Ethernet cable. A single run of yellow cable (called a *segment*) can be as long as 500 meters.

- ✔ The way yellow cable is attached to individual computers is weird. Usually, a long length of yellow cable is run along a path that takes it near each computer on the network. Each computer must be connected to the yellow cable via a device called a *transceiver*. The transceiver usually includes a *vampire tap*, a clamp-like thingamabob that taps into the yellow cable without cutting and splicing it. The transceiver is connected to the network interface card by means of an *AUI* cable. (*AUI* stands for *attached unit interface*, not that it matters.)

- ✔ I think you can see why the yellow stuff isn't used much anymore.

- ✔ It's really too bad, because the yellow stuff would coordinate so well with this book.

Thinnet

The most common type of cable used for small networks is thin coaxial cable, usually called *thinnet*. Thinnet is less expensive than yellow cable, not only because the cable itself is less expensive, but also because separate transceivers aren't required to attach computers to the cable. (Thinnet does use transceivers, but the transceiver is built into the adapter card.) Figure 9-1 shows a typical thinnet cable.

- ✔ Thinnet is about ⅕ inch in diameter, so it's much lighter and more flexible than the yellow stuff. You can easily wrap it around corners, drape it over doorways, around potted plants, and so on.

- ✔ You attach thinnet to the network interface card by using a goofy twist-on connector called a *BNC* connector. You can purchase preassembled cables with BNC connectors already attached in lengths of 25 or 50 feet, or you can buy bulk cable on a big spool and attach the connectors yourself by using a special tool.

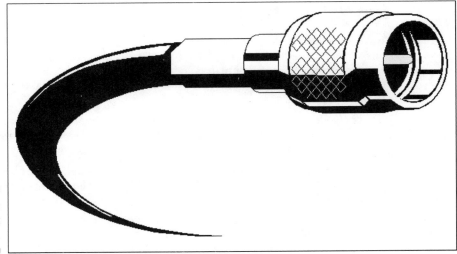

Figure 9-1:
A thinnet
cable.

✔ Whereas yellow cable is usually wired with a single length of cable that is
tapped into using vampire taps, thinnet is run with separate lengths of
cable. At each computer, a tee-connector is used to connect two cables to
the network interface card. Figure 9-2 shows a typical thinnet arrangement.
One length of thinnet connects Ward's computer to June's, a second length
connects June's to Wally's, and a third length connects Wally's to Beaver's.

✔ A special plug called a *terminator* is required at each end of a series of
thinnet cables. In Figure 9-2, a terminator is required at Ward's computer
and at Beaver's. The terminator prevents data from spilling out the end of
the cable and staining the carpet.

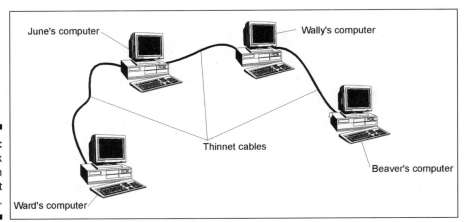

Figure 9-2:
A network
wired with
thinnet
cable.

✔ The cables strung end to end from one terminator to the other are collectively called a *segment*. The maximum length of a thinnet segment is 185 meters. You can connect as many as 30 computers on one segment. To span a distance greater than 185 meters or to connect more than 30 computers, you must use two or more segments with a funky device called a *repeater* to connect each segments.

Unshielded twisted-pair (UTP) cable

In recent years, a new type of cable has become popular with Ethernet networks: unshielded twisted-pair cable, or UTP. UTP cable is even cheaper than thin coax cable, and, best of all, many modern buildings are already wired with twisted pair, because this type of wiring is often used with modern phone systems. Figure 9-3 shows a twisted-pair cable.

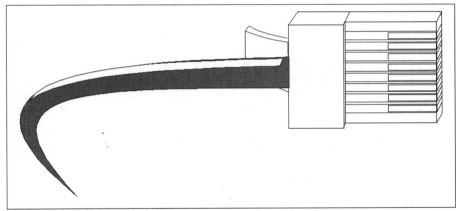

Figure 9-3:
Unshielded
twisted pair
cable.

When you use UTP cable to construct an Ethernet network, you connect the computers in a star arrangement, as Figure 9-4 illustrates. In the center of this star is a device called a *hub*. Depending on the model, Ethernet hubs let you connect from 4 to 24 computers using twisted-pair cable. Most hubs have connectors for 8 or 12 cables. Hubs are sometimes called *concentrators*.

An advantage of this star arrangement is that if one cable goes bad, only the computer attached to that cable is affected; the rest of the network continues to chug along. With thinnet, a bad cable affects not only the computer it's connected to, but all computers unfortunate enough to lie beyond the bad cable.

✔ UTP cable consists of pairs of thin wire twisted around each other; several such pairs are gathered up inside an outer insulating jacket. Ethernet uses two pairs of wires, or four wires all together. The number of pairs in a UTP cable varies but is often more than two. UTP with four pairs can be used for both a phone system and a computer network.

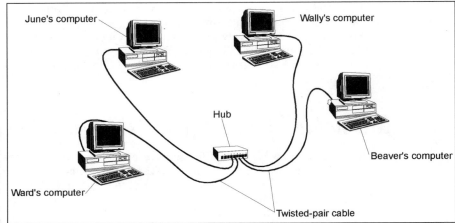

Figure 9-4: A
network
wired with
twisted-pair
cable.

✔ UTP cable comes in five grades, level 1 through level 5. The higher the level number, the greater the amount of protection the cable provides from outside electrical interference. Of course, higher-level cables are also more expensive. Ethernet networks should be cabled with level 3 or better. Level 5 is preferable.

✔ UTP cable connectors look like modular phone connectors but are slightly different. UTP connectors are officially called *RJ-45 connectors*.

✔ Unlike thinnet, UTP cable is rarely sold in prefabricated lengths. You must buy bulk cable, cut it to the length you want, and attach the connectors with a special tool.

✔ The maximum allowable cable length between the hub and the computer is 100 meters.

Working with Hubs

The biggest difference between using thinnet and UTP cable is that when you use UTP, you also must use a separate device called a *hub*. Working with a hub is not difficult, but it is one extra piece of an already complicated puzzle, so many do-it-yourself networkers opt for thinnet to avoid dealing with hubs altogether.

If your network has more than 6 or 8 computers, you may find it's worth it to purchase a hub and use UTP instead of thinnet, especially if it's likely that your networking needs will change periodically. With UTP, it's easier to add new computers to the network, to move computers, to find and correct cable problems, and to service computers that need to be removed from the network temporarily.

Ten base what?

The IEEE, in its infinite wisdom, has decreed that the following names shall be used to designate the three types of cable used with 802.3 networks (in other words, with Ethernet):

- *10base5* is thick coax cable (the yellow stuff).

- *10base2* is thin coax cable (thinnet).

- *10baseT* is unshielded twisted-pair cable (UTP).

In each moniker, the *10* means that the cable operates at 10Mbps, and *base* means the cable is used for baseband networks as opposed to broadband networks (don't ask). The *5* in *10base5* is the maximum length of a yellow cable segment: 500 meters; the *2* in *10base2* stands for 200 meters, which is about the 185-meter maximum segment length for thinnet (for a group of engineers, the IEEE is odd; I didn't know the word "about" is in an engineer's vocabulary); and the *T* in *10baseT* stands for "twisted."

Of these three official monikers, 10baseT is the only one that's frequently used; 10base5 and 10base2 are usually just called *thick* and *thin*.

If you do decide to use UTP, you need to know some of the ins and outs of using 10baseT hubs:

- Because you must run a cable from each computer to the hub, find a central location for the hub to which the cables can be easily routed.

- The hub requires electrical power, so make sure there's an electrical outlet handy.

- When you purchase the hub, purchase one with at least half as many connections as you need. Don't buy a four-port hub if you want to network four computers; when (and not if) you add the fifth computer, you'll have to buy another hub.

- You can connect hubs to one another as shown in Figure 9-5; this is called *daisy-chaining*. When you daisy-chain hubs, you connect a cable to a standard port on one of the hubs and the daisy-chain port on the other hub. Be sure to read the instructions that came with the hub to make sure that you daisy-chain them properly.

- You can daisy-chain no more than three hubs together. If you have more computers than can be accommodated by three hubs, don't panic. Most hubs have a BNC connection on the back so that you can connect them together via thinnet cable. The three-hub limit doesn't apply when you connect the hubs using thinnet cable.

- When you shop for network hubs, you may notice that the expensive ones have network-management features that support something called *SNMP*. Unless your network is very large and you know what SNMP is, don't bother with the SNMP hubs. You'd be paying for a feature you'd never use.

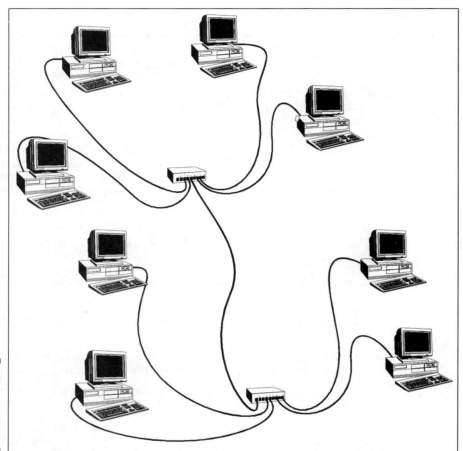

Figure 9-5:
You can
daisy-chain
hubs
together.

Network Interface Cards

Now that you know far more about network cable than you really need to, I want to point out a few things about network interface cards you should consider before you buy:

- ✔ The network interface cards you use must have a connector that matches the type of cable you use. If you plan on wiring your network with thinnet cable, make sure that the network cards have a BNC connector. For twisted pair wiring, make sure that the cards have an RJ-45 connector.

- ✔ Some network cards provide two or three connectors. I've seen them in every combination: BNC and AUI, RJ-45 and AUI, BNC and RJ-45, and all three. It's not a bad idea to select a card that has both BNC and RJ-45 connectors. That way, you can switch from thinnet to twisted pair or vice-versa without buying new network cards. It should cost only $10-$20 more per card to get both types of connectors. Don't worry about the AUI connector, though. You'll probably never need it. Figure 9-6 shows Ethernet cards with various connectors; these particular cards are from Artisoft's NodeRunner series.

✔ The standard of compatibility for network interface cards is the NE2000, which used to be manufactured by Novell but is now made by Eagle. If a card is NE2000 compatible, you can use it with just about any network.

✔ When you purchase a network card, make sure that you get one that's compatible with your computer. Most computers can accommodate cards designed for the standard 16-bit ISA bus. But if you have an IBM PS/2 with its proprietary Micro Channel bus, you must purchase network cards designed for Micro Channel.

✔ Some newer network cards let you configure various settings by using software. This is easier than the tedious configuration gyrations most cards demand. The NodeRunner cards shown in Figure 9-6 use software configuration.

✔ Network cards can be a bit tricky to set up, and each one has its nuances. You'll simplify your life a bit if you pick one card and stick with it. Try not to mix and match network cards.

Figure 9-6:
Four
Ethernet
cards.

✔ If you see Ethernet cards advertised on late-night television for an unbelievably low price (like $19.95 or something), make sure that the cards are
16-bit cards. You won't be satisfied with the slow performance of bargain-
basement 8-bit cards unless your computer is also of the bargain-base-
ment variety. If you have a 386 or 486 computer, don't even think about
using 8-bit cards.

✔ If you're stuck in the dark ages with an ancient 8088-based computer (such
as an original IBM PC or XT), you have two alternatives: (1) You can
purchase an 8-bit network adapter card or (2) you can sell the computer to
Sanford & Son (like for $19.95 or something). Don't get a 16-bit network
adapter card, though, because it won't work. 8088-based computers don't
have a 16-bit bus, so they can't accommodate 16-bit cards.

Professional Touches

If most of the stuff I've presented so far makes sense to you, and if you want to
impress your friends, consider adding the following extra touches to your network
installation. They'll make the job look like it was done by a professional. (If
you've found this chapter to be hopelessly confusing so far, you should probably concentrate on just getting your network up and running. Worry about
making it look pretty later.)

These professional touches are shown in Figure 9-7.

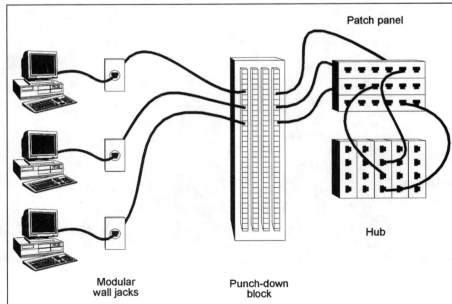

Figure 9-7:
A
professional
touch.

Modular wall jacks · Punch-down block · Patch panel · Hub

✔ Use 10baseT wiring; that's what most network pros are doing these days.

✔ Run the wiring through the ceiling and walls instead of along the floor, and mount a wall jack near each computer. Then plug each computer into the wall jack by using a short (10-foot or so) *patch cable*.

✔ To really do it right, run 10baseT cable to every possible computer location in your office, even if you don't yet have a computer there. That way, when you do move a computer to that location, the hard wiring (up in the ceiling and through the wall) already will have been done. All you'll have to do is attach the computer to the wall jack with a patch cord.

✔ Designate a corner of a closet or storeroom to be your *wiring closet*. Bundle all the cables together and attach them to a *punch-down block*. Run wires from the punch-down block to a patch panel, which is nothing more than a series of RJ-45 jacks mounted neatly in a row.

✔ Connect the appropriate jacks in the patch panel to your network hub with short patch cables. The whole thing will look a bit like a rat's nest, but you'll be able to easily reconfigure the network at a moment's notice. If someone changes locations, all you have to do is adjust the patch cables in the wiring closet accordingly.

✔ A full-fledged patch panel like this is usually used only with large networks. For smaller networks, you can get small self-contained units that contain a punch-down block that's already connected to six or eight RJ-45 blocks. These boxes are a slick way to give a professional look to a small network setup.

✔ Be careful about making your network look too good. People will assume that *you* are a network geek, and they'll start offering you Cheetos to solve their problems.

Reading a Network Ad

If you're willing to purchase your network components from a mail-order supplier, you can probably save a bunch of money. Just go to the supermarket and pick up a copy of *Computer Shopper* and browse through it until you find several companies that specialize in networking products. Figure 9-8 shows a typical mail-order advertisement for network stuff.

You can probably figure out most of this ad, but I want to point out a few things:

✔ The lines that have two prices are either listing the price if you buy one item or the price if you buy five or more, or the price for two similar items configured differently. For example, the NE2000-Compatible network card with a BNC and 10baseT connector is $119 if you buy one, but $109 each if you buy five or more. The Artisoft AE2 and AE2T Ethernet adapters are both $209.

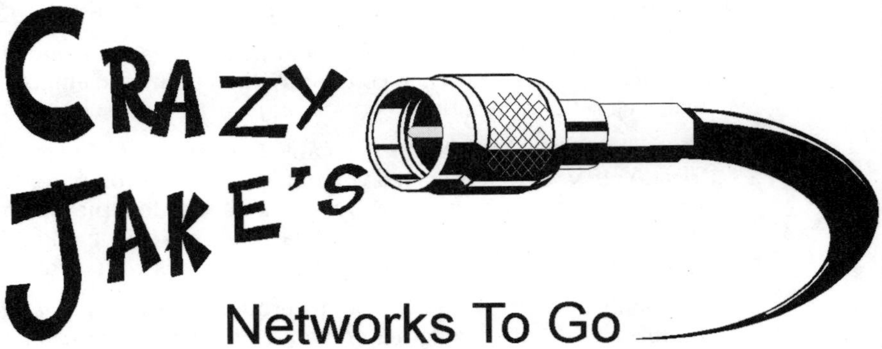

ETHERNET CARDS

NE2000 Compatible-BNC ea/5+	109/99
NE2000 Compatible-BNC+10baseT ea/5+	119/109
NE2000 Compatible-BNC+10baseT+AUI ea/5+	149/129

HUBS

12 port+BNC+AUI 10baseT Cascadable Hub	499
Thomas Conrad 8 Port	389

NETWARE

NetWare 3.11 5 User	579
NetWare 3.11 50/100 User	$CALL
NetWare 2.2 5 User	479
NetWare 2.2 10/50 User	1,099/2,099
NetWare Lite	69

ARTISOFT

NodeRunner Starter Kit	449
NodeRunner Starter Kit w/Windows	549
AE2 Ethernet Adapter BNC+AUI/AE2T BNC+10baseT	209/209
AE3 Ethernet Adapter BNC+10baseT+AUI	239
Lantastic 5.0 Adapter Independent NOS	69

CABLE

Thinnet 25' Assy	15
Thinnet 50' Assy	25
Thinnet 1000' Spool	199
10baseT 4 pair 1000' Spool	139
BNC Crimp Connector	3
BNC T-Connector	4
BNC Crimp Tool	39
RJ45 Connector	75¢
RJ45 Crimp Tool	39

Figure 9-8: A mail-order add for network stuff.

✔ You can't tell from the ad what's included in the NodeRunner Starter Kit; you'll have to call to find out.

✔ If you're building a LANtastic network and you buy the inexpensive Ethernet cards, you'll also have to buy one copy of the LANtastic 5.0 Adapter Independent NOS for each card.

✔ The price of a 50- or 100-user license of NetWare 3.11 changes too often to print, so you have to call to find out.

✔ Most mail-order networking companies are very willing to answer questions on the phone. If you're not sure what you need, give the company a call.

✔ Make sure that you understand the shipping costs and the conditions for returning damaged goods. Before you buy anything, make sure that they have it in stock and can ship it the same day, or the next day if you call late.

Chapter 10

Putting It Together
(or, Insert Tab A into Slot B)

....

....

Now comes the fun part: putting your network together. Get ready to roll up your sleeves and dig in to the bowels of your computers. Make sure that you scrub thoroughly first.

Tools You'll Need

Of course, to do a job right, you must have the right tools.

Start with a basic set of computer tools, which can be had for about $15 from any computer store or large business-supply store. These kits include the right screwdrivers and socket wrenches to open up your computers and insert adapter cards. (If you don't have a computer tool kit, make sure that you have several flathead and Phillips screwdrivers of various sizes.)

If all your computers are in the same room, and you're going to run the cables along the floor, and you're using prefabricated cables, the computer tool kit should contain everything you need.

If you're using bulk cable and plan on attaching your own connectors, you need:

- ✔ Wire cutters. Big ones for thinnet cable; smaller ones are okay for 10baseT cable. If you're using yellow cable, you need the Jaws of Life.

- ✔ A crimp tool appropriate to your cable type. You need the crimp tool to attach the connectors to the cable.

- ✔ If the crimp tool does not include a wire stripper, you need a separate wire stripper. For thinnet, a special wire-stripper-doohickey is required because the cable's inner conductor, outer conductor, and outer insulation must be cut at precise lengths.

If you plan on running cables through walls, you need additional tools:

- ✔ A hammer.

- ✔ A keyhole saw, if you plan on cutting holes through walls to route your cable.

- ✔ A flashlight.

- ✔ A ladder.

- ✔ Possibly a *fish tape*. A fish tape is a coiled-up length of stiff metal tape. To use it, you feed the tape into one wall opening and "fish" it towards the other opening, where a partner is ready to grab it when it arrives. Next, your partner attaches the cable to the fish tape and yells something like "Let 'er rip!" or "Bombs away!" Then you reel in the fish tape and the cable along with it. (Fish tape can be found in the electrical section of most well-stocked hardware stores.)

- ✔ If you plan on routing cable through a concrete subfloor, you need to rent a jackhammer and a backhoe and hire someone to hold a yellow flag while you work.

Configuring and Installing Your Network Cards

You have to install a network card in each of your computers before you can connect the network cables. Installing a network card is a manageable task, but you have to be willing to roll up your sleeves.

Unfortunately, most network cards must be *configured* before you install them. This is probably the most confusing part of installing a network, and it's also the most troublesome if you don't get it just right. So be sure to pay attention when you're configuring your network cards. Make sure that you've had your morning coffee.

✔ It's not your fault that this is so confusing. Blame it on the guys and gals who designed the original IBM PC many moons ago. They had no idea that so many companies would make so many different kinds of add-on devices for the PC, such as modems, scanners, tape drives, CD-ROM drives, mice, and, of course, network cards. So they didn't put enough engineering muscle into the design of the PC's expansion slots. The result is that you have to manually configure your network card to make sure that its electronic signals don't crash into electronic signals used by the other manually-configured cards already in your computer.

✔ To change the configuration settings on most cards, you must change DIP switches or jumper blocks. Figure 10-1 shows what a DIP switch and a jumper block look like.

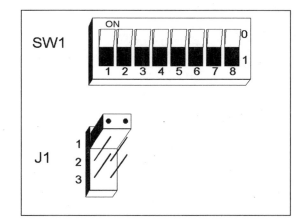

Figure 10-1:
A DIP switch and a jumper block.

✔ A straightened-out paper clip is the ideal tool for setting DIP switches.

✔ To change a jumper block, you move the "plug" from one set of wires to another. You need fingernails to do it properly.

✔ If you're lucky, your network cards have been preconfigured for you with the most likely settings. You need to double-check, though, because (1) the factory settings are not always appropriate, and (2) sometimes they make mistakes at the factory and configure the card incorrectly.

✔ If you're even luckier, your cards don't use DIP switches or jumper blocks at all. These cards still have to be configured, but the configuration is done with software rather than with a paper clip or your fingernails.

✔ Most network cards have two configuration settings: IRQ number and I/O port address. Some also let you configure a DMA channel. These settings are described under separate headings on the next few pages. It's technical and boring, so make sure that you're wide awake.

  ✔ Network cards that support more than one type of cable connector also have to be configured for the proper cable type. For example, if your card supports both 10baseT and AUI connectors, you have to configure the card depending on the type of cable you use. Normally, the card will be configured at the factory for thinnet or 10baseT (if the card supports both thinnet *and* 10baseT, it's usually configured for thinnet). So you have to change the configuration only if you're not using the preconfigured cable type.

  ✔ When you configure a network card, write down the settings you select. You'll need these settings later when you install the workstation software. Store your list of network card settings in your network binder.

  ✔ It would be too easy to add a joke about DIP switches here. Insert your own joke if you are so inclined.

Configuring the IRQ number

IRQ stands for "Interrupt ReQuest." You don't need to know that; I showed you only because I think it's funny that the Q is capitalized in the middle of the word. Each computer has 16 different IRQ numbers, and each I/O device — such as a printer port, modem, mouse, and so on — must be assigned a separate IRQ number. It's not always easy to find an IRQ number that's not already used. (On old XT computers, there are only eight IRQ numbers. That makes it even harder to avoid IRQ conflicts.)

The trick to setting the IRQ number is knowing what IRQ numbers are already being used by the computer. Table 10-1 shows the usual IRQ settings.

Table 10-1	Typical IRQ Assignments
IRQ Number	*What It's Used For*
IRQ0	The computer's internal timer
IRQ1	The keyboard
IRQ2	Not usable
IRQ3	Serial port COM2, often a mouse or modem
IRQ4	Serial port COM1, often a mouse or modem
IRQ5	Parallel port LPT2
IRQ6	Floppy disk
IRQ7	Parallel port LPT1
IRQ8	Internal clock
IRQ9-13	Usually available
IRQ14	Hard disk
IRQ15	Usually available

✔ Some network interface cards support only a few IRQ numbers, such as IRQ 3, 4, or 5. IRQ5 is usually a safe choice unless the computer has two printers. However, if you've installed a device such as a CD-ROM drive or a scanner, make sure that IRQ5 isn't already in use.

✔ IRQ3 and 4 are used by the serial ports COM1 and COM2. If you have a modem and a serial-port mouse, don't use IRQ3 or 4 for the network card.

✔ If your computer is loaded up with extra devices, you should check which IRQs are available *before* you buy your network cards. Make sure that the cards you buy can be configured to an IRQ number you can use.

✔ If you're not sure what IRQ numbers are in use and you have DOS version 6.0 or 6.2 or Windows 3.1, run the MSD program. Press Q to display the IRQs that are in use.

Configuring the I/O port address

The I/O port address is a doorway the network card uses to transfer information to and from the network. It's usually set to a number such as 300, 310, 320, and so on. The only trick to setting the I/O port is making sure that it doesn't conflict with the port setting used by another device.

✔ Unlike IRQ lines, I/O port conflicts are less common. There are lots of I/O port addresses to choose from, so it's easier to avoid conflicts. It's likely that the factory I/O port address setting is acceptable.

✔ The factory certainly won't ship out a network card with an I/O port setting that conflicts with your printer port, mouse, disk drive, or other common components. You're likely to see a conflict only if you have other unusual stuff attached to your computer, such as a sound card, CD-ROM drive, or scanner. When you configure a network card, just make sure the I/O port setting isn't the same as the setting you used for some other device.

✔ I/O port addresses are hexadecimal numbers that include the letters A-F along with the digits 0-9. For example, 37C is a valid I/O port address number. Be thankful that you don't have to understand hexadecimal numbering to set the port address correctly; just follow the instructions that come with the card, and the hex monsters won't bite you.

✔ The *h* that's sometimes added to the end of the I/O address — like 300h or 37Ch — is just to remind you that the number is hexadecimal, as if it mattered.

Configuring the DMA channel

Some network cards use DMA channels for faster performance. (*DMA* stands for "Direct Memory Access," but that's not important now.) If your card uses a DMA channel, you may have to change the default setting to avoid conflicting with some other add-on card that also might use DMA, such as a CD-ROM adapter or a scanner.

Not all network cards use DMA. If yours doesn't, you get to skip this step.

Installing the card

If you've installed one adapter card, you've installed them all. In other words, installing a network card is just like installing a modem, a new video controller card, a sound card, or any other type of card. If you've ever installed one of these cards, you can probably install a network card blindfolded.

If you haven't installed a card, here's a step-by-step procedure.

1. **Turn the computer off and unplug it.**

   Never work in your computer's insides with the power on or the power cord plugged in!

2. **Remove the cover from your computer.**

   Figure 10-2 shows the screws you must typically remove to open the cover. Put the screws someplace where they won't wander off.

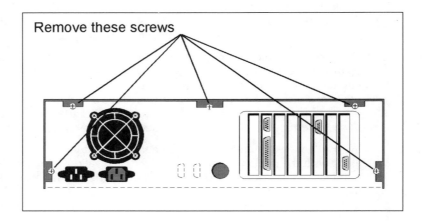

Figure 10-2:
Removing your computer's cover.

Remove these screws

3. **Find an unused expansion slot inside the computer.**

   The expansion slots are lined up in a neat row near the back of the computer; you can't miss 'em.

   Some older computers have both 8-bit slots and 16-bit slots. You can tell the difference by looking at the connectors: Each 16-bit slot has two connectors, whereas 8-bit slots have only one connector. Since 16-bit cards have two connectors, you can't possibly put a 16-bit card into an 8-bit slot. If you have an 8-bit card and your computer has both an 8-bit slot and a 16-bit slot free, slide the card into the 8-bit slot. There's no point in wasting a perfectly good 16-bit slot on a wimpy 8-bit card if you can avoid it.

4. **When you've found a slot that doesn't have a card in it, remove the metal slot protector from the back of the computer's chassis.**

   There's a small retaining screw holding the slot protector in place. Remove it, pull the slot protector out, and put the slot protector in a box with all your other old slot protectors. Don't lose the screw. (After a while, you'll collect a whole bunch of slot protectors. Keep them as souvenirs.)

5. **Insert the network card into the slot.**

   Line up the connectors on the bottom of the card with the connectors in the expansion slot, and then press the card straight down. Sometimes you have to press uncomfortably hard to get the card to slide into the slot.

6. **Secure the network card with the screw you removed in Step 4.**

7. **Put the computer's case back together.**

   Watch out for the loose cables inside the computer; you don't want to pinch them with the case as you slide it back on. Secure the case with the screws you removed in Step 2.

Working with Cable

The hardest part about working with network cable is attaching the cable connectors. That's why the easiest way to wire a network is to buy prefabricated cables, with the connectors already attached. Thinnet cable is commonly sold in prefabricated lengths of 25, 50, or 100 feet. Twisted-pair cable isn't usually sold prefabricated, but its connectors are easier to attach than thinnet connectors.

Before I show you how to attach cable connectors, here's a few general tips for working with cable:

- ✔ Always use more cable than you need, especially if you are running cable through walls. Leave plenty of slack.

- ✔ When running cable, avoid sources of interference like fluorescent lights, big motors, and so on. The most common source of interference for cables run behind fake ceiling panels are fluorescent lights; be sure to give light fixtures a wide berth as you run your cable. Three feet should do it.

- ✔ If you must run cable across the floor where people will be walking, cover the cable so that no one will trip over it. Inexpensive cable protectors are available from most hardware stores.

- ✔ When running cables through walls, label each cable at both ends. Most electrical supply stores carry pads of cable labels that are perfect for the job. These pads contain 50 sheets or so of precut labels with letters and numbers. They're much better than wrapping a loop of masking tape around the cable and writing on it with a marker.

✔ When several cables come together, tie them with plastic cable ties. Avoid masking tape if you can; the tape doesn't last, but the sticky glue stuff does. It'll be a mess a year later. Cable ties are available from electrical supply stores.

Attaching a BNC connector to thinnet cable

Properly connecting a BNC connector to thinnet cable is an acquired skill. You need two tools: A wire stripper that can cut through the various layers of the coax cable at just the right location, and a crimping tool that crimps the connector tightly to the cable once you get it into position. BNC connectors have three separate pieces, as shown in Figure 10-3.

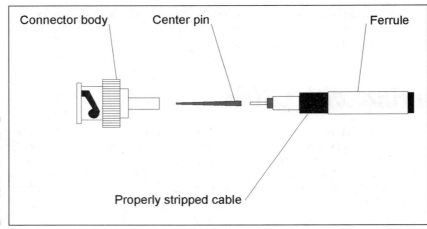

Figure 10-3:
Attaching a
BNC
connector to
thinnet
cable.

Here's the procedure, in case you ignore my advice and try to attach the connectors yourself.

1. **Slide the hollow tube portion of the connector (lovingly called the *ferrule*) over the cable.**

    Let it slide back a few feet to get it out of the way.

2. **Cut the end of the cable off cleanly.**

3. **Use the stripping tool to strip the cable.**

    The outer jacket should be stripped back ½ inch from the end of the cable, the braided shield should be stripped back ¼ inch from the end, and the inner insulation should be stripped back ³⁄₁₆ inch from the end.

4. **Twist the strands of the center conductor tightly, and then insert them into the center pin.**

    Slide the center pin down until it seats against the inner insulation.

5. **Use the crimping tool to crimp the center pin.**

6. **Slide the connector body over the center pin and inner insulation but under the braided shield.**

   When you've pushed the body back far enough, the center pin will click into place.

7. **Now slide the ferrule forward until it touches the connector body.**

   Crimp it with the crimping tool.

Attaching an RJ-45 connector to UTP cable

RJ-45 connectors for UTP wiring are much easier to connect than thinnet connectors. The only trick is making sure that you attach each wire to the correct pin. Each pair of wires in a UTP cable has complementary colors: One pair consists of one white wire with an orange stripe and an orange wire with a white stripe, and the other pair has a white wire with a green stripe and a green wire with a white stripe.

Here are the proper pin connections:

Pin Number	Proper Connection
Pin 1	White/green wire
Pin 2	Green/white wire
Pin 3	White/orange wire
Pin 6	Orange/white wire

Figure 10-4 shows an RJ-45 plug properly connected.

Here's the procedure for attaching an RJ45 connector:

1. **Cut the end of the cable to the desired length.**

   Make sure that you make a square cut, not a diagonal cut.

2. **Insert the cable into the stripper portion of the crimp tool so that the end of the cable is against the stop.**

   Squeeze the handles and slowly pull the cable out, keeping it square. This should strip off the correct length of outer insulation without puncturing the insulation on the inner wires.

3. **Arrange the wires so that they lay flat in the following sequence from lift to right: white/orange, orange/white, white/green, green/white.**

   Pull the green/white wire a bit to the right, then insert cable into the back of the plug so that each wire slides into the channel for the correct pin.

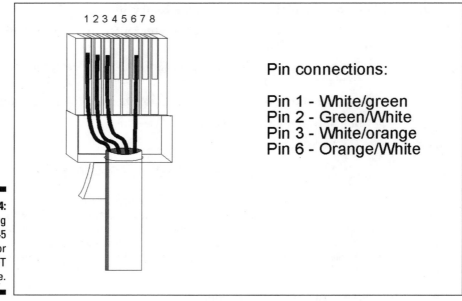

1 2 3 4 5 6 7 8

Pin connections:

Pin 1 - White/green
Pin 2 - Green/White
Pin 3 - White/orange
Pin 6 - Orange/White

Figure 10-4:
Attaching
an RJ-45
connector
to 10baseT
cable.

4. **Make sure that the wires are in the correct pin channels; especially make sure that the green/white cable is in the channel for pin 6.**

5. **Insert the plug and wire into the crimping portion of the tool and squeeze the handles to crimp the plug.**

   Remove the plug from the tool and double-check the connection.

   • The pins on the RJ-45 connectors are not numbered, but you can tell which is pin 1 by holding the connector so that the metal conductors are facing up, as in Figure 10-4. Pin 1 is on the left.

   • Some people wire 10baseT cable differently, using the green and white pair for pins 1 and 2 and the orange and white pair for pins 3 and 6. This doesn't affect the operation of the network (the network is color-blind), *so long as the RJ-45 connectors on both ends of the cable are wired the same!*

   • Yes, I know that any normal person would have set up the RJ-45 connectors using pins 1 through 4, not pins 1, 2, 3, and 6. But remember, computer people are not *normal* in any particularly relevant sense, so why would you expect the fourth wire to connect to the fourth pin? That's pretty naive, don't you think?

Installing the Network Software

Having installed the network cards and cable, all that remains is installing the network software. The procedures for doing this vary considerably depending on the network you're using, so you need to consult your network software's manual for the details. I'll just describe some general things to keep in mind here.

Installing the server software

Start by setting up your network server. It's the centerpiece of your network, and you won't know whether your workstations are working until you have a working server they can log on to.

If you're using NetWare, installing the server software is the most difficult part of setting up the network. Read the manual carefully, place it ceremoniously on your highest bookshelf, and pick up a copy of *NetWare For Dummies*.

Installing a network server if you're using a peer-to-peer network system is much easier. With most systems, you just insert the installation disk into drive A:, type **INSTALL**, and answer a few questions.

It's even easier with Windows for Workgroups. There's no separate procedure for installing the server's software; you just install Windows for Workgroups as you normally would, then set up your shared disks. Sharing a disk is what makes a Windows for Workgroups computer a server.

- ✔ After you've installed the network software, you must define the server resources that will be shared on the network. This is where you assign the network names for your shared disk drives and printers.

- ✔ You also must build the user list. For each user on the system, you supply the user ID, password (if any), and access rights. More information about setting up the user list and managing network security is found in Chapter 12.

- ✔ You also should modify the server computer's AUTOEXEC.BAT file so that the network is started automatically every time the computer starts. That way, if a power failure occurs, the network will automatically resume when power is restored. (If a power failure does occur, it's a good idea to turn off all the computers. Then, when the power comes back on, restart the server first. Wait until the server has come back on-line before turning the workstations back on.)

Installing workstation software

Installing network software for a workstation is easier than installing server software, especially for NetWare.

Two programs are required on a network workstation. One is the *network shell*, or *redirector*, which keeps an eye on application programs and jumps in when they do something that requires access to the network. The other is a driver program that can communicate directly with your network card to access the network.

- ✔ With NetWare, the network shell is called NETX.COM, and the driver is called IPX.COM. You must generate a specific IPX.COM file for each computer by running the WSGEN program and supplying it with information about your network card, including the IRQ number, I/O address, and so on. This probably doesn't make any sense to you here, but that's OK. *NetWare For Dummies* explains all.

- ✔ To install workstation software for NetWare Lite, run the INSTALL program from the NetWare Lite disk. INSTALL asks for information about the network card. Then it sets up NetWare Lite, copying the necessary files to the hard disk and creating a STARTNET.BAT file that contains the commands needed to start the network. With NetWare Lite, the network redirector program is called CLIENT.EXE. The network driver actually consists of three files: LSL.COM, IPXODI.COM, and a driver file that's unique to each particular network card (NE2000.COM works with any NE2000-compatible network card).

- ✔ To install the workstation software for LANtastic, you run INSTALL from the installation disks and answer the questions. This copies the necessary files to the hard disk and, like NetWare Lite, creates a STARTNET.BAT file that loads the programs necessary to access the network. The network redirector for LANtastic is called REDIR.EXE, and the network driver is split into two files: AEX.EXE and AILANBIO.EXE. You need them both.

- ✔ Installing Windows for Workgroups is more time-consuming than installing other peer-to-peer networks because Windows for Workgroups is not only a network operating system, but also, well, Windows. You install it by inserting the first installation disk in drive A: and running SETUP. Along the way, you must supply information Windows needs to activate the network driver file: the adapter type, IRQ, and so on.

Testing Your Network Installation

Your network isn't finished until you've tested it to make sure that it works. Hold your breath as you fire up your computers, starting with the server then proceeding to the workstations. Watch for error messages as each computer starts up. Then log on to the network to see whether it works.

- ✔ If you have a problem, the first culprit to suspect is your network cable. Check all your connections, especially any connections you crimped yourself. If you're using thinnet, make sure that the terminators are attached properly. If you're using UTP, make sure that the hub is plugged in and turned on.

✔ If you're using UTP, you can find a bad cable by checking the light on the back of each network card and each hub connection. The light should be glowing steadily; if it's not glowing at all or if it's glowing intermittently, replace the cable or reattach the connector.

✔ Double-check your network card configuration to make sure that there aren't any conflicts with other devices. Also, make sure that your network software configuration agrees with the way your network cards are actually set.

Part III
The Dummy's Guide to Network Management

The 5th Wave   By Rich Tennant

Alice in WonderLAN

In this part...

You learn that there's more to networking than installing the hardware and software. Once you get the network up and running, you have to *keep* it up and running. That's called *network management*. Bother.

The chapters in this section will show you how to set up your network's security system, how to improve its performance, and how to protect your network from disaster. There's a bit of technical stuff here, but no one said life was easy.

Chapter 11

Help Wanted (A Network Manager's Job Description)

*H*elp wanted. Network manager to help small business get control of a
network run amok. Must have sound organizational and management skills.
Only moderate computer experience required. Part-time only.

Does this sound like an ad your company should run? Every network needs a
network manager, whether the network has 2 computers or 200. Of course,
managing a 200-computer network is a full-time job, whereas managing a
2-computer network isn't. At least, it shouldn't be.

This chapter introduces you to the boring job of network management.
Oops...you're probably reading this chapter because you've been elected to be
the network manager, so I'd better rephrase that: This chapter introduces you
to the wonderful, exciting world of network management!

The Network Manager: A Closet Computer Geek

Most small companies can't afford and don't need a full-time computer geek. So
the network manager is usually just a part-time computer geek. The ideal
network manager is a closet computer geek: someone who has a secret interest
in computers, but doesn't like to admit it.

The job of managing a network requires some computer skills, but it isn't entirely a technical job. Much of the work done by the network manager is routine housework. Basically, the network administrator dusts, vacuums, and mops the network periodically to keep it from becoming a mess.

✔ The network manager should be an organized person. Conduct a surprise office inspection and place the person with the neatest desk in charge of the network. (Don't warn them in advance, or everyone will mess up their desks intentionally the night before the inspection.)

✔ Allow enough time for network management. For a small network (like 3 or 4 computers), an hour or two each week is enough. More time will be needed up front as the network manager settles into the job and learns the ins and outs of the network. But after an initial settling-in period, network management for a small office network shouldn't take more than an hour or two per week. (Of course, larger networks take more time to manage.)

✔ Make sure that everyone knows who the network manager is, and that your network manager has authority to make decisions about the network — such as what files can and cannot be stored on the server, how often backups are done, and so on.

✔ In most cases, the person who installs the network will also be the network manager. That's as it should be, because no one will understand the network better than the person who designed and installed it.

✔ The network manager should make sure that he or she has an understudy, someone who knows almost as much about the network, is eager to make a mark, and smiles when the worst network jobs are "delegated."

✔ The network manager should have some sort of official title, like Network Boss, Network Czar, Vice President in Charge of Network Operations, or Dr. Network. A badge, personalized pocket protector, or set of Spock ears helps too.

Throw the Book at It

One of the network manager's main jobs is keeping the network book up-to-date. In Chapter 6, I suggested that you keep all of the important information about your network in a ½-inch binder. Call this binder your *Network Bible* or *The Good Book*.

✔ Include an up-to-date diagram of the network. This can be in the form of a detailed floor plan, showing the actual location of each computer, or it can be in a more abstract, Picasso-like format. Any time you change the network layout, update the diagram. And include a detailed description of the change, the date the change was made, and the reason for the change.

✔ A detailed inventory of your computer equipment. Here is a sample form you can use to keep track of your computer equipment:

Computer Equipment Checklist

Computer location: _____

User: _____

Manufacturer: _____

Model number: _____

Serial number: _____

Date purchased: _____

CPU type & speed: _____

Memory: _____

Hard disk size: _____

Video type: _____

Printer type: _____

Other equipment: _____

_____

_____

DOS version: _____

Software & version: _____

_____

_____

Network card type: _____

Connector (BNC/RJ45): _____

IRQ: _____

I/O Port Address: _____

DMA Channel: _____

✔ Keep a detailed list of network resources and drive assignments in the binder.

✔ If you use LANtastic or Novell Lite, keep a copy of each computer's STARTNET.BAT file in the binder. For Novell, keep copies of the login scripts.

✔ Keep in the binder whatever other information you think will be useful, such as details about how a particular application program must be configured to work with the network.

Managing the Network

The most obvious duty of the network manager is managing the network itself. The network's hardware — the cables, network adapter cards, hubs, and so on — need oversight, as does the network operating system. On a big network, these responsibilities can themselves become full-time jobs. Large networks tend to be volatile: Users come and go, equipment fails, cables break, and life in general seems to be one crisis after another.

Smaller networks are much more stable. After you get your network up and running, you probably won't have to spend much time managing its hardware and software. An occasional problem will pop up, but with only a few computers on the network, problems should be few and far between.

✔ The network manager must put on the pocket protector whenever a new computer is added to the network. It's the network manager's job to consider what changes need to be made to the cabling configuration, what computer name and user ID should be assigned to the new user, what security rights the user will have, and so on.

✔ Every once in a while, your trusty network vendor will release a new version of your network operating system. It's the network manager's job to read about the new version and decide whether its new features are beneficial enough to warrant an upgrade. Keep in mind that switching to an upgraded network version is usually an all-or-nothing proposition: You can't have some computers running version *X* and others running version *Y*. Upgrading to a new network version is a bit of a chore, so you need to carefully consider the advantages the new version will bring.

✔ One of the easiest traps to get sucked into is the quest for network speed. The network is never fast enough, and your users will always blame the hapless network manager. So the manager spends hours and hours tuning and tweaking the network to squeeze out that last 2 percent of performance. You don't want to get caught in this trap, but in case you do, Chapter 13 can help. It clues you in to the basics of tuning your network for best performance.

Routine Stuff You Hate to Do

Much of the network manager's job is routine stuff, the equivalent of vacuuming, dusting, and mopping. It's boring, but it has to be done.

- It's the network manager's job to make sure that the network is properly backed up. If something goes wrong and the network isn't backed up, guess who gets the blame? On the other hand, if disaster strikes but you're able to recover everything from yesterday's backup with only a small amount of work lost, guess who gets the pat on the back, the fat bonus, and the vacation in the Bahamas? Chapter 14 describes the options for network backups. You'd better read it soon.

- Chapter 14 also describes another routine network chore: checking for computer viruses. If you don't know what a virus is, you'll have to read Chapter 14 to find out.

- Users think the network server is like the attic: They want to throw files up there and leave them there forever. The network manager gets the fun job of cleaning up the attic once in a while. Oh, joy. The best advice I can offer is to constantly complain about how messy it is up there, and warn your users that spring cleaning is coming up.

Managing Network Users

Managing network technology is the easiest part of network management. Computer technology can be confusing at first, but computers are not nearly as confusing as people. The real challenge of managing a network is managing the network's users.

The difference between managing technology and managing users is obvious: You can figure out computers, but you can never really figure out people. The people who use the network are much less predictable than the network itself.

- Training is a key part of the network manager's job. Make sure that everyone who uses the network understands it and knows how to use it. If the network users don't understand the network, they'll do all kinds of weird things to it without meaning to.

- Never treat your network users like idiots. If they don't understand the network, it's not their fault. Explain it to them. Offer a class. Buy them each a copy of this book and tell them to read the first five chapters. Hold their hands. But don't treat them like idiots.

✔ Make up a network cheat sheet that has everything the users need to know about using the network on one page. Make sure that everyone gets a copy.

✔ Be as responsive as you can when a network user complains of a network problem. If you don't fix the problem soon, the user will try to fix it. You probably don't want that.

Tools for Network Managers

Network managers need certain tools to get their jobs done. Managers of big, complicated, and expensive networks need big, complicated, and expensive tools. Managers of small networks need small tools.

Some of the tools the manager needs are hardware tools like screwdrivers, cable crimpers, and hammers. But the tools I'm talking about here are software tools.

✔ Many of the software tools you need to manage a network come with the network itself. As the network manager, you should read through the manuals that come with your network software to see what management tools are available. For example, LANtastic comes with a program called LANCHECK, which you can use to test to make sure that all the computers on a network are able to communicate with one another.

✔ The DOS MSD program I've mentioned in several chapters is a useful utility for network managers. It comes with MS-DOS versions 6.0 and 6.2, as well as Microsoft Windows 3.1.

✔ I suggest you get one of those 100-in-1 utility programs like *The Norton Utilities* or *PC Tools*. Both of these utility packages include invaluable utilities for repairing damaged disk drives, rearranging the directory structure of your disk, gathering information about your computer and its equipment, and so on. These programs are useful on NetWare networks, but they're even more useful on peer-to-peer networks because you can use them on the server computer as well as on the workstations.

✔ More software tools are available for NetWare networks than for peer-to-peer networks. This is not only because NetWare is more popular than peer-to-peer networks, but also because NetWare networks tend to be larger and more in need of software management tools than peer-to-peer networks.

Chapter 12

Who Are You? (or, Big Brother's Guide to Network Security)

In This Chapter

▶ Deciding how much security you need
▶ Setting up user IDs and passwords
▶ Protecting network resources
▶ Simplifying network security by using groups

*B*efore you had a network, computer security was easy. You just locked your door when you left work for the day. You could rest securely in the knowledge that the bad guys would have to break down the door to get to your computer.

The network changes all of that. Now, anyone with access to any of the computers on the network can break into the network and steal *your* files. Not only do you have to lock your door, but you also have to make sure that everyone else locks their doors, too.

Fortunately, just about every network operating system known to humankind has built-in provisions for network security. This makes it difficult for someone to steal your files even if they do break down the door. The networks covered in this book all provide security measures that are more than adequate for all but the most paranoid users.

And when I say *more* than adequate, I mean it. Most networks have security features that would make even Maxwell Smart happy. Using all these security features is kind of like Smart insisting that the Chief lower the "Cone of Silence." Sure, no one else can hear them talking. But they can't hear each other, either! Don't make your system so secure that even the good guys can't get their work done.

Do You Need Security?

Most small networks are in small businesses or departments where everyone knows and trusts everyone else. They don't lock up their desks when they take a coffee break, and although everyone knows where the petty cash box is, money never disappears.

Network security isn't necessary in an idyllic setting such as this, is it? You bet it is. No network should be set up without at least some minimal concern for security.

✔ Even in the most friendly of office environments, some information is and should be confidential. If this information is stored on the network, it should be stored in a directory that's available only to authorized users.

✔ Not all security breaches are malicious. A network user may be routinely scanning through his or her files and discover a file whose name isn't familiar. The user then may call up the file, only to discover that it contains confidential personnel information, juicy office gossip, or your résumé. Curiosity rather than malice is often the source of security breaches.

✔ Sure, everyone at the office is trustworthy now. But what if someone becomes disgruntled, a screw pops loose, and he or she decides to trash the network files before jumping out the window? Or what if that same person decides to print a few $1,000 checks before packing off to Tahiti?

✔ Sometimes the mere opportunity for fraud or theft can be too much for some people to resist. Give people free access to the payroll files, and they may decide to vote themselves a raise when no one is looking.

✔ Finally, remember that not everyone on the network knows enough about how DOS and the network work to be trusted with full access to your network disks. One careless use of **DEL *.*** can wipe out an entire directory of network files. One of the best reasons for activating your network's security features is to protect the network from mistakes made by users who don't know what they're doing.

User Accounts

The first level of network security is the use of *user accounts* to allow only authorized users access to the network. Without an account, a computer user can't log in and therefore can't use the network.

✔ Each account is associated with a *user ID*, which the user must enter when logging in to the network.

✔ Each account also has other network information associated with it, such as the user's password, the user's full name, and a list of *access rights* that tell the network what the user is and isn't allowed to do on the network. More about access rights later.

✔ Most networks let you specify that certain users can log in only during certain times of the day. This lets you restrict your users to normal working hours so that they can't sneak in at 2:00 a.m. to do unauthorized work. It also prevents your users from working overtime, so use this feature judiciously.

✔ Some networks let you use wildcards in the user ID. For example, LANtastic lets you specify SALES* as the user ID in an account for all workers in the SALES department. Then, any user who enters a user ID that begins with SALES, such as SALES-BOB or SALESRUP, is granted access to the network, using the SALES* account.

This sounds like a convenient way to assign the same access rights to several users, but it's not a good idea. The problem is that all users of the wildcard account have the same password. Because the effectiveness of your security system depends on the privacy of your users' passwords, using wild-card accounts defeats the purpose of having separate user accounts.

✔ Beware of the all-encompassing "*" wildcard. If your network has an account whose user ID is simply "*", delete it as soon as you've created your permanent accounts. The "*" account allows anyone to access the system, no matter what user ID he or she enters.

✔ Some networks have a better way to set up several accounts that share access rights: *group accounts*. When you use up a group account, each user still has an individual account with a user ID and password, but all user accounts that belong to a particular group "inherit" the group account's access rights. This is better than using wildcards because it allows each user to have an individual password.

Passwords

One of the most important aspects of network security is the use of passwords. User IDs are not usually considered secret. In fact, it's often necessary that network users know one another's user IDs. For example, if you use your network for electronic mail, you have to know your colleagues' user IDs in order to address your mail properly.

Passwords, on the other hand, are top secret. Your network password is the one thing that keeps an impostor from logging in to the network using your user ID and therefore receiving the same access rights that you ordinarily do. *Guard your password with your life.*

- Don't use obvious passwords, like your last name, your kid's name, or your dog's name. Don't pick passwords based on your hobbies, either. A friend of mine is into boating, and his password is the name of his boat. Anyone who knows him could guess his password after a few tries. Five lashes for naming your password after your boat.

- Store your password in your head, not on paper. Especially bad: writing your password down on a post-it note and sticking it on your computer's monitor. Ten lashes for that. (If you must write your password down, write it on digestible paper you can swallow after you've memorized the password.)

- Don't put your password in a batch file, either. Sure, it saves you time because you don't have to type it every time you log in. But if you put your password in a batch file, you may as well not have a password. Anyone can display the batch file to see your password, or easier still, run the batch file to log in as you. Twenty lashes for adding your password to a batch file.

- Most network operating systems let you set an expiration time for passwords. For example, you can specify that passwords expire after 30 days. When a user's password expires, the user must change it. Your users may consider this a hassle, but it helps limit the risk of someone swiping a password and then trying to break into your computer system later.

- Some network managers opt against passwords altogether. This is often appropriate on small networks where security is not a major concern. This is especially true when sensitive data isn't kept on a file server or when the main reason for the network is to share access to a printer. (Even if you don't use passwords, it's still possible to impose basic security precautions like limiting certain users' access to certain network directories. Just remember that if passwords are not used, there's nothing to prevent a user from signing on using someone else's user ID.)

A Password Generator for Dummies

How do you come up with passwords that no one can guess but that you can remember? Most security experts say that the best passwords do not correspond to any words in the English language, but consist of a random sequence of letters, numbers, and special characters. But how in the heck are you supposed to memorize a password like *DKS4%DJ2*? Especially when you have to change it three weeks later to something like *3PQ&X(D8*?

Here's a compromise solution that lets you create passwords that consist of two four-letter words back to back. Take your favorite book (if it's this one, you need to get a life) and turn to any page at random. Find the first four-letter word on the page. Let's say it's WHEN. Then repeat the process to find another four-letter word; let's say you pick MOST the second time. Now combine the words to make your password: WHENMOST. I think you'll agree that WHENMOST is easier to remember than 3PQ&X(D8 and is probably just about as hard to guess. I probably wouldn't want the folks at NORAD using this scheme, but it's good enough for most of us.

- ✔ If the words end up being the same, pick another word. And pick different words if the combination seems too commonplace, like WESTWIND or FOOTBALL.

- ✔ For an interesting variation, pick one four-letter word and one three-letter word, and randomly pick one of the keyboard's special characters (like *, &, or >) to separate the words. You'll end up with passwords like INTO#CAT, BALL$AND, or TREE>DIP.

- ✔ If your network lets you use passwords that are longer than eight characters, use longer words. For example, if your passwords can be 10 characters long, use a five-letter word, a four-letter word, and a separator, as in RIGHT)DOOR, HORSE!GONE, or CRIME^MARK.

- ✔ To further confuse your friends and enemies, use medieval passwords by picking words from Chaucer's *Canterbury Tales*. Chaucer is a great source for passwords because he lived before the days of word processors with spelling checkers. He wrote *seyd* instead of *said*, *gret* instead of *great*, *welk* instead of *walked, litel* instead of *little.* And he used lots of seven- and eight-letter words suitable for passwords: *glotenye* (gluttony), *benygne* (benign), and *opynyoun* (opinion).

- ✔ If you use any of these password schemes and someone breaks into your network, don't blame me. You're the one who's too lazy to memorize D#SC$H4@.

Privileges

User accounts and passwords are only the front line of defense in the game of network security. After a user has gained access to the network by typing a valid user ID and password, the second line of security defense comes into play: privileges.

In the harsh realities of network life, all users are created equal, but some are more equal than others. *Privileges* are what separate the snobs from the wannabes.

The specific privileges you can assign to users depends on the network operating system you use. Here are some of the privileges LANtastic lets you assign:

Super ACL	The user has unlimited access to all files on all network drives, regardless of any access rights that have been established for those files. (See the following section, "Access Rights.") This privilege gives the user godlike status to do anything he or she pleases; only a few users should have it.
Super Queue	The user can control all jobs in the print queue, not just his or her own.
Super Mail	The user can access anyone's electronic mail. Usually best reserved for the network manager who likes to snoop through other people's private stuff.
System Manager	Lets the user do server stuff like forcing other users to log off, shutting down the server, and so on.
Operator	Any messages that require action from an operator (like "Change the paper, idiot!") will be sent to users with this privilege. Some "privilege," eh?

✔ Most users are not assigned any of these privileges. Privileges are reserved for those users who have supervisory functions that require them to have control over other users' network files, print documents, mail, and so on.

✔ Limit especially the number of users who have the Super ACL privilege. These users are not subject to any of the restrictions set up by access rights, as described later in this chapter.

Network privileges we'd like to see

The network privileges allowed by most network operating systems are pretty boring. Here are a few privileges I wish would be allowed:

Priviledge	Description
Sublimer	Allows the user to send subliminal messages to any other network user. These messages flash on the screen for only a few milliseconds, but have been proven to enable complete mind control. (An option to display subliminal messages backwards to enhance the effect would be a nice touch.)
Whiner	Automatically sends E-mail messages to other users that explain how busy, tired, or upset the user is.
Gamer	Provides access to all computer games located on all computers connected to the network.
Super ATM	Allows the user's computer to double as an ATM, with full access to any network user's bank account.

Access Rights (Who Gets What)

Privileges control what a user can do on a network-wide basis. Access rights let you fine-tune your network security by controlling specific file operations for specific users. For example, you can set up access rights to allow users in the accounting department to access files in the server's \ACCTG directory. Access rights also can allow some users to read certain files but not modify or delete them.

Each network operating system manages access rights in a different way. Whatever the details, the effect is that each user can be given certain rights to certain files, directories, or network drives. The specific rights that can be given vary from network to network, but the following list is typical:

Right	What the User Can Do
R	The user can read files.
W	The user can write files; that is, the user is allowed to retrieve a file, make changes to it, and save the resulting changes.
C	The user is allowed to create new files.
M	The user is allowed to create (make) new subdirectories.
L	The user is allowed to list the name of the file, as in a DIR listing.
D	The user is allowed to delete files.
K	The user is allowed to delete subdirectories.
N	The user is allowed to rename files.
E	The user is allowed to execute program files.

✔ These operations usually are controlled on a directory-by-directory basis, though you can apply them to a single file or to a group of files by specifying a wildcard filename (like **ACCT*.*** to refer to all files that begin with ACCT).

✔ With most networks, rights specified for a directory are applied automatically to any of that directory's subdirectories, unless a different set of rights is explicitly specified for the subdirectory.

Breeze right past this stuff about DOS file attributes

DOS has always provided a very rudimentary form of access rights through it's directory *attributes*. Every file stored on your disk has one or more of the following attributes:

Attribute	Definition
R	*Read-only.* The file may be read but not changed, renamed, or deleted.
H	*Hidden.* The file doesn't show up in DIR listings.
S	*System.* The file is a part of DOS and should not be disturbed. System files usually also have the Hidden attribute.
A	*Archive.* The file has been modified since it was last backed up and should be backed up again.

You can change these attribute settings by using the DOS ATTRIB command, but you normally shouldn't. In particular, don't try to use the DOS attributes to make a file read-only. The read-only access right managed by your network software is much more flexible than the DOS read-only attribute.

The main difference between DOS file attributes and network access rights is that after you assign a DOS attribute to a file, that attribute is in effect for everyone who uses the file. In contrast, network access rights to particular files are assigned on a user-by-user basis, so that a file may be read-only to one user, but another user can have full rights to the file.

God (a.k.a the Supervisor)

It stands to reason that at least one network user must have the authority to use the network without any of the restrictions imposed upon other users. This user is called the *supervisor* or *system administrator*. The supervisor is responsible for setting up the network's security system; that's why the supervisor is exempt from all security restrictions.

Many networks automatically create a supervisor user account when you install the network software. The user ID and password for this initial supervisor are published in the network's documentation and are the same for all networks that use the same network operating system. One of the first things you should do after getting your network up and running is change the password for this standard supervisor account. Otherwise, all of your elaborate security precautions will be a farce; anyone who knows the default supervisor user ID and password can access your system with full supervisor rights and privileges, bypassing the security restrictions you so carefully set up.

If you didn't read the last one, you REALLY should skip this one

One of the reasons Novell decided to write NetWare from scratch rather than build it atop DOS is the limitations of DOS file attributes. NetWare provides 14 different file attributes rather than the 4 provided by DOS. You don't need to know what they are, but you wouldn't bother reading this sidebar if you didn't want to know. So here they are, just so you won't lie awake tonight wondering:

Attribute	Description	Attribute	Description
A	Archive needed (same as DOS)	Ro	Read only
C	Copy inhibit; the file cannot be copied	R	Rename inhibit; the file cannot be renamed
D	Delete inhibit; the file cannot be deleted	S	Shareable
X	Execute only (program files)	Sy	System (same as DOS S)
H	Hidden file (same as DOS)	T	Transactional; the file uses NetWare's advanced transaction-tracking features to ensure accuracy
I	Indexed file		
P	Purge when deleted	Wa	Write audit
Ra	Read audit		

✔ Most network administrators use a boring user ID for the supervisor account, like ADMIN, MANAGER, or SUPRVSOR. Some network administrators like to pretend they're creative by using a more clever user ID for the supervisor account. Here are some suitable user IDs for your supervisor account:

GOD	R2D2
ALLAH	C3PO
ALADDIN	PICARD
GENIE	DATA
TITAN	BORG
ZEUS	HUGH
SKIPPER	HAL
GILLIGAN	M5

✔ ***Do not forget the password for the supervisor account!*** If a network user forgets his or her password, you can log in as the supervisor and change that user's password. But if you forget the supervisor's password, you're stuck.

Too Many Lists! (How to Manage Multiple Servers)

One of the problems you'll encounter as your network grows is that each file server on the network has its own list of user accounts. If you set up a five-computer network in which every computer is both a workstation and a server, you have to keep a separate user account list on each server. These lists can quickly get out of control if you don't manage them properly.

✔ Be consistent with user IDs. If a user's user ID is BARNEY on one server, it should be BARNEY on all servers.

✔ Not every user needs access to every server. One of the best security techniques is to create accounts for users only on the servers they need to access.

✔ Some networks have a feature that lets you copy the user list from one server to another. This makes it easier to manage user accounts on several servers. After you get your user list set up the way you want it, you just copy it to all your servers. When you need to change a user account, you change it on just one server and copy the updated user list to the rest of the servers.

✔ Some networks, like NetWare 4.0 and Windows for Workgroups, maintain just one user list for the entire network. With these networks, you don't have to maintain a separate user list for each server. LANtastic 5.0 has a similar feature, called *remote accounts*, which lets you store your user list on one server. All the other servers are then set up so that they look to this *account server* for their user accounts.

Other Ways to Keep Bad Guys Out

So far, we've only talked about the security features built into your network software. Some of the best security techniques have nothing to do with your network software. Here are some low-tech security issues you may not have thought about:

✔ Make sure that all the computers on the network are in secure locations. It amazes me whenever I walk into the reception area of an accounting firm and see an unattended computer sitting on the receptionist's desk logged in to the network. Computers that are logged in to the network should not be left unattended; if you must leave your computer, log out of the network first.

✔ If your office has a door that can be locked, by all means lock it. Don't be lulled into a false sense of security, though. Anyone who knows your user ID and password can access the network from any computer on the network. Locking your door doesn't necessarily prevent the bad guys from snooping through your computer files.

✔ Don't overlook the lack of privacy at the printer. Your sensitive files may be protected by access rights, but the stacks of printed output lying on the floor behind the printer aren't protected. If you send something confidential to a network printer, make sure that you're at the printer when it is printed so that you can promptly remove the output. If the printer is in a busy location, cover up the printer with a sheet while your sensitive data is being printed. Or make everyone in the room cover their eyes or lie on the floor face-down until your print job finishes.

✔ If your network has a modem that's set up to allow users to access the network by dialing in from a remote computer, don't forget that unauthorized users may gain access to your network through this modem. Did you ever see "War Games"? If you have a setup like this, it's time to become paranoid. Make sure that every user ID is password protected.

Chapter 13

Fast as Fast Can Be (or, The Jackalope's Guide to Network Performance)

- -

In This Chapter

▶ Understanding network bottlenecks

▶ Tuning your network

▶ Making your network server faster

▶ Making your network workstations faster

- -

*I*t really is true that there's no such thing as a free lunch. When you network your computers, you reap the benefits of being able to share information and resources such as disk drives and printers. But there are also many costs. There is the cost of purchasing network cards, cable, and software, plus the cost of the time required to install the network, learn how to use it, and keep it running.

There's another cost of networking you may not have considered yet: the performance cost. No matter how hard you try, you can't hide the ugly truth that putting a computer on a network slows it down. It takes a bit longer to retrieve a word processing document from a network disk than it does to retrieve the same document from your local disk drive. Sorting that big database file takes a bit longer. And printing a 300-page report also takes a bit longer.

Notice that I've used the word "bit" three times now. Lest my editor chide me for Overuse of a Three-Letter Word, I'd better point out that I used the word three times to make a point. The network inevitably slows things down, but only a bit. If your network has slowed things down to a snail's pace—so that your users are routinely taking coffee breaks whenever they save a file— you've got a performance problem you can probably solve.

What Exactly Is a Bottleneck?

The term *bottleneck* does not in any way refer to the physique of your typical computer geek. (Well, I guess it *could*, in some cases.) It is, rather, a phrase coined by computer geeks when they discovered that the tapered shape of a bottle of Jolt Cola limited the rate at which they could consume the beverage. "Hey," a computer geek said one day, "the narrowness of this bottleneck limits the rate at which I can consume the tasty caffeine-laden beverage contained within. This draws to mind an obvious analogy to the limiting effect that a single slow component of a computer system can have upon the performance of the system as a whole."

"Fascinating," replied all the other computer geeks who were fortunate enough to be present at that historic moment.

The phrase stuck and is used to this day to draw attention to the simple fact that a computer system is only as fast as its slowest component. It's the computer equivalent of the old truism that a chain is only as strong as its weakest link.

For a simple demonstration of this concept, consider what happens when you print a word processing document on a slow dot-matrix printer. Your word processing program reads the data from disk and sends it to the printer. Then you sit and wait while the printer prints the document.

Would buying a faster CPU or adding more memory make the document print faster? No. The CPU is already much faster than the printer driver, and your computer already has more than enough memory to print the document. The printer itself is the bottleneck, so the only way to print the document faster is to replace the slow printer with a faster one.

- ✔ A computer system always has a bottleneck. Buying a faster printer makes the bottleneck less severe, but the printer will still be a bottleneck. In some extreme cases, a printer can process information faster than the computer can send it. In this case, the printer is not the bottleneck; the parallel port the printer is attached to has become the bottleneck. There is still a bottleneck, but it's been moved around. Since you can't eliminate bottle-necks, the best you can do is limit their effect.

- ✔ One way to limit the effect of a bottleneck is to avoid waiting for the bottleneck. For example, you can use WordPerfect's print spooling feature to avoid waiting for the printer. This doesn't speed up the printer, but it does free you up to do other work while the printer chugs along. Network print spooling works the same way.

- ✔ One of the reasons computer geeks are switching from Jolt Cola to Snapple is that Snapple bottles have wider necks.

What Are the Ten Most Common Network Bottlenecks?

Funny you should ask. Here they are, in no particular order:

1. **The CPU in the file server.** If the file server will be used extensively, it should have a powerful CPU — 386 or better. This is especially true if you're using NetWare.

2. **The amount of memory in the file server.** You can set up the file server to take advantage of lots of extended memory. A few extra megabytes of server memory can almost always be put to good use.

3. **The file server computer's bus.** Oops...this is kind of technical, so I'll put the details in a sidebar you can skip. The nontechnical version is this: Buy a server computer that has an EISA bus if you can afford it.

4. **The network card.** Use 16-bit network cards; cheaper 8-bit cards slow things down. And don't even think about using Artisoft's proprietary 2Mbs cards for a LANtastic network. Use standard Ethernet cards instead.

I almost forgot to tell you about memory

It's time to face up to the harsh reality that you can't successfully tune a network server unless you know the differences between four basic types of computer memory. Here we go:

Conventional Memory. The memory DOS uses to run programs is called conventional memory. A computer can have up to 640K of conventional memory. Any memory the computer has in addition to the standard complement of 640K is either *upper memory, extended memory,* or *expanded memory.* Each is defined in the following paragraphs.

Upper Memory. The portion of memory between 640K and 1M is called upper memory. Upper memory is used mostly by I/O devices like monitors and disk drives. However, bits and pieces of upper memory can be used by programs if you have a 386 or 486 computer and DOS 5.0 or a later version.

Expanded Memory. Expanded memory is memory that lives on a special expansion card. Expanded memory is the only way to use extra memory on an 8088-based computer. It's not used much anymore, because extended memory is a whole lot better.

Extended Memory. Extended memory is memory beyond the first 1MB in a 286, 386, or 486 computer. DOS can't directly access extended memory, but Windows can. The Windows craze has given extended memory a big boost. Extended memory can be used to simulate expanded memory for older programs that know how to use expanded memory but are clueless about extended memory.

You can never have too much extended memory in a file server. There are lots of good ways to put it to use to make your network run faster.

If you have DOS 5.0 or a later version, you can find out how much of each type of memory you have by typing **MEM** at the command prompt.

Warning! Reading this may be hazardous to your sanity

Every computer has a *bus*, which is basically a row of slots into which you can plug expansion cards such as disk controllers, modems, video controllers, and network adapter cards. Four different types of buses are generally available today:

ISA. ISA stands for "Industry Standard Architecture." It is the most common type of expansion bus. It was designed many years ago, when IBM introduced its first computers based on the 80286 processor. The ISA bus sends data between the CPU and the expansion cards 8 or 16 bits at a time, depending on whether you use it with 8-or 16-bit adapter cards. The ISA bus runs at 8MHz.

MCA. MCA stands for "MicroChannel Architecture." It was introduced by IBM for its PS/2 systems. MCA sends data 32 bits at a time. MCA never really caught on, though, so it's not used as much. MCA runs a bit faster than ISA, clocking in at 10MHz.

EISA. EISA, which stands for "Extended Industry Standard Architecture," is a 32-bit version of the basic ISA bus with a few bells and whistles added

in. It's widely available and is often used for network servers because the 32-bit bus can make disk and network more efficient if special 32-bit disk controllers and network adapter cards are used. To stay compatible with standard ISA cards, the EISA bus runs at 8MHz.

Local Bus. Local bus is a technique that overcomes the speed limitation that's inherent in each of the other three types of buses: The local bus runs at the same clock speed as the CPU. For example, if you have a 33MHz CPU, the local bus also runs at 33MHz. Most new 486-based computers now come with two or three local bus slots in addition to a standard ISA or EISA bus. Local bus is used mostly to improve video performance for Windows users, but also can be used to improve disk performance. Local bus network adapter cards should be available soon. (Two types of local bus are currently available: VESA, which stands for "Video Electronics Standards Association" and is pronounced like the credit card, and PCI, which stands for "Peripheral Component Interconnect.")

5. **The file server's disk drive.** If you use an old computer for your file server, watch out: Its disk drive may be of the slower ST-506 variety. Newer IDE drives are faster, but the fastest are the new SCSI-2 drives. Sorry! I went technical on you again. Time for another sidebar.

6. **The file server's disk controller card.** All disks must be connected to the computer via a controller card, and sometimes the bottleneck isn't the disk itself, but the controller card. A beefed-up controller card can do wonders for performance.

7. **The configuration options setup for the server.** Even simple peer-to-peer networks have all sorts of options you can configure. Some of these options can make the difference between a pokey network and a network that zips. Unfortunately, there aren't any hard-and-fast rules for setting these options. Otherwise, they wouldn't be options.

8. **Windows!** If you use a peer-to-peer network, don't run Windows on the server. You'll just bog things down. (Of course, you can't avoid running Windows on the server computer if you use Windows for Workgroups.)

Technical Stuff

Just say no to technical stuff about drive interfaces

Disk drives come in several varieties, and not all of them are made equal. Here's the Lowe-down on the most common drive types:

ST-506. ST-506 drives are really old, but there are still lots of them around. They're pretty slow by today's standards, so they don't make very good network drives.

ESDI. ESDI was a popular drive type during the early days of 386 computers, but its popularity was eclipsed by IDE drives. ESDI stands for "Enhanced System Device Interface," and it's pronounced EZ-dee or ES-dee.

IDE. IDE, which stands for "Integrated Drive Electronics" (as if that mattered), is the most common drive type used today. Most IDE drives have a capacity of 500M or less. Don't embarrass yourself by trying to pronounce this in any way other than spelling out the letters.

SCSI. SCSI stands for "Small Computer System Interface" but is pronounced Scuzzy. SCSI drives have several advantages over IDE drives but are also a bit more expensive. SCSI is the most common choice for drives larger than 500M. It also wins the prize for Best Computer Acronym, hands down.

---

9. **DOS!** No matter how hard they try, peer-to-peer networks will never be as fast as NetWare networks because the peer-to-peer networks run DOS on the server computers. NetWare has a built-in advantage because it is written specifically to take advantage of the fast features of 386 and 486 processors. DOS is not.

10. **The network itself.** If you have too many users, the network can become bogged down. The solution is to divide the network into two smaller networks connected with a cool little black box called a *bridge*.

The hardest part about improving the performance of a network is determining what the bottlenecks are. With sophisticated test equipment and years of experience, network gurus can make pretty good educated guesses. Without the equipment and experience, you can still make pretty good uneducated guesses.

The Compulsive Way to Tune Your Network

There are two ways to tune your network. The first is to think about it a bit, take a guess at what may improve performance, try it, and see whether the network seems to run faster. This is the way most people go about it.

Then there's the compulsive way, suitable for people who organize their sock drawers by color and their food cupboards alphabetically by food groups, or worse, alphabetically within food groups. The compulsive approach to tuning a network goes something like this:

1. **Establish a method for objectively testing the performance of some aspect of the network.**

   This is called a *benchmark*. For example, if you want to improve the performance of network printing, use a stopwatch to time how long it takes to print a fairly large document.

2. **Now, change one variable of your network configuration and rerun the test.**

   For example, if you think increasing the size of the disk cache will improve performance, change the cache size, restart the server, and run the benchmark test. Note whether the performance improved, stayed the same, or became worse.

3. **Repeat Step 2 for each variable you want to test.**

   If possible, test each variable separately—in other words, reverse the changes you've made to other network variables before proceeding.

   - Write down the results of each test so that you'll have an accurate record of the impact each change has on your network's performance.

   - It's important that you change only one aspect of the network each time you run the benchmark. If you make several changes, you won't know which one resulted in the change. Or it could be that one change improved performance, but the other change worsened performance so that the changes canceled each other out — kind of like offsetting penalties in a football game.

   - Make sure that no one else is using the network when you conduct the test; otherwise, the unpredictable activities of other network users will spoil the test.

   - To establish your baseline performance, run your benchmark test two or three times to make sure that the results are repeatable. If the print job takes one minute the first time, three minutes the second time, and 22 seconds the third time, there's something wrong with the test. A variation of just a few seconds is acceptable, though.

   - Standardized benchmark tests are available from on-line services such as CompuServe. These tests aren't as good as tests you devise yourself, because the tests you come up with are likely to reflect the type of work you do on your network. Nevertheless, they are useful if you can't come up with any realistic tests on your own.

Tuning a Peer-To-Peer Server

When you use a peer-to-peer network such as LANtastic or NetWare Lite, there are lots of options you can fiddle around with to improve the performance of your server computers. The time spent is worthwhile to a point, because the effect of a more efficient server computer is noticed by all users of the network.

When you first install your network, make no attempt to tune the server for efficient performance. In fact, do what you can to make sure that the server runs as inefficiently as possible. Then, after the network has been running a week or two, announce that you're sick and tired of lackluster network performance and you're not going to take it any more. Apply the basic performance-tuning techniques described here, and you'll be a hero.

Using a disk cache

The numero uno thing you can do to boost the performance of a server is to use a program called a *disk cache*. A disk cache dramatically improves the performance of your disk drives. Here's how it works. (This is a bit complicated, so make sure that you're sitting down before you continue.)

It's a given that computer memory (that is, RAM) can be accessed faster than disk storage, right? A disk cache works by setting aside a portion of memory to hold disk data that's frequently accessed. Whenever a network user tries to read data from the disk, the cache program checks first to see whether the data is already in the cache memory. If so, the data is read directly from memory, much faster than if it had to be accessed from the disk.

The more memory you set aside for the cache, the more likely it is that when a network user needs to retrieve data from the server's disk, the data can be retrieved quickly from cache memory instead. So the general rule is this: Set aside as much memory as humanly possible for the disk cache. The cache is the reason you can never have too much memory in a network server.

- A disk-caching program isn't something you have to run out and buy. In fact, you probably already own two cache programs. Most peer-to-peer networks come with a caching program that's designed to work specifically with the network software. LANtastic comes with a caching program called LANcache, and NetWare Lite comes with a caching program called NLCACHE. In addition, recent versions of MS-DOS also come with a disk caching program called SMARTDRV.

- If you're using DOS 5.0 or an earlier version, the cache that came with your networking software is probably more sophisticated than your version of SMARTDRV. However, the DOS 6.0 and 6.2 versions of SMARTDRV are as powerful as LANcache or NLCACHE. Which one you use is a matter of preference.

- PC Tools and The Norton Utilities also come with powerful disk-caching programs. If you own one of these utilities, you have even more caches to choose from.

- Computer geeks tend to have strong "opynyouns" about which cache is better. Although it's true that one cache program may achieve better scores in benchmark tests than another, the truth of the matter is that any cache is better than no cache, and the differences between caches are relatively minor. Don't fret too much over which cache to use, so long as you use one.

✔ A hot topic of debate among cache aficionados (called *cacheoholics*) is whether or not to enable the risky but speedy *delayed write* feature. This feature, found in LANcache, NLCACHE, and the DOS 6.0 and 6.2 versions of SMARTDRV, caches disk writes as well as disk reads. This significantly speeds up disk performance, but at some risk: If a power failure, an earthquake, or the rapture occurs between the time that data is written to the cache and the time that the cache program decides to write the data to disk, there's a good chance that you'll lose data.

✔ The command to start your disk cache should be included in the server computer's AUTOEXEC.BAT file. That way, the cache starts automatically when you turn on the server computer.

✔ If you use a disk-caching program, you should reduce the BUFFERS setting in your CONFIG.SYS file to 2. Find the BUFFERS line in CONFIG.SYS and change it to this:

```
buffers=2
```

LANcache details to ignore

If you use LANtastic, you should add a LANCACHE command to each computer's AUTOEXEC.BAT file. Place the LANCACHE command as close to the top of the AUTOEXEC.BAT file as possible, preferably right after the PATH command, like this:

```
path c:\dos;c:\lantasti
lancache
```

If you use the LANCACHE command with no parameters, it will figure out how much memory your computer has and set aside an appropriate amount to use for cache memory, up to 2MB.

If the server computer has more than 2MB of available memory, you may want to tell LANcache to create a larger cache. Then you have to add

a switch to the LANCACHE command, something along these lines:

```
path c:\dos;c:\lantasti
lancache /cache_size=4096
```

This command tells LANcache to create a 4MB cache. (The number you type in this command specifies the number of *kilobytes* you want to use for cache memory; 4MB is the same as 4096K.)

LANcache uses the risky delayed-write feature unless you add the /NODELAYED_WRITES switch to the LANCACHE command, like this:

```
path c:\dos;c:\lantasti
   lancache /cache_size=4096
   /nodelayed_writes
```

Stop! You already know too much about SMARTDRV!

If you have DOS Version 6.0 or 6.2, you have the latest and greatest version of Microsoft's disk-caching program, affectionately known as SMARTDRV. To activate SMARTDRV, add a command to your AUTOEXEC.BAT like this one:

```
smartdrv
```

You should place the command near the top of AUTOEXEC.BAT, preferably immediately after the PATH command.

SMARTDRV checks the amount of memory your computer has to decide how much memory to use for the cache. If your computer has 4MB of memory or less, SMARTDRV uses 1MB of memory for the cache. If more than 4MB is available, SMARTDRV creates a 2MB cache.

You can change the size of the cache SMARTDRV creates by typing the size of the cache you want to use on the command line:

```
smartdrv 4096
```

This command tells SMARTDRV to create a 4MB cache. (The number you type in this command specifies the number of *kilobytes* you want to use for cache memory; 4MB is the same as 4096K.)

Like LANcache, SMARTDRV uses the risky delayed-write feature unless you specifically tell it not to. With DOS 6.0, you tell SMARTDRV to forget about the delayed-write feature by listing all the drives you want cached, following each drive letter with a plus sign. If you have two hard disks — C and D — you type the SMARTDRV command like this:

```
smartdrv c+ d+
```

Confusing? Yup. Microsoft saw the error of its ways and decided that DOS 6.2 would let you disable delayed-write simply by adding /X to the command:

```
smartdrv /x
```

The FASTOPEN command

When DOS accesses a file, at least three separate disk operations are required: The first reads the file's directory information; the second accesses a special area on the disk called the *File Allocation Table* (lovingly known as the *FAT*) to determine where the file is located on the disk; and the third actually accesses the file's data.

If you add a FASTOPEN command to your server computer's AUTOEXEC.BAT file, you often can eliminate the first two of these disk operations. FASTOPEN sets aside a portion of your computer's memory to keep track of each file's location on the disk. Whenever DOS accesses a file, it adds the file's name and disk location to this memory area. Then if DOS needs the file again, it looks in the FASTOPEN memory to see whether the file's location is already on record. If so, the directory and FAT information doesn't have to be read from disk.

- To use FASTOPEN, just add the command FASTOPEN without any parameters, switches, or other junk to your AUTOEXEC.BAT file. You can insert it anywhere in AUTOEXEC.BAT, as long as it's after the PATH statement. For example:

```
path c:\dos;c:\lantasti

fastopen
```

- FASTOPEN normally keeps track of up to 48 files for each drive. You can increase this number, like this:

```
path c:\dos;c:\lantasti

fastopen c:=200 d:=200
```

This one sets up FASTOPEN so that it keeps track of 200 files on drives C: and D:. FASTOPEN can track no more than 999 files altogether, so don't overdo it.

- Once upon a time, when IBM and Microsoft were working on DOS 4.0, some sadistic programmers got a hold of the FASTOPEN command and decided its syntax wasn't confusing enough. They thought it would be funny to make you specify not just the number of files to let FASTOPEN track, but also the number of "continuous space buffers," whatever the heck that is. They thought parentheses would be a nice touch, too. The result is that if you have DOS 4.0, you have to type the FASTOPEN command like this:

```
fastopen c:=(50,200) d:=(50,200)
```

This command sets up FASTOPEN so that it tracks 50 files on drives C: and D:, and it has enough room for 200 continuous space buffers.

The programmers who slipped in these extra options were caught red-handed and sent to programmer's prison, and Microsoft reverted to the old FASTOPEN format with MS-DOS 5.0. There *is* a God.

- LANtastic has its own built-in equivalent of FASTOPEN, called the *seek cache*. If you use LANtastic's seek cache, don't use FASTOPEN.

Server start-up parameters

Most peer-to-peer networks let you play around with several variables that affect the performance of a file server. The standard settings for these options aren't always the best settings for the majority of systems, so it almost always pays to read about what options are available and make a few adjustments.

Figure 13-1 shows the settings you can change for a LANtastic server. Other networks have similar settings. I won't describe each of these configuration options here; instead, I'll zero in on the ones that are most likely to improve your network's performance if you adjust them.

Notice that the screen in Figure 13-1 is titled "Server Startup Parameters." That's because these settings are read by the network server program when you start it. You can change these settings while the network is running, but the new values you specify won't take effect until you restart the server.

Because adjusting these settings requires that you frequently restart the server, you have to ask everyone to stay off the network for a while so that you can experiment with various settings. If you're really dedicated, you may want to do this on a Saturday or in the evening.

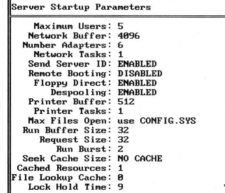

```
Server Startup Parameters

      Maximum Users: 5
     Network Buffer: 4096
    Number Adapters: 6
      Network Tasks: 1
     Send Server ID: ENABLED
     Remote Booting: DISABLED
      Floppy Direct: ENABLED
         Despooling: ENABLED
     Printer Buffer: 512
      Printer Tasks: 1
     Max Files Open: use CONFIG.SYS
    Run Buffer Size: 32
       Request Size: 32
          Run Burst: 2
    Seek Cache Size: NO CACHE
   Cached Resources: 1
  File Lookup Cache: 0
     Lock Hold Time: 9
```

Figure 13-1:
LANtastic's
server
start-up
parameters.

Try adjusting the following options, as you think they are appropriate to your situation:

Maximum Users. This option says how many users can be logged in to the server at one time. The default is five; if you have more than five users on the network, you should increase this value. Increasing this value takes memory away from other functions, so you should set it to just a few more than the actual number of users you have.

Network Buffer. This option tells LANtastic how much data should be transferred from the server to the workstations each time a workstation requests disk data. The default setting for this option is 4096 (that's 4K). Most networks run better if you increase this value to 8192 (that's 8K). Try it and see. If not, you can always change it back to 4096.

If you change the server's Network Buffer setting, you also should change the /size parameter on the REDIR command found in each computer's STARTNET.BAT file. The /size value and the Network Buffer setting should be the same.

Network Tasks. This setting tells LANtastic how many network requests the server can handle simultaneously. The default is 1, which means that network requests are handled one at a time. If a user requests data from the server while the server is busy handling another user's request, the second user will just have to wait.

Your network's performance will almost surely improve if you increase this setting to 3. The benefit of additional network tasks beyond 3 is usually small.

Each task requires a separate network buffer, so if you specify 3 network tasks and an 8K network buffer, a total of 24K is set aside for the network buffers.

Printer Buffer. This option specifies the size of the buffer used for network printing. The default is a paltry 512 bytes. You almost always can improve printing performance by specifying a larger value, especially if you have a relatively fast printer. Try specifying 4096 or 8192 and see what happens.

Printer Tasks. You should set this option to the number of printers that are attached to the server. Most servers have only one printer, so the default setting of 1 is appropriate. A separate printer buffer is created for each printer task.

Run Buffer Size. This option sounds important, but it's not. It only affects the seldom-used NET RUN command, so don't worry about it.

Request Size. When a workstation requests some action from the server, the request is held in a small area of the server's memory called a *request buffer* until the server can process it. The default size of this request buffer is 32 bytes. Increasing this value often can improve performance, though not usually dramatically. Try increasing the request size to 512 and see what happens.

A separate request buffer is created for each network user allowed by the Maximum Users setting.

Run Burst. This setting lets you tell the server whether to place more emphasis on servicing network tasks or local tasks. The default setting of 2 means that the server will concentrate solely on network tasks for 2 "clock ticks" before checking to see whether there is any non-network processing to be done. Each clock tick is 1/18th of a second, so a run burst of 2 means that the server stops processing network tasks 9 times every second.

If a server operates as a dedicated file server, you should increase this value. I like to set it to 18 so that the server checks for local work once per second. The maximum value for this setting is 255.

LANtastic considers print despooling to be a local task. Therefore, if a server functions as both a file server and a print server, increasing the Run Burst setting improves file I/O at the expense of printer I/O. This is one of the main reasons it is best to have separate file servers and print servers if possible. To set this value appropriately for a combined file/print server, you must do what Mr. Miyagi says in the Karate Kid movies: "Find balance."

Seek Cache Size. The seek cache duplicates the function provided by the DOS FASTOPEN command: It keeps track of the locations of files on disk. The default setting is "NO CACHE," but you can change it by specifying a cache size from 1 to 64K. Most networks will benefit from FASTOPEN or a modest seek cache (16-32K), but there's no point in using both FASTOPEN and a seek cache.

Cached Resources. Information about each network resource (shared disk drive, printer, and so on) can be stored in cache memory to improve performance. This option sets the number of resources that are held in memory. You should set it to the number of resources defined for the server @md that is, the **number of shared disk drives and printers.**

File Lookup Cache. Use this only if the server has a CD-ROM drive.

Dedicating the server

Both LANtastic and NetWare Lite come with programs you can run to improve the performance of a dedicated network server. The LANtastic program is called ALONE; the NetWare Lite program is called DEDICATE.

Both ALONE and DEDICATE do essentially the same thing: They temporarily prevent you from running any other program at the server. The server is then free to concentrate on running the network.

✔ To dedicate a server, add the ALONE or DEDICATE command as the last line of the STARTNET.BAT file. That way, ALONE or DEDICATE automatically runs when the server is started.

✔ You can exit the ALONE or DEDICATE programs at any time to run programs at the server. Even if the server is not used as a workstation, you need to do this periodically. For example, you may need to run the NET program to manage the printer queue. You have to exit ALONE or DEDICATE to do that.

To exit the ALONE program, press Esc. To exit the DEDICATE program, you can press any key.

Tuning a NetWare Server

Tuning a NetWare server is both easier and more difficult than tuning a peer-to-peer server. It's easier because NetWare is an inherently more efficient network operating system. Because it doesn't run under DOS, you don't have to worry about the built-in limitations of DOS, such as the 640K limit on conventional memory. It's more difficult because NetWare provides more options you can adjust.

- NetWare has an optional mode of transmitting data over the network cable, called *burst mode*. Burst mode can significantly improve network performance, but it's a little tricky to set up. For burst mode to work, you must install a program module on the server called PBURST.NLM and a program named BNETX.COM on each workstation. Burst mode doesn't work with all network cards, so you have to test it carefully before relying on it.

- Many NetWare configuration options are controlled with SET commands that you should place in the AUTOEXEC.NCF file or the STARTUP.NCF file. For example, SET lets you specify the amount of memory to use for file caching, the size of each cache buffer, the size of packet receive buffers, and a whole bunch of other stuff that's way too low-level and detailed to go into in a proud book such as this one.

- Some of the best techniques for tuning NetWare are suitable only for larger networks. For example, you can dramatically improve disk performance by using a special type of disk-drive gizmo called *RAID* (which stands for "Redundant Array of Inexpensive Disks"). You improve server performance by using "superservers" that have more than one CPU. And NetWare networks are often tuned by using devices such as bridges and routers to manage "traffic" on the network.

Tuning a Workstation

The biggest network performance benefits are gained by tuning the network servers because the effort you spend tuning one computer results in improved performance for every user who uses that server. Still, you shouldn't neglect performance tuning for the individual workstations on the network.

- All workstations should use some sort of local disk cache: LANcache, NLCACHE, SMARTDRV, or some other caching program. A local disk cache can't cache network drives, but it can still improve performance when accessing nonnetwork drives.

✔ Speaking of local drives, you can reduce the traffic on the network dramatically by storing frequently used data on local disks rather than on a server disk. Of course, files that have to be shared should be stored on a server drive so that the users who share the file all have access to the same copy of the file. But many files don't actually have to be shared. For example, consider placing a copy of frequently used program files on each computer rather than forcing each user to access program files from the server. This can improve network performance considerably. (Of course, you must make sure that each user has a legal copy of the software.)

✔ Many application programs can be customized to specify the location of temporary files. Always set these programs up so that the temporary files are stored on a local drive. This is especially important for database files that are used to sort information.

The 5th Wave
By Rich Tennant
FROM THE DEPARTMENT OF DEFENSE COMES...
©RICH TENNANT
THE STEALTH PC
THE STEALTH LAN
THE STEALTH MAINFRAME
NO SMOKING
THE STEALTH LAPTOP

Chapter 14

Things That Go Bump in the Night (How to Protect Your Network Data)

- -

- -

*I*f you're the hapless network manager, the safety of the data on your network is your responsibility. You get paid to lay awake at night worrying about your data. Will it be there tomorrow? If it's not, will you be able to get it back? And — most importantly — if you can't get it back, will *you* be there tomorrow?

This chapter covers the ins and outs of being a good, responsible, trustworthy network manager. They don't give out merit badges for this stuff, but they should.

Disaster Planning

On April Fool's Day a few years ago, my colleagues and I discovered that some kook had broken into the office the night before and pounded our computer equipment to death with a crowbar. (I'm not making this up.)

Sitting on a shelf right next to the mangled piles of what used to be a Wang minicomputer system was an undisturbed disk pack that contained a complete backup of all the information that was on the destroyed computer. The vandal didn't realize that one more swing of the crowbar would have escalated this major inconvenience into a complete catastrophe. Sure, we were up a creek until we could get the computer replaced. But after we had a new computer, a simple restore from the backup disk brought us right back to where we were on March 31. Without that backup, it would have taken months to get back on track.

I've been paranoid about disaster planning ever since. Before then, I thought that disaster planning meant doing good backups. That's a part of it, but I'll never forget the day we came within one swing of the crowbar of losing it all. Vandals are probably much smarter now: They know to smash the backup disks as well as the computers themselves. There's more to being prepared for disasters than doing regular backups.

Don't think it can happen to you? As I write this, the news is filled with stories of fires in Los Angeles that destroyed 400 homes. How many computers do you think were lost to hurricane Andrew? to the floods along the Mississippi in 1993? to the San Francisco earthquake in 1989? (Not too many computers were lost in the 1906 earthquake.)

Most disasters are of the less spectacular variety. You should make at least a rudimentary plan for how you will get your computer network back up and running should a major or minor disaster strike.

- ✔ The cornerstone of any disaster/recovery plan is a program of regular backups. Much of this chapter is devoted to helping you get a backup program started. Keep in mind, though, that your backups are only one swing of the crowbar from being useless. Don't leave your backup disks or tapes sitting on the shelf next to your computer: Store them in a fireproof box or safe, and store at least one set at another location.

- ✔ Your network binder is an irreplaceable source of information about your network. You should have more than one copy of it. I suggest you take a copy home so that if the entire office burns to the ground, you'll still have a copy of your network documentation. Then you'll be able to decide quickly what equipment you need to purchase and how you need to configure it so that you can get your network back up and running again.

- ✔ When your computers are completely destroyed by fire, vandalism, or theft, how will you prove to your insurance adjuster that you really had all that equipment? A frequently overlooked part of planning for disaster is keeping a detailed record of what computer equipment you own. Keep copies of all invoices for computer equipment and software in a safe place. And consider making a videotape or photographic record of your equipment, too.

- ✔ Another aspect of disaster planning that's often overlooked is expertise. In many businesses, one person takes charge of all the computers, and that one person is the only one who knows anything more than how to start WordPerfect and print a letter. What if that person should become ill, move, or decide to go work for the competition? Don't let any one person at the office form a computer dynasty that only he or she can run. Spread the computer expertise around as much as possible.

Backing Up Your Data

The main goal of backups is simple: Make sure that no matter what happens, you'll never lose more than one day's work. The stock market may crash, and the Canadians may win the series again, but you'll never lose more than one day's work if you stay on top of your backups.

Now that we agree on the purpose of backups, let's get to the good stuff: how to do it.

Use a decent backup program

DOS comes with a backup program called, appropriately, BACKUP. If your network has only a few megabytes of important data, BACKUP may be a reasonable program to use. If you have more than a few megabytes of data, however, BACKUP is unacceptable. Life is too short to spend it waiting for the BACKUP command to toss your data off to disk one byte at a time when programs that are four times as fast are readily available. Which would you prefer: spending 5 minutes backing up your data every day, or spending 20 minutes to do the same job?

✔ Besides being faster than BACKUP, other backup programs use special techniques to squeeze your data so that fewer floppy disks are required to store your backups. Compression factors of 2:1 are common, so a backup that takes 20 disks with the BACKUP command can be done with 10 disks using another backup program.

✔ MS-DOS 6.0 and 6.2 came with an improved backup program called MSBACKUP. MSBACKUP isn't quite as good as backup programs you purchase separately, but it's good enough for most. The only drawback to MSBACKUP is that you can't use it with a tape drive. If you buy a tape drive, you'll have to use some other program.

✔ My favorite program for backing up small networks is Central Point Backup, by Central Point Software. Figure 14-1 shows Central Point Backup's main display. You can purchase Central Point Backup separately, or you can get it by purchasing the complete PC Tools package. PC Tools comes with several other utility programs that are useful to network managers, so I suggest you get the complete package.

✔ To be fair (although no one said I had to be fair; this is my book and I can say what I want), there are other good backup programs around, too. Two of them are The Norton Backup by Symantec and Fastback Plus from Fifth Generation Systems.

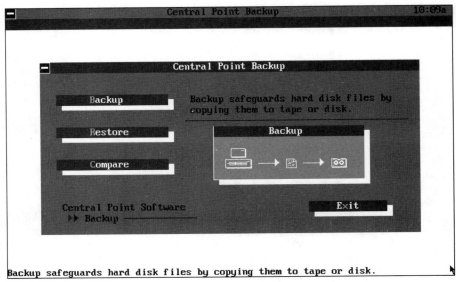

Figure 14-1:
Central
Point
Backup.

> ✔ If you buy a tape drive, you'll get backup software designed specifically for that drive. You can use the software that comes with the tape drive, but you also can use any of the three backup programs I've mentioned with most tape drives.

Why you should buy a tape drive

Diskettes are OK for backing up a few megabytes of data, but if you have a large amount of data to back up, you should at least consider purchasing a tape drive. With an inexpensive tape drive, you can copy as much as 250M of data to a single tape.

The beauty of a tape drive is that you can start your backups and leave. You don't have to baby-sit your computer, feeding it disk after disk and reading a bad novel in between disk swaps. A tape drive makes it possible to run your backups unattended.

> ✔ The most common type of tape drives used for small networks are called *QIC* tapes, which stands for "quarter-inch cartridge." QIC tape drives are available in two sizes: 120MB and 250MB. Just before I wrote this chapter, I checked a couple of mail-order advertisements and discovered that a 120MB tape drive could be purchased for as little as $145, but a 250MB drive cost only $20 more. Buy the 250MB drive even if you don't need the extra capacity yet. You won't regret it.
>
> ✔ The 120MB/250MB capacity claimed by the folks who make these tape drives relies on the backup software's capability to compress data as it

copies it to the tape. Because some files compress better than others, you may be able to store more or less than 120MB or 250MB on a single tape, depending on your files.

✔ Tapes cost about $20 each. It takes about two hours to format a tape, but you can buy them preformatted for a few dollars extra.

✔ For larger networks, you can get higher capacity digital audiotape (DAT) drives. For example, you can buy a drive that can back up 2GB to a single tape for about $1,000, or a 4GB drive for about $1,500.

You don't have to back up every file every day

If you have a tape drive and all your network data can fit on one tape, the best approach to backups is to back up all your data every day. If you have more data than can fit on one tape, or if you are using disks for backup, and a complete backup takes more than a few disks, you should consider using *incremental* backups instead.

An incremental backup backs up only the files that you have modified since the last time you did a backup of any sort. Incremental backups are a lot faster than full backups because you probably only modify a few files each day. Even if a full backup takes 50 disks, you can probably fit each day's incremental backups on one or two disks.

✔ The easiest way to use incremental backups is to do a full backup every Monday and then do an incremental backup on Tuesday, Wednesday, Thursday, and Friday.

✔ When you use incremental backups, the complete backup consists of the full backup disks and all the incremental backup disks you've made since you did the full backup.

✔ A variation of the incremental backup idea is the *differential* backup. A differential backup backs up all the files that have been modified since the last time you did a *full* backup. When you use differential backups, the complete backup consists of the full backup disks plus the disks from your most recent differential backup.

Server versus workstation backups

When you back up on a peer-to-peer network, there are two basic approaches to running the back-up software: You can run the backup software on the file server itself, or you can run the backups from one of the network's workstations. If you run the backups from the file server, you'll probably have to shut down the network in order to run backups. You can run backups from a workstation without taking down the server.

Stop me before I get carried away

The Archive Bit is not an old Abbott & Costello routine ("All right, I wanna know who modified the archive bit." "What." "Who?" "No, what." "Wait a minute...just tell me what's the name of the guy who modified the archive bit!" "Right.").

The archive bit is a little flag that's tucked into each file's directory entry, right next to the file name. Any time a program modifies a file, DOS sets the file's archive bit to the "ON" position. Then, when a backup program backs up the file, it sets the file's archive bit to the "OFF" position.

Because backup programs reset the archive bit when they back up a file, they can use the archive bit to select just the files that have been modified since the last backup. Clever, eh?

Differential backups work because they don't reset the archive bit. When you use differential backups, each differential backup backs up all the files that have been modified since the last full backup.

Even though you can run backups from a workstation while the network is running, it's not a good idea to do backups while the network is being used. The backup program will skip over any files that have been opened by other users, so your backup will not include those files. Ironically, those are the files that need backing up the most, because they're the files that are being used and probably modified.

- ✔ Backing up from a workstation enables you to select network drives from more than one server. If you back up from the server and shut down the network, you'll only be able to access the drives on that server.

- ✔ You may think that backing up directly from the server would be more efficient than backing up from a workstation because data doesn't have to travel over the network. Actually, this usually isn't the case, because most networks are faster than most tape drives. The network probably won't slow down backups unless you back up during the busiest time of the day, when hordes of network users are storming the network gates.

- ✔ It's best to set up a special user ID for the user who does backups. This user ID will require access to all of the files on the server. If you're worried about security, you should worry about this user ID. Anyone who knows it — and its password — can log in and bypass any security restrictions you've placed on that user's normal user ID.

You can counter this by restricting the backup user ID to a certain workstation and a certain time of the day. If you're really clever (and paranoid), you can probably set up the backup user's account so that the only program it can run is the backup program.

How many sets of backups should you keep?

Don't try to cut costs by purchasing one backup tape and reusing it every day. What happens if you accidentally delete an important file on Tuesday and don't discover your mistake until Thursday? Because the file didn't exist on Wednesday, it won't be on Wednesday's backup tape. If you have only one tape that's reused every day, you're outta luck.

The safest scheme is to use a new backup tape every day and keep all your old tapes in a vault. Pretty soon, though, your tape vault would start to look like the warehouse where they stored the Ark of the Covenant at the end of *Raiders of the Lost Ark.*

As a compromise between these two extremes, most users purchase several tapes and rotate them. That way, you always have several backup tapes to fall back on in case the file you need isn't on the most recent backup tape. This technique is called *tape rotation*, and there are several variations of it in common use.

- ✔ The simplest approach is to purchase three tapes and label them A, B, and C. You use the tapes on a daily basis in sequence: A, B, C, A, B, C, and so on. On any given day, you have three *generations* of backups: today's, yesterday's, and the day-before-yesterday's. Computer geeks like to call these the *grandfather*, *father*, and *son* tapes.

- ✔ Another simple approach is to purchase five tapes and use one each day of the week.

- ✔ A variation of this scheme is to buy eight tapes. Take four of them and write *Monday* on one label, *Tuesday* on another, *Wednesday* on the third, and *Thursday* on the fourth label. On the other four tapes, write *Friday 1*, *Friday 2*, *Friday 3*, and *Friday 4*. Now, tack a calendar up on the wall near the computer and number all the Fridays in the year: 1, 2, 3, 4, 1, 2, 3, 4, and so on.

  On Monday through Thursday, you use the appropriate daily backup tape. When you do backups on Friday, you consult the calendar to decide which Friday tape to use. With this scheme, you always have four week's worth of Friday backup tapes, plus individual backup tapes for the past five days.

- ✔ If bookkeeping data lives on the network, it's a good idea to make a backup copy of all your files (or at least all your accounting files) immediately before closing the books each month and to retain those backups for each month of the year. Does that mean you should purchase 12 additional tapes? Not necessarily. If you back up just your accounting files, you probably can fit all 12 months on a single tape. Just make sure that you back up with the "append to tape" option rather than the "erase tape" option so that the previous contents of the tape aren't destroyed. And treat this "accounting backup" as completely separate from your normal daily backup routine.

A word about tape reliability

From experience, I've found that although tape drives are very reliable, once in a while they run amok. Problem is, they don't always tell you they're not working. A tape drive can spin along for hours, pretending to back up your data, when in reality your data isn't being written reliably to the tape. In other words, a tape drive can trick you into thinking your backups are working just fine, but when disaster strikes and you need your backup tapes, you may just discover that the tapes are worthless.

Don't panic! There's a simple way to assure yourself that your tape drive is working. Just activate the "compare after backup" feature of your backup software. Then, as soon as your backup program finishes backing up your data, it will rewind the tape, read each backed up file, and compare it with the original version on disk. If all files compare, you know your backups are trustworthy.

- ✔ The compare function doubles the time required to do a backup, but that doesn't matter if your entire backup fits on one tape. You can just run the backup after hours. It doesn't matter whether it takes one hour or ten, as long as it's finished by the time you arrive at work the next morning.

- ✔ If your backups require more than one tape, you may not want to run the compare-after-backup option every day. But be sure to run it periodically to check that your tape drive is working.

- ✔ All back-up programs have a compare function, but not all of them have a "compare after backup" option that automatically compares data immediately after a backup. If yours doesn't, you can construct a batch file that has two commands: one to back up your data, the other to run the backup program's compare function. This will have the same effect. Such a batch file might look something like this:

```
TAPE C:\*.* /S /BACKUP
TAPE C:\*.* /S /COMPARE
```

Here, I use a backup program called TAPE to back up all the files on drive C:, including files in subdirectories (that's what the /S does). Then, the next command runs the TAPE program again, this time using the /COMPARE switch to do a comparison instead of a backup.

Change the Oil Every 5,000 Miles

Like cars, disk drives need periodic maintenance. All versions of DOS come with a command called CHKDSK, which does some of this checking for you. MS-DOS 6.2 comes with an improved disk-maintenance command called ScanDisk.

Chckng yr dsk wth th chkdsk cmmnd

A friend of mine who is an authority on the origins of DOS claims that the CHKDSK command was conceived by a group of biblical scholars, which is why the word CHKDSK has no vowels. (Ancient Hebrew was written without vowels, and I really reached for that one, didn't I? Sorry.)

CHKDSK stands for "check disk," and that's sort of what it does. It checks your disk for problems, but unfortunately it checks for only a certain class of problems and not all types of disk problems. Hence, the CHKDSK command is flawed: It lulls you into a false sense of security, leaving you thinking that it's checking the reliability of your disk drive, when in fact it is not.

CHKDSK tests for the types of problems that occur when DOS becomes confused about where your files are stored on the disk. These types of problems usually occur when the dog steps on your computer's power cord while you are saving a file. If you run CHKDSK with the /F switch, it happily corrects these problems so that you can go on your merry way.

But CHKDSK does *not* in any way check to see whether your disk is doing a good job of storing data. It won't tell you if part of your disk has gone south for the winter.

- ✔ With MS-DOS 6.2, Microsoft finally realized that the CHKDSK command had outlived its usefulness, so they added a new command called ScanDisk to do more thorough disk checking. If you have MS-DOS 6.2, you should use ScanDisk instead of CHKDSK.

- ✔ With MS-DOS 6.2, Microsoft also made a dramatic improvement to CHKDSK: It uses commas when it displays big numbers, so now you can tell that 18374368 is 18,374,368 without squinting at the screen while trying to count the digits. Of course, this is a so-what-who-cares improvement, because you'll be using ScanDisk from now on.

- ✔ If you don't have MS-DOS 6.2, you shouldn't rely on the CHKDSK command to thoroughly test your disk. Get a utility program like PC Tools or The Norton Utilities and use it instead.

Scanning your disk with, you guessed it, the ScanDisk command

With MS-DOS 6.2, Microsoft introduced a new command called ScanDisk. ScanDisk does everything the old CHKDSK command does, plus more: It actually checks the reliability of your disk drive by trying to write something into every sector on your disk and then reading it back to see whether it took. (Don't worry — it does this without upsetting any of the existing data on your disk.)

Unlike the other new programs that were introduced with MS-DOS 6.0, the ScanDisk program really is easy to use. Just type **SCANDISK** and let it go. Figure 14-2 shows ScanDisk's friendly and uncluttered display, which shows the progress of the various tests.

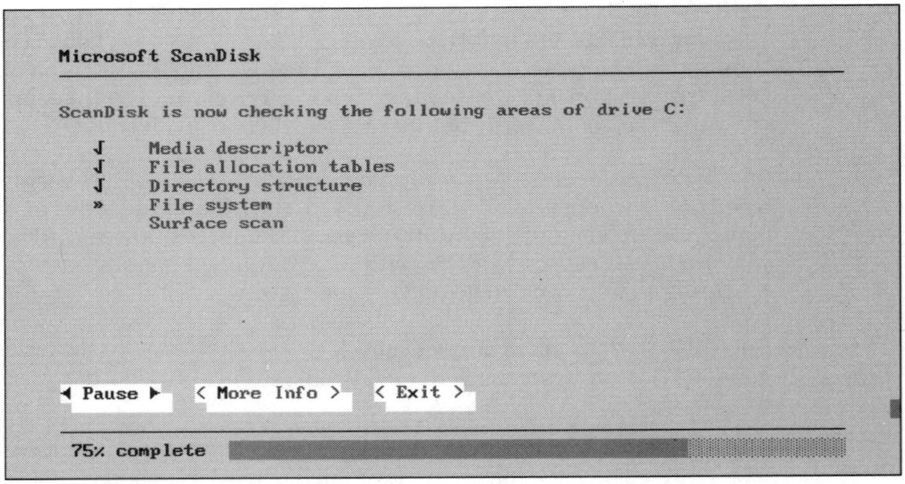

```
Microsoft ScanDisk


ScanDisk is now checking the following areas of drive C:

    √     Media descriptor
    √     File allocation tables
    √     Directory structure
    »     File system
          Surface scan












  ◄ Pause ►      < More Info >     < Exit >


  75% complete  ▓▓▓▓▓▓▓▓▓▓▓▓▓▓▓▓▓▓▓▓▓▓▓▓▓▓▓░
```

Figure 14-2:
ScanDisk's friendly and uncluttered display.

After ScanDisk does some preliminary checks, it asks whether you want to proceed with the time-consuming surface analysis. Press Enter to proceed, or press Tab and then Enter to skip the surface analysis.

- ✔ If ScanDisk detects a problem, it displays a message that describes the problem and offers to fix it for you. Read the instructions on the screen, and select the "More Info" function if you don't understand what's going on.

- ✔ If you want ScanDisk to blast straight through its tests without asking you whether it should do the surface scan or correct errors, add the /SUR-FACE, /AUTOFIX, and /NOSUMMARY switches so that the command looks like this:

```
scandisk /surface /autofix /nosummary
```

It's totally unreasonable to expect anyone to type a command like this, but you can easily put this command in a one-line batch file named SCAN.BAT. Then you just type **SCAN** to invoke the command.

✔ Aren't you glad (but a little bit surprised) that they didn't name this new command SCNDSK?

✔ If you don't have MS-DOS 6.2, you can get programs that are similar to ScanDisk, and a bit more exhaustive in their tests, in utility packages such as PC Tools or The Norton Utilities.

Guarding against the Dreaded Computer Virus

Viruses are one of the most misunderstood computer phenomena around these days. What is a virus? How does it work? How does it spread from computer to computer? I'm glad you asked.

What is a virus?

Make no mistake, viruses are real. They're not as widespread as the news media may lead you to believe, but they are very real nonetheless. Every computer user is susceptible to attacks by computer viruses, and using a network increases your vulnerability.

Viruses don't just spontaneously appear out of nowhere. Viruses are computer programs that are created by malicious programmers who've lost a few screws and should be locked up.

What makes a virus a virus is its capability to make copies of itself that can be spread to other computers. These copies, in turn, make still more copies that spread to still more computers, and so on, ad nauseam.

Then, on a certain date or when you type a particular command or press a certain key, the virus strikes, sometimes harmlessly displaying a "gotcha" message, sometimes maliciously wiping out all the data on your hard disk. Ouch.

Viruses move from computer to computer mostly by latching themselves onto floppy disks, which are frequently exchanged between computers. But viruses also can travel over the network cables that connect the computers in your network. That's why networked computers are especially vulnerable to virus attack.

Keep in mind that the network can't be infected by a virus unless the virus enters the network through some other means, typically through an infected floppy disk. But after one computer on the network has become infected, it's not unlikely that all the computers on the network will soon be infected, as well.

- ✔ The term *virus* is often used to refer not only to true virus programs (which are able to replicate themselves), but also to any other type of program that's designed to harm your computer. These include so-called *trojan horse* programs that usually look like games, but are in reality hard disk formatters.

- ✔ There are several thousand "strains" of viruses that computer-virus experts have identified. Many of them have colorful names, such as the Stoned Virus, the Jerusalem Virus, and the Michelangelo Virus.

- ✔ Antivirus programs are able to recognize known viruses and remove them from your system, and they're able to spot the telltale signs of unknown viruses. However, the idiots who write viruses aren't idiots (in the intellectual sense), so they're constantly developing new techniques to evade detection by antivirus programs. New viruses are frequently discovered, and the antivirus programs are periodically updated to detect and remove them.

Using an antivirus program

The best way to protect your network from virus infection is to use an antivirus program. These programs have a catalog of several thousand known viruses that they can detect and remove. In addition, they can spot the types of changes viruses typically make to your computer's files, decreasing the likelihood that some previously unknown virus will go undetected.

MS-DOS 6 comes with a basic antivirus program called MSAV. MSAV scans disk drives to determine whether any known viruses are present. How often you use MSAV depends on factors unique to your network (that's a clever way of not telling you you should do it once a week, which you probably should, but you'd write me off as a paranoid lunatic if I actually said it). Figure 14-3 shows MSAV's opening screen.

- ✔ To run MSAV so that it automatically checks all drives, including network server drives, add the /A switch to the command, like this:

```
msav /a
```

To scan all your local drives but not the network drives, use the /L switch:

```
msav /l
```

MSAV has a bunch of other command-line switches, all of which are worth ignoring.

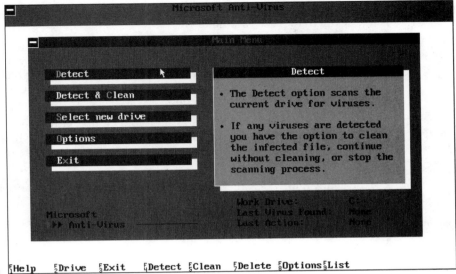

Figure 14-3:
MSAV,
brave
defender
against evil
computer
viruses.

✔ Both PC Tools and The Norton Utilities come with more advanced antivirus programs that have additional features for network users, such as the capability to notify network users of virus infections. In addition, Central Point sells a version of its antivirus program that can run as an NLM on a NetWare server.

✔ The good folks who make antivirus programs periodically issue updates that allow them to capture newly discovered viruses. Consult the documentation (ugh!) that came with your antivirus program to find out how you can obtain these updates.

✔ DOS 6, as well as antivirus programs, comes with programs you can run to constantly monitor your computer for signs of virus infection. The DOS 6 command for this purpose is VSAFE; run it, and an alert message pops up whenever VSAFE smells a virus sneaking into your computer. To use VSAFE, add this line to your AUTOEXEC.BAT file:

```
\dos\vsafe
```

Safe computing

Besides using an antivirus program, there are a few additional precautions you can take to ensure virus-free computing. If you haven't talked to your kids about these safe computing practices, you'd better do it soon.

✔ Regularly back up your data. If you do get hit by a virus, you may need the backup to recover your data.

✔ If you buy software from a store and discover that the seal has been broken on the disk package, take the software back. Don't try to install it on your computer. You don't hear about tainted software as often as you hear about tainted beef, but if you buy software that's been opened, it may well be laced with a virus infection.

✔ Scan your disk for virus infection after your computer has been to a repair shop or worked on by a consultant. These guys don't intend harm, but they occasionally spread viruses accidentally simply because they work on so many strange computers.

✔ Scan any floppy disk that doesn't belong to you before you access any of its files.

✔ And above all, do not leave strange disks in your disk drives overnight. The most common way for computer viruses to spread is by starting a computer with an infected disk in drive A.

Chapter 15

How to Stay on Top of Your Network and Keep the Users off Your Back

• •

In This Chapter

▶ Training your users

▶ Organizing a library

▶ Sources for help

▶ Great excuses for network managers

• •

*N*etwork administrators really have a rotten deal. Users come to you whenever anything goes wrong, regardless of whether the problem has anything to do with the network. They'll knock on your door if they can't log in, if they've lost a file, or if they can't remember how to use the microwave. They'll probably even ask you to show them how to program their VCRs.

This chapter brushes over a few basic things you can do to simplify your life as a network manager.

Training Your Users

When you first get your network up and running, you should invite all the network users to Network Obedience School so that you can train them in how to behave on the network. Teach them the basics of accessing the network, make sure that they understand about sharing files, and explain the rules to them.

A great way to prepare your users for this session is to have each of them read the first five chapters of this book. Remember, those chapters are written with the network *user* in mind, so they explain the basic facts of network life. If your users read those chapters first, they'll be in a much better position to ask good questions during obedience school.

- ✔ Write up a summary of what your users need to know about the network, on one page if possible. Include everyone's user ID, the names of the servers, network drive assignments and printers, and the procedure for logging in to the network. Make sure that everyone has a copy of this Network Cheat Sheet.

- ✔ Emphasize the etiquette of network life. Make sure that everyone understands that all the free space on the network drive isn't their own personal space. Explain the importance of treating other people's files with respect. Suggest that it might be nice to check with your fellow users before sending a three-hour print job to the network printer.

- ✔ Don't bluff your way through your role as network manager. If you're not a computer genius, don't pretend to be one just because you know a little more than everyone else. Be up front with your users; tell them that you're all in over your collective heads, but that you're in this together and you're going to do your best to try to solve any problems that might come up.

- ✔ If you have your users read the first five chapters of this book, place special emphasis on Chapter 5, especially the part about bribes. Subtly suggest which ones are your favorites.

Organizing a Library

One of the biggest bummers about being the network manager is that every network user expects you to be an expert at every computer program they use. That's a manageable enough task when you have only two network users and the only program they use is WordPerfect. But if you have a gaggle of users who use a bevy of programs, it's next to impossible to be an expert at all of them.

The only way around this dilemma is to set up a well stocked computer library that has all the information you'll need to solve problems that come up. When a user bugs you with some previously undiscovered bug, you'll be able to say with confidence, "I'll get back to you on that one."

Your library should include:

- ✔ A copy of your network binder, containing all the information you need about the configuration of your network.

- ✔ A copy of the manuals for every program that's used on the network. Most users ignore the manuals, so they won't mind if you "borrow" it for the library. If a user won't part with the manual, at least make a note of the manual's location so you'll know where to find it.

- ✔ A DOS manual for every version of DOS that's being used on the network. With luck, all the computers will be running the same version, so only one manual will be needed. But if you have several DOS versions on your network, you'll need a copy of the manual for each version.

✔ A copy of the network software manual or manuals.

✔ At least 20 copies of this book (hey, I have bills to pay). Seriously, your library should contain books appropriate to your level of expertise. Of course, *...For Dummies* books are available on just about every major computer subject. It's not a bad idea to devote an entire shelf to these yellow-and-black books.

Keeping Up with the Computer Industry

The computer business changes fast, and one of the things your users probaby will expect is for you to be abreast of all the latest trends and developments. "Hey, Ward," they'll ask, "what do you think about the new version of SkyWriter? Should we upgrade, or should we stick with version 23?"

"Hey, Ward, we'd like to get into desktop publishing. What's the hottest desktop publishing program nowadays for under $200?"

"Hey, Ward, my kid wants me to buy a sound card. Which one is better, the SoundSmacker Pro or the BlabberMouth 9000?"

The only way to give halfway intelligent answers to questions like these is to read about the industry. Visit your local newsstand and pick out a few computer magazines that appeal to you.

✔ Subscribe to at least one general-interest computer magazine and one magazine specifically written for network users. That way, you'll keep abreast of general trends plus the specific stuff that applies just to networks.

✔ Look for magazines that have a mix of good how-to articles and reviews of new products.

✔ Don't overlook the value of the advertisements in many of the larger computer magazines. Some people (myself included) subscribe to certain magazines because of the number of mail-order advertisements the magazines carry.

✔ Keep in mind that most computer magazines are very technical. Try to find magazines that seem to be written to your level. You may discover that after a year or two, you outgrow one magazine and are ready to replace it with one that's more technical.

✔ Subscriptions to some of the most popular computer magazines are available through Publishers Clearinghouse. Who knows, you may win $10,000,000. Then you'll be able to quit your job as network manager, and you won't need the computer magazines after all!

The Guru Needs a Guru, Too

No matter how much you know about computers, there are plenty of people who know more than you do. This rule seems to apply at every rung of the ladder of computer experience. I'm sure there's a top rung somewhere, occupied by the world's best computer guru. But I'm not sitting on that rung, and neither are you.

As the local computer guru, one of the most valuable assets you can have is a knowledgeable friend who's a notch or two above you on the geek scale. That way, when you run into a real stumper, you've got a friend you can call for advice.

- ✔ When it comes to your own guru, don't forget the Computer Geek's Golden Rule: "Do unto your guru as you would have your own users do unto you." Don't pester your guru with simple stuff that you just haven't spent the time to think through. But if you have thought it through, give your guru a call. Most computer experts welcome the opportunity to tackle an unusual computer problem. It's a genetic defect.

- ✔ If you don't already know someone who knows more about computers than you do, consider joining your local PC users' group. The group may even have a subgroup that specializes in your networking software, or there may be a user group devoted entirely to local folks who use the same networking software you do. Odds are, you're sure to make a friend or two at a users' group meeting. And you can probably convince your boss to pay any fees required to join the group.

- ✔ If you can't find a real-life guru, try to find an on-line guru. Join CompuServe and check in to the support forum for your networking software. There, you'll find lots of people willing to answer your questions, help with your problems, and shoot the electronic breeze. (And make sure your boss pays for your CompuServe account, too.)

- ✔ Remember that the bribes listed way back in Chapter 5 can be used on your own guru. The whole point of these bribes is to make your guru feel loved and appreciated.

Network Manager BS

As network manager, sometimes you just won't be able to solve a problem, at least not immediately. There are two things you can do in this situation. The first is to explain that the problem is particularly difficult and that you'll have a solution as soon as possible. The second is to lie. Here are some of my favorite excuses and phoney explanations:

- Blame the problem on sunspots. You see, sunspots are associated with solar flares, which unleash a tremendous amount of solar radiation upon the earth. Up until a few years ago, we were protected from that radiation by the ozone layer. But now, with the hole in the ozone growing bigger and bigger each year, the solar radiation occasionally gets through and causes unpredictable computer glitches.

- Blame it on the version of whatever software you're using.

- Blame it on cheap imported memory chips. Next time, buy American.

- Let's hope the problem wasn't caused by stray static electricity. Those types of problems are very difficult to track down.

- You don't have enough memory to do that.

- You don't have a big enough disk to do that.

- You need a Pentium to do that.

- You can't do that under Windows.

- You can only do that under Windows.

- You're not using DoubleSpace are you?

- Sounds like a virus.

- Your mind is fuzzy. You'll have to think about it over a round of golf.

Part IV
The Part of Tens

The 5th Wave   By Rich Tennant

"OOPS, I FORGOT TO LOG OFF AGAIN."

In this part...

*1*f you keep this book in the bathroom, the chapters in this section are the ones that will get read most. Each of these chapters consists of ten (more or less) things that are worth knowing about various aspects of networking. Without further ado, here they are, direct from the home office in Fresno, California.

Chapter 16

Ten Big Network Mistakes

*J*ust about the time you figure out how to avoid the most embarrassing computer mistakes, such as folding a 5¼" disk in half to make it fit in a 3½" drive, the network lands on your computer. Now there's a whole new list of dumb things you can do, mistakes that will give your average computer geek a belly laugh because they seem so basic to him. Well, that's because he's a computer geek. Nobody had to tell him not to fold the disk — he was born with an extra gene that gave him an instinctive knowledge of such things.

Here's a list of some of the most common basic mistakes made by network novices. Avoid these mistakes, and you'll deprive your local computer geek of the pleasure of a good laugh at your expense.

Turning Off or Restarting a Server Computer While Users Are Logged On

The fastest way to blow your network users to kingdom come is to turn off a server computer while users are logged on. Restarting it by pressing its reset button or giving it the three-finger salute (Ctrl+Alt+Del) can have the same disastrous effect.

If your network is set up with a dedicated file server, you probably won't be tempted to turn it off or restart it. But if your network is set up as a true peer-to-peer network, where each of the workstation computers — including your own — also doubles as a server computer, be careful about the impulsive urge to turn your computer off or restart it. Someone may be accessing a file or printer on your computer at that very moment.

Before turning off or restarting a server computer, find out whether anyone is logged on. If so, politely ask them to log off.

Deleting Important Files on the Server

Without a network, you can do anything you want to your computer, and the only person you can hurt is yourself. Kind of like the old "victimless crime" debate. Put your computer on a network, though, and you take on a certain amount of responsibility. You must learn to live like a responsible member of the network society.

That means you can't capriciously delete files from a network server just because you don't need them. They may not be yours. You wouldn't want someone deleting your files, would you?

Be especially careful about files that are required to keep the network running. For example, every LANtastic server has a directory named LANTASTI.NET. Delete the files in this directory and poof! — the server is history.

Copying a File from the Server, Changing It, and Then Copying It Back

Sometimes it's easier to work on a network file if you first copy the file to your local disk. Then you can access it from your application program more efficiently because you don't have to use the network. This is especially true for large database files that have to be sorted to print reports.

You're asking for trouble, though, if you copy the file to your PC's local hard disk, make changes to the file, and then copy the updated version of the file back to the server. Why? Because there's no guarantee somebody else didn't try the same thing at the same time. If that happens, the updates made by one of you — the one who copies the file back to the server first — will be lost.

Copying a file to a local drive is an OK thing to do, but not if you plan on updating the file and copying it back.

Sending Something to the Printer Again Just Because It Didn't Print the First Time

What do you do if you send something to the printer and nothing happens? Right answer: Find out why nothing happened and fix it. Wrong answer: Send it again and see whether it works this time. Some users keep sending it over and over again, hoping that one of these days, it will take. The result is rather embarrassing when someone finally clears the paper jam and then watches 30 copies of the same letter print.

Unplugging a Cable While the Computer Is On

Bad idea! If for any reason you need to unplug a cable from behind your computer, turn your computer off first. You don't want to fry any of the delicate electronic parts inside your computer, do you?

If you need to unplug the network cable, it's a good idea to do it when all the computers on the network are off. This is especially true if your network is wired with thinnet coax cable; it's not such a big deal with twisted-pair cable.

Note: With thinnet cable, it's OK to disconnect the T connector from your computer, as long as you don't disconnect the cable itself from the T connector.

Assuming That the Server Is Safely Backed Up

Some users make the unfortunate assumption that the network somehow represents an efficient and organized bureaucracy worthy of their trust. Far from the truth. Never assume that the network jocks are doing their jobs backing up the network data every day. Check up on them. Conduct a surprise inspection one day: Burst into the computer room wearing white gloves and demand to see the backup tapes. Check the tape rotation to make sure that more than one day's worth of backups are available.

If you're not impressed with your network's backup procedures, take it upon yourself to make sure that *you* will never lose any of *your* data. Back up your most valued files to floppy disks frequently.

Thinking You Can't Work Just Because the Network Is Down

A few years back, I realized that I cannot do my job without electricity. Should a power failure occur and I find myself without electricity, I can't even light a candle and work with pencil and paper because the only pencil sharpener I have is electric.

Some people have the same attitude about the network: They figure that if the network goes down, they may as well go home. That's not always the case. Just because your computer is attached to a network doesn't mean that it won't work when the network is down. If the wind flies out of the network sails, it's true that you can't access any network devices. You can't get files from network drives, and you can't print on network printers. But you can still use your computer for local work, accessing files and programs on your local hard disk and printing on your local printer (if you're lucky enough to have one).

Always Blaming the Network

Some people treat the network kind of like the village idiot who can be blamed whenever anything goes wrong. Networks do cause problems of their own, but they are not the root of all evil.

If your monitor displays only capital letters, it's probably because you pressed the Caps Lock key. Don't blame the network.

If you spill coffee on the keyboard, well, that's your fault. Don't blame the network.

Your three-year-old sticks Play Doh in the floppy drive — hey, kids will be kids. Don't blame the network.

Get the point?

Chapter 17
Ten Networking Commandments

- -

In This Chapter

▶ Thou shalt back up thy hard disk religiously

▶ Thou shalt not drop thy guard against the unholy viri

▶ Remember thy network disk, to keep it clean of old files

▶ Thou shalt not tinker with thine AUTOEXEC.BAT, CONFIG.SYS, and STARTNET.BAT files unless thou knowest what thou art doing

▶ Thou shalt not covet thy neighbor's network

▶ Thou shalt schedule downtime before doing major work upon thy server

▶ Thou shalt keep an adequate supply of spare parts

▶ Thou shalt not steal thy neighbor's program without license

▶ Thou shalt train thy users in the way in which they should go

▶ Thou shalt write down thy network configuration upon tablets of stone

- -

"*B*lessed is the network manager who walks not in the council of the ignorant, nor stands in the way of the oblivious, nor sits in the seat of the greenhorn, but delights in the Law of the Network, and meditates on this Law day and night."

— Networks 1:1

And so it came to pass that these Ten Networking Commandments were passed down from generation to generation, to be worn as frontlets between the computer geeks' eyes and written upon their doorposts. Obey these commandments and it shall go well with you, with your children, and with your children's children.

I. Thou shalt back up thy hard disk religiously

Prayer is a wonderful thing, but when it comes to protecting the data on your network, nothing beats a well-thought-out schedule of backups followed religiously.

II. Thou shalt not drop thy guard against the unholy viri

Remember Col. Flagg from *M*A*S*H*, who hid in trash cans looking for commies? You don't exactly want to become him, but on the other hand, you don't want to ignore the possibility of getting zapped by a virus. Start by making sure that every user realizes that any floppy disk from the outside could be infected, and after one computer on the network is infected, the entire network is in trouble. Then show the users how easy it is to scan suspicious disks before using them.

III. Remember thy network disk, to keep it clean of old files

Don't wait until your 300MB network drive is down to just one cluster of free space before thinking about cleaning it up. Set up a routine schedule for disk housekeeping, where you wade through the files and directories on the network disk to remove old junk.

IV. Thou shalt not tinker with thine AUTOEXEC.BAT, CONFIG.SYS, and STARTNET.BAT files unless thou knowest what thou art doing

The AUTOEXEC.BAT, CONFIG.SYS, and STARTNET.BAT files contain weird-looking commands your computer can't do without. Don't mess around with these files unless you know what you're doing. And be especially careful if you think you know what you're doing. It's people who think they know what they're doing who get themselves into trouble!

V. Thou shalt not covet thy neighbor's network

Network envy is a common malady among network administrators. If your network uses LANtastic and it works, there's nothing to be gained by coveting someone else's NetWare network. If you run NetWare 2.2, resist the urge to upgrade to 3.11 unless there really is a good reason. And if you run NetWare 3.11, fantasizing about NetWare 4.0 is a venial sin.

You're especially susceptible to network envy if you're a gadget freak. There's always a better hub to be had or some fancy network protocol gizmo to lust after. Don't give in to these base urges! Resist the devil, and he will flee!

VI. Thou shalt schedule downtime before working upon thy network

As a courtesy, try to give your users plenty of advance notice when you intend to take down the network to work on it. Obviously, you can't predict when random problems will strike. But if you know you're going to add a new computer to the network on Thursday morning, you'll earn points if you tell everyone about the inconvenience two days before rather than two minutes before.

VII. Thou shalt keep an adequate supply of spare parts

There's no reason your network should be down for two days just because a cable breaks. You should always make sure that you have at least a minimal supply of network spare parts on hand. As luck would have it, the next chapter suggests ten things you should keep in your parts drawer.

VIII. Thou shalt not steal thy neighbor's program without license

How would you like it if Inspector Clouseau barged into your office and looked over your shoulder as you ran Lotus 1-2-3 from a network server, and asked, "Do you have a liesaunce?"

"A liesaunce?" you reply, puzzled.

"Yes of course, liesaunce, that is what I said. The law specifically prohibits the playing of a computer program on a network without a proper liesaunce."

You don't want to go against the law, do you?

IX. Thou shalt train thy users in the way in which they should go

Don't blame the users if they don't know how to use the network. It's not their fault.

X. Thou shalt write down thy network configuration upon tablets of stone

If you kick the bucket, who else will know diddly-squat about the network if you don't write it down somewhere? The back of a napkin won't cut it. Write down everything and put it in an official binder labeled "Network Bible" and protect it as if it were sacred.

Your hope should be that 2,000 years from now, when archaeologists are exploring caves in your area, they find your network documentation hidden in a jar and marvel at how meticulously the people of our time recorded their network configurations.

They'll probably draw ridiculous conclusions such as we offered sacrifices of burnt data packets to a deity named NOS, but that makes it all the more fun.

Chapter 18

Ten Things You Should Keep in the Closet

*W*hen you first networkize your office computers, you need to find a closet where you can stash some network goodies. If you can't find a whole closet, shoot for a shelf, a drawer, or at least a sturdy cardboard box.

Here's a list of what stuff to keep on hand.

Tools

You should have at least a basic computer tool kit, the kind you can pick up for $15 from just about any office supply store. You also should have wire cutters, strippers, and cable crimpers that work for your network cable type.

Extra Cable

When you buy network cable, you should never buy exactly the amount you'll need. In fact, it's not a bad idea to buy at least twice as much cable as you'll need, so half of the cable will be left over in case you need it later. You will. Something will go wrong and you'll suspect a cable problem, so you'll need extra cable to replace the bad cable. Or you'll add a computer or two to the network and need extra cable.

If you glue your entire network together with preassembled 25' lengths of thinnet coax cable, it's a good idea to have at least one 25' segment lying around in the closet.

Extra Connectors

Don't run out of connectors, either. If you use twisted-pair cabling, you'll find that connectors go bad more often than you'd like. Buy the connectors 25, 50, or 100 at a time so that you'll have plenty of spares lying around.

If you use thinnet cable, keep a few spare BNC connectors handy, plus a few T connectors and a few terminators. Terminators have been known to mysteriously disappear. Rumor has it that they are sucked through some kind of time vortex into the 21st century, where they are refabricated and returned to our time in the form of Arnold Schwarzenegger.

Preassembled Patch Cables

If you wired your network the professional way, with wall jacks in each office, keep a few preassembled patch cables of various lengths in the closet. That way, you won't have to pull out the cable crimpers every time you need to change a patch cable.

Twinkies

If left sealed in their little individually wrapped packages, Twinkies will keep for years. In fact, they'll probably outlast the network itself. You can give 'em to future network geeks, ensuring continued network support for generations to come.

An Extra Network Card

Ideally, you want to use identical network cards in all your computers. But if the boss's computer is down, you'll probably settle for whatever network card the corner network street vendor is selling today. That's why you should always keep at least one spare network card in the closet. You'll rest easy knowing that if a network card fails, you have an identical replacement card sitting on the shelf, just waiting to be installed — and you won't have to buy one from someone who also sells imitation Persian rugs.

Obviously, if you have only two computers on your network, it's hard to justify spending the money for a spare network adapter card. With larger networks, it's easier to justify.

Complete Documentation of the Network, on Tablets of Stone

I've mentioned several times in this book the importance of documenting your network. Don't spend hours documenting your network and then hide the documentation under a pile of old magazines behind your desk. Put the binder in the closet with the other network supplies so that you and everyone else will always know where to find it.

Don't you dare chisel passwords into the network documentation, though. Shame on you for even thinking about it!

If you do decide to chisel the network documentation in stone tablets, consider using sandstone. It's attractive, inexpensive, and easy to update (just rub out the old info and chisel in the new). Keep in mind, however, that sandstone is subject to erosion from spilled Jolt Cola or Snapple. Oh, and make sure you store it on a reinforced shelf.

The Network Manuals and Disks

In the land of Oz, a common lament of the Network Scarecrow is "If I only had the manual." True, the manual probably isn't a Pulitzer prize candidate, but that doesn't mean you should toss it in a landfill, either. Put it where it belongs: in the closet with all the other network tools and artifacts.

Likewise the disks. You may need them someday, so keep them with the other network stuff.

Ten Copies of This Book

Obviously, you'll want to keep an adequate supply of this book on hand to distribute to all your network users. The more they know, the more they'll stay off your back. Sheesh, 10 copies may not be enough — 20 may be closer to what you need . . ..

Chapter 19

Ten Network Gizmos Only Big Networks Need

- -

- -

*P*eople who compile statistics on things, such as the ratio of chickens to humans in Arkansas and the likelihood of the Mets losing when the other team shows up, report that more than 40 percent of all networks have fewer than 10 computers and that this percentage is expected to increase in coming years. A Ross Perot-style pie chart would be good here, but my editor tells me I'm running long, so we'll have to pass on that.

The point is that if you're one of the lucky 40 percent with fewer than 10 computers on your network, you can skip this chapter altogether. It's a brief description of various network gizmos you should know about if your network is really big. How big is big? There's no hard-and-fast rule, but the soft-and-slow rule is that you should look into this stuff when your network grows to about 25 computers.

The exceptions to the soft-and-slow rule are: (1) Your company has two or more networks that you want to hook together, and these networks were designed by different people who refused to talk to each other until it was too late; (2) your network needs to connect computers that are more than a few hundred yards apart, perhaps in different buildings.

Repeaters

A *repeater* is a gizmo that's designed to give your network signals a boost so that they can travel farther. It's kind of like the Gatorade stations in a marathon. As they travel past the repeater, the network signals pick up a cup of Gatorade, take a sip, splash the rest of it on their heads, toss the cup, and hop in a cab when they're sure no one is looking.

Repeaters are used when the total length of your network cable is larger than the maximum allowed for your cable type:

Cable	Maximum Length
Thick coax (Yellow Stuff)	500 meters, or 1640 feet
Thin coax (cheapernet)	185 meters, or 606 feet
10baseT (Twisted Sister)	100 meters, or 328 feet

For coax cable (thick and thin), the preceding cable lengths apply to cable *segments*, not individual lengths of cable. A segment is the entire run of cable from one terminator to another and may include more than one computer. In other words, if you have 10 computers and you connect them all with 25-foot lengths of thin coax cable, the total length of the segment is 225 feet. (Made you look! Only *nine* cables are required to connect 10 computers — that's why it's not 250 feet.)

For 10baseT cable, the 100-meter length limit applies to the cable that connects a computer to the hub. In other words, each computer can be connected to the hub with no more than 100 meters of cable.

Figure 19-1 shows how a repeater might be used to connect two groups of computers that are too far apart to be strung on a single segment. When you use a repeater like this, the repeater divides the cable into two segments. The cable length limit still applies to the cable on each side of the repeater.

✔ Repeaters are used only with Ethernet networks wired with coax cable. 10baseT networks don't use repeaters, nor do ARCnet or Token Ring networks.

Actually, that's not quite true: 10baseT, ARCnet, and Token Ring networks do use repeaters. It's just that the repeater isn't a separate device. In a 10baseT network, the hub is actually a multiport repeater. That's why the cable used to attach each computer to the hub is considered to be a separate segment. Likewise for ARCnet networks: The active hubs are actually repeaters. In a Token Ring network, each computer acts like a repeater, listening to the token and sending it to the next computer in line.

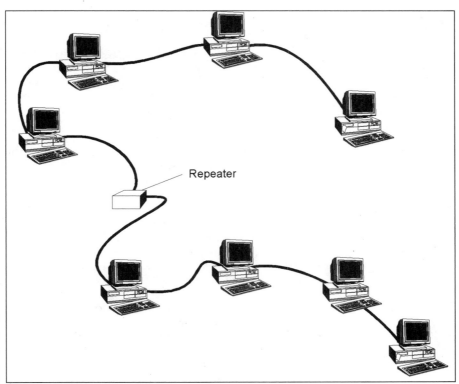

Figure 19-1:
Using a
repeater.

✔ Most 10baseT hubs have a BNC connector on the back. This BNC connector is a thinnet repeater that enables you to attach a full 185-meter thinnet segment. The segment can attach other computers, 10baseT hubs, or a combination of both.

✔ A basic rule of Ethernet life is that a signal cannot pass through more than three repeaters on its way from one node to another. That doesn't mean you can't have more than three repeaters or hubs, but if you do, you have to carefully plan the network cabling so that the three-repeater rule isn't violated.

✔ Two-port thinnet repeaters can be had for about $300 from mail-order suppliers.

✔ Repeaters are legitimate components of a by-the-book Ethernet network. They don't extend the maximum length of a single segment; they just let you tie two segments together. Beware of the little black boxes that claim to extend the segment limit beyond the standard 185-meter limit for thinnet or 500-meter limit for the yellow stuff. These usually work, but it's better to play by the rules.

Bridges

A *bridge* is a device that's used to connect two networks so that they act as if they're one network. Bridges can be used to connect two different types of networks, such as an Ethernet network and a Token Ring network, but they're more often used to partition one large network into two smaller networks for performance purposes.

A bridge is kind of like a smart repeater. Repeaters listen to signals coming down one network cable, amplify them, and send them down the other cable. They do this blindly, paying no attention to the content of the messages they repeat.

In contrast, a bridge is a little smarter about the messages that come down the pike. For starters, most bridges have the capability to listen to the network and automatically figure out the address of each computer on both sides of the bridge. Then the bridge can inspect each message that comes from one side of the bridge and broadcast it on the other side of the bridge only if the message is intended for a computer that's on the other side.

This is the key feature that enables bridges to partition a large network into two smaller, more efficient networks. Bridges work best in networks that are highly segregated. For example (humor me here), suppose that the Sneetches networked all their computers and discovered that, although the Star-Bellied Sneetches' computers talked to each other frequently and the Plain-Bellied Sneetches' computers also talked to each other frequently, it was a rare occasion that a Star-Bellied Sneetch computer talked to a Plain-Bellied Sneetch computer.

A bridge could be used to partition the Sneetchnet into two networks: the Star-Bellied network and the Plain-Bellied network. The bridge would automatically learn which computers were on the Star-Bellied network and which were on the Plain-Bellied network. It would forward messages from the Star-Bellied side to the Plain-Bellied side (and vice versa) only when necessary. The overall performance of both networks would improve, although the performance of any network operation that had to travel over the bridge would be slowed down a bit.

- As I mentioned, some bridges also have the capability to translate the messages from one format to another. For example, if the Star-Bellied Sneetches built their network with Ethernet and the Plain-Bellied Sneetches used Token Ring, a bridge could be used to tie the two together.

- A basic bridge to partition two Ethernet networks can be had for about $1,500 from mail-order suppliers. More sophisticated bridges can cost as much as $6,000.

- If you're not confused yet, don't worry. Read on.

Routers

A *router* is kind of like a super-intelligent bridge for really big networks. Bridges know the addresses of all the computers on each side of the bridge and can forward messages accordingly. But routers know even more about the network. A router not only knows the addresses of all the computers but also about other bridges and routers on the network and can decide the most efficient path to send each network message. In fact, the router knows everything about you and your little network.

One of the best tricks routers can do is to listen in on the entire network to see how busy various parts of it are. If one part of the network is busy, the router may decide to forward a message by using a less busy route. In this respect, the router is kind of like a traffic reporter up in a helicopter. The router knows that 101 is bumper-to-bumper through Sunnyvale, so it takes 280 instead.

✔ Routers aren't cheap. But for big networks, they're worth it.

✔ The functional distinctions between bridges and routers get blurrier all the time. As bridges become more sophisticated, they're able to take on some of the chores that used to require a router, thus putting many routers out of work. (Ross Perot blames this on NAFTA.) Bridges that perform routing functions are sometimes called *brouters*.

✔ Some routers are nothing more than computers with several network interface cards and special software to perform the router functions. In fact, NetWare comes with a router program that lets a NetWare server act as a router.

✔ Routers can also be used to connect networks that are geographically distant from one another via modems. You can't do that with a bridge.

✔ If you're confused about the distinction between bridges and routers, join the club. The technical distinction has to do with the OSI Reference Model network layer the devices operate at. Bridges operate at the MAC layer (MAC stands for "Media Access Control"); whereas, routers operate at the next level up: the network layer.

Gateways

No, not the Bill Gates way. This kind of gateway is a super-intelligent router, which is a super-intelligent bridge, which is a super-intelligent repeater. Notice a pattern here?

Gateways are designed to connect radically different types of networks together. They do this by translating messages from one network's format to another's, much like the Universal Translator that got Kirk and Spock out of so many jams.

Gateways usually are used to connect a network to a mainframe or minicomputer. If you don't have a mainframe or minicomputer, you probably don't need a gate.

✔ Gateways are necessary only because of the mess computer manufacturers got us into by insisting on using their own proprietary designs for networks. If computer manufacturers had talked to each other 20 years ago, we wouldn't have to use gates to make their networks talk to each other today.

✔ Gateways come in several varieties. My favorite is ornamental wrought iron.

Superservers

A funny thing happened to personal computers when networks became popular. They turned into mainframe computers.

As networks grew and grew, some organizations found that they had to have dozens of PCs functioning as dedicated file servers. Some networks had 50 or 100 dedicated servers! You can imagine the network management nightmares you'd have to contend with on a network that large.

To ease the burdens of managing a gaggle of file servers, some network managers are turning to *superservers*, unbelievably high-powered computers that can single-handedly take on the duties of half a dozen or more mere mortal computers. These superservers have huge cabinets that can hold stacks of disk drives, specialized high-speed disk controllers, room for more memory than Col. Hathi, and — get this — more than one CPU.

Superservers aren't cheap — they sell for tens of thousands of dollars. But they're often less expensive than an equivalent number of ordinary computers, they're more efficient, and they're easier to manage.

✔ One common argument against the use of superservers is the old "don't put all your eggs in one basket" line. What if the superserver breaks? The counter to this argument is that superservers are loaded with state-of-the-art fault-tolerance gizmos that make it unlikely that they'll ever break. In contrast, if you use ten separate file servers, you actually increase the likelihood that one of them will fail, probably sooner than you'd like.

It's RAID!

In most small networks, it's a hassle if a disk drive goes south and has to be sent to the shop for repairs. In some large networks, a failed disk drive is more than a hassle: It's an outright disaster. Big companies don't know how to do anything when the computer goes down. Everyone just sits around, looking at the floor, silently keeping vigil 'til the computers come back up.

A RAID system is a fancy type of disk storage that hardly ever fails. It works by lumping several disk drives together and treating them as if they were one humongous drive. RAID uses some fancy techniques devised by computer nerds at Berkeley that guarantee that if one of the disk drives in the RAID system fails, no data is lost. The disk drive that failed can be removed and repaired, and the data that was on it can be reconstructed from the other drives.

- ✔ RAID stands for "Redundant Array of Inexpensive Disks", but that doesn't matter. You don't have to remember that for the test.

- ✔ A RAID system is usually housed in a separate cabinet that includes its own RAID disk controller. It is sometimes called a *disk subsystem*.

- ✔ In the coolest RAID systems, the disk drives themselves are *hot swappable*. That means that you can shut down and remove one of the disk drives while the RAID system continues to operate. Network users won't even know that one of the disks has been removed, since the RAID system reconstructs the data that was on the removed disk using data from the other disks. When the failed disk has been replaced, the new disk is brought on-line without a hitch.

Chapter 20

Ten Layers of the OSI Model

*O*SI sounds like the name of a top-secret government agency you hear about only in Tom Clancy novels. What it really stands for, as far as this book is concerned, is "Open System Interconnection," as in the "Open System Interconnection Reference Model," affectionately known as the *OSI model*.

The OSI model breaks the various aspects of a computer network into seven distinct layers. These layers are kind of like the layers of an onion: Each successive layer envelopes the layer beneath it, hiding its details from the levels above. The OSI model is also like an onion in that if you start to peel it apart to have a look inside, you're bound to shed a few tears.

The OSI model is not itself a networking standard in the same sense that Ethernet and Token Ring are. Rather, the OSI model is a framework into which the various networking standards can fit. The OSI model specifies what aspects of a network's operation can be addressed by various network standards. So in a sense, the OSI model is sort of a standard's standard.

Although there are seven layers to the OSI model, the bottom two are the ones that have the most practical impact on smaller networks. Networking standards like Ethernet and Token Ring are layer-1 and layer-2 standards. The higher layers of the OSI model have not resulted in widespread standards.

Don't read this if you're dyslexic

The OSI standard was developed by a group known as *ISO*, for "International Standards Organization." So technically, it can be called the *ISO OSI* standard. Hold that up to a mirror and see what happens.

ISO develops standards for all sorts of stuff, like the size of sprinkler pipes and machine screws. Other ISO standards include SOI, SIO, OIS, and IOS.

Layer 1: The Physical Layer

The bottom layer of the OSI model is the *physical layer*. It addresses the physical characteristics of the network: the types of cables that will be used to connect devices, the types of connectors that will be used, how long the cables can be, and so on. For example, the Ethernet standard for 10baseT cable specifies the electrical characteristics of the twisted-pair cables, the size and shape of the connectors, the maximum length of the cables, and so on.

Another aspect of the physical layer is the electrical characteristics of the signals used to transmit data over the cables from one network node to another. The physical layer does not define any meaning to those signals other than the basic binary values 0 and 1. It's up to higher levels of the OSI model to assign meanings to the bits that are transmitted at the physical layer.

Layer 2: The Data Link Layer

The *data link layer* is the layer at which meaning is assigned to the bits that are transmitted over the network. A standard for the data link layer must address things such as the size of each packet of data to be sent, a means of addressing each packet so that it is delivered to the intended recipient, and a way to ensure that two or more nodes don't try to transmit data on the network at the same time.

The data link layer also provides basic error detection and correction to ensure that the data sent is the same as the data received. If an uncorrectable error occurs, the data link standard must specify how the node is to be informed of the error so that it can retransmit the data.

You don't really care how Ethernet fits into the OSI model, do you?

Ethernet is a standard published by the *IEEE* (if you pronounce that *eye-triple-ee*, people will think you know what you're talking about). It's official title is "802.3," pronounced *eight-oh-two-dot-three*. The 802.3 standard addresses both the physical layer of the OSI model and the data link layer.

You can blame the portion of the 802.3 that addresses the physical layer for the need to attach terminators to each end of a segment of thinnet coax, for the fact that BNC connectors are a pain in the rumpus to attach, and for the limit on the number of hubs that can be daisy-chained together when twisted-pair cabling is used. The physical-layer portion of the 802.3 standard is also responsible for the colorful terms *10base5*, *10base2*, and *10baseT*.

The portion of 802.3 that deals with the data link layer actually deals only with one portion of the data link layer, called the "Media Access Control Sublayer," or *MAC sublayer*. The MAC portion of 802.3 spells out how the CSMA/CD operation of Ethernet works...how Ethernet listens for network traffic, sends data if the network appears to be free of traffic, and then listens for collisions and resends the information if necessary.

The other portion of the data link layer of the OSI model is called the "Logical Link Control Sublayer," or (you guessed it) the *LLC sublayer*. The LLC sublayer spells out the basics of sending and receiving packets of information over the network and correcting errors. The LLC standard used by Ethernet is called 802.2.

None of this really matters unless you plan on building network interface cards in your garage.

Layer 3: The Network Layer

The *network layer* addresses the interconnection of networks by routing packets from one network to another. The network layer is most important when you use a router to link two different types of networks, such as an Ethernet network and a Token Ring network. Because the network layer is one step above the data link layer, it doesn't matter whether the two networks use different standards at the data link and physical layers.

Layer 4: The Transport Layer

The *transport layer* is the basic layer at which one network computer communicates with another network computer. The transport layer identifies each node on the computer with a unique address and manages connections between nodes. The transport layer also breaks large messages into smaller messages that are sent in sequence and reassembles the messages at the receiving node.

The transport layer and the OSI layers above it are implemented differently by various network operating systems. You can thank the OSI model for the capability to run NetWare, LANtastic, Windows for Workgroups, or just about any other network operating system on a standard Ethernet network. Ethernet addresses the lower layers of the OSI model. As long as the network operating system's transport layer is able to interface with Ethernet, you're in business.

Layer 4a: The Lemon-Pudding Layer

The *lemon-pudding layer* is squeezed in between the rather dry and tasteless transport and session layers to add flavor and moisture.

Layer 5: The Session Layer

The *session layer* establishes "sessions" between network nodes. A session must be established before data can be transmitted over the network. The session layer makes sure that these sessions are properly established and maintained.

Layer 6: The Presentation Layer

The *presentation layer* is responsible for converting the data sent over the network from one type of representation to another. For example, the presentation layer can apply sophisticated compression techniques so that fewer bytes of data are required to represent the information when it is sent over the network. At the other end of the transmission, the transport layer then uncompresses the data.

The presentation layer also can scramble the data before it is transmitted and unscramble it at the other end, using a sophisticated encryption technique that even Sherlock Holmes would have trouble breaking.

Layer 7: The Application Layer

The highest layer of the OSI model, the *application layer* deals with the techniques that application programs use to communicate with the network. The name of this layer is a little confusing. Application programs like Lotus 1-2-3 and WordPerfect are not a part of the application layer. Rather, it's the network operating system itself that works within the application layer.

The 5th Wave   By Rich Tennant

"IT TURNED OUT TO BE A TWO HOUR LECTURE ON A NEW COMMUNICATIONS PROTOCOL."

Chapter 21

Ten Tips for Networking Windows

*I*t used to be that when you wrote a networking book, you could put the considerations for networking Windows in a separate chapter somewhere around page 912 or maybe in an appendix. Not any more. Windows is too common to treat as an afterthought, so I've incorporated information about networking Windows throughout this book wherever possible.

Even so, it's nice to gather together some of the more useful tips for running Windows on a network. So here we go.

Consider Installing a Shared Version of Windows

If you use Windows on a network — especially a NetWare network — you must make a basic decision: Will you install a separate copy of Windows on each user's local hard disk, or will you install a shared copy of Windows on the network server? There are advantages and disadvantages to each approach.

The advantage of installing a separate copy of Windows for each user is that the user will have more control over his or her Windows setup, and you won't have to contend with many of the special Windows setup options for installing a shared copy. The disadvantage of separate Windows installations is that you have to support each user's customized setup. And if you need to make a change to the way Windows is set up, you have to repeat the change for each user's copy of Windows.

The advantage of installing a shared copy of Windows on the server is that you save about 10MB of disk space on each user's workstation, and you have to maintain just one copy of Windows rather than a separate copy for each workstation. The disadvantage is that Windows will not perform as efficiently.

If you opt to install a shared version of Windows on the server, here's the general procedure:

1. Insert the Windows Setup disk #1 into a floppy drive, log to that drive, and type this command:

```
SETUP /A
```

This command copies all the files from the Windows setup disks to a network directory. When Setup asks for the drive and directory to copy the files to, specify a network drive.

2. To install a shared copy of Windows for a workstation, log in to the network for that workstation, log to the network drive that contains the Windows files, and type this command:

```
SETUP /N
```

This command installs just the files that are required to configure Windows for this workstation. When Setup asks for the drive and directory to copy these files to, specify either a local drive or a private network directory. Do *not* copy these files to a shared network directory!

If you decide to install a shared copy of Windows on a server, you still must have a separate license for each workstation that will run Windows. You cannot legally buy just one copy of Windows and use it for every computer on the network!

If You Use LANtastic, Get LANtastic for Windows

LANtastic can be used with Windows without purchasing the slightly more expensive LANtastic for Windows, but it's not worth the inconvenience. LANtastic for Windows includes Windows versions of the NET and NET_MGR programs, as well as a Windows e-mail capability and a really slick network clipboard that lets you copy data from an application on one computer and paste it into an application running on another computer. Very cool!

If All of Your computers Run Windows, Consider Windows for Workgroups

Windows for Workgroups is a great network choice for small networks on which all the computers run Windows. With Windows for Workgroups, all the networking support you could ever dream of is built right in to Windows. No need to install a separate program, read two manuals, or get on a conference call with Microsoft and your network software vendor to decide whether you have discovered a Windows bug or a network bug.

Windows for Workgroups comes with an enhanced version of File Manager that lets you manage network drive connections, an enhanced version of Print Manager for network printing, and a really cool network Hearts game.

For a Peer-to-Peer Network with a Dedicated Server, Do Not Run Windows on the Server

If you run LANtastic, NetWare Lite, or some other peer-to-peer network (other than Windows for Workgroups) and you have set up a computer to run as a dedicated server, don't run Windows on that computer. You'll just tie up a hefty portion of that computer's memory and CPU cycles displaying the pretty Windows user interface. Because no one is using the dedicated server computer to run application programs, the memory can be better used for a larger disk cache, and the CPU cycles can be put to better use servicing network I/O requests.

Create a Permanent Swap File on Each User's Local Disk

One of the most important things you can do to improve the performance of Windows on a network is to make sure that every user is set up with a permanent swap file on a local disk.

Windows uses the swap file to make up for not having enough memory. Basically, the swap file acts as an extension to your computer's RAM so that Windows can pretend that your computer has more RAM than it really does.

Window's normal configuration is to use a temporary swap file, and if that temporary swap file is set up on a network disk, Windows slows to a crawl. A permanent swap file allows Windows to access this RAM-extension area more efficiently. Here's the procedure to switch to a more efficient permanent swap file on a local drive:

1. Double-click the Control Panel icon in the Main Program Manager group.

2. In the Control Panel window, double-click the 386 Enhanced icon.

3. Click the Virtual Memory button.

4. Click the Change button.

5. Change the Type field to Permanent and the Drive field to a local drive (usually C:). If you want, you can specify a size for the swap file. The bigger the better, as long as you remember that the swap file uses disk space. I usually set up a 4,096K or 8,192K swap file.

6. Click OK to change the settings, and then restart Windows so that they take effect.

Set Up Your Network Connections before Starting Windows

As much as humanly possible, set up your login script or STARTNET.BAT file so that your network drive and printer assignments are set up before Windows is started.

Depending on your networking software, you may be able to specify that any changes to your network configuration you make while running Windows should remain in effect when you quit Windows. Although this feature sounds attractive, I usually disable it. That's because I prefer to rely on the login script or STARTNET.BAT file to set up my standard network assignments. Then any changes I make during a Windows session will be temporary; I can easily return to my standard network setup at any time just by restarting Windows.

Disable Print Manager

All networks employ some form of print spooling. Windows' own Print Manager is also a form of print spooling. Using both the network's print spooling and Windows' print spooling wastes time and leads to errors.

Here's the procedure for disabling Print Manager:

1. Double-click the Printers icon in the Main Program Manager group.

2. In the Printers window, click the Use Print Manager check box to uncheck it.

3. Click the Close button to activate the change.

Create a Shared Program Manager Group for Shared Network Applications

Here's a tricky technique that makes it easier to maintain programs that are shared on a network: Create a Program Manager group that can be shared by all network users. Then put your shared programs in this group. Any changes you make to this group — adding a program, changing an icon, and so on — automatically appear on each user's workstation.

Here's the procedure:

1. In Program Manager, choose the New command from the File menu.

2. When Program Manager asks whether you want to create a group or a program item, choose Program Group.

3. Type a description for the group, such as **Network Applications**. Then, in the Group File field, specify a file on a network drive, such as H:\NETAPPS.GRP.

4. On each workstation, edit the user's PROGMAN.INI file (in the \WINDOWS directory) and add a line similar to this one to the [groups] section:

    Group9=H:\NETAPPS.GRP

The group number depends on the groups that already exist in PROGMAN.INI. The drive letter (H: in this case) specifies a network drive so that all users access the same copy of the program group file.

Buy the Windows Resource Kit

That last one was a little tricky, wasn't it? That's why you should buy Microsoft's *Windows Resource Kit*, a $20 book, which has exhaustive documentation of Windows details like what goes in the PROGMAN.INI file, and a disk that contains a few interesting utility programs. If you get the Resource Kit, you'll know how to edit PROGMAN.INI.

Most Windows users don't need the *Windows Resource Kit*. But if you're responsible for setting up and maintaining Windows on a network, you'd better get it. You can get it at most software stores or you can order it directly from Microsoft.

Chapter 22

Ten Things to Know about Networking Macintoshes

*T*his book has dwelt on networking PCs as if IBM were the only game in town. To be politically correct, I should at least acknowledge the existence of an altogether different breed of computer: Apple's Macintosh computers.

Apple prides itself on its ability to include stuff in its Macintosh operating system that DOS users have to purchase separately. Windows is the classic example of that; Macintosh users don't have to purchase a graphical user interface separately because the Macintosh operating system *is* a graphical user interface. Network support is another example. Every Macintosh ever manufactured has come with built-in networking support. All you have to do to network your Macintosh computers is buy network cable.

Well, there's actually a lot more to it than that. This chapter presents some basic things you need to know before you try to network your Macintoshes. It's not comprehensive — if you want more information, you can pick up IDG's humongoid book, *Macworld Networking Handbook* by Dave Kosiur, Ph.D., and Nancy E. H. Jones.

This chapter presents roughly 10 things you need to know about networking Macintoshes. To make these snippets of information easier to digest, I've gathered them into three groupings: what you need to know to hook up a Macintosh network, what you need to know to use a Macintosh network, and what you need to know to mix Macintoshes and PCs on the same network.

What You Need to Know to Hook Up a Macintosh Network

Hooking up a small Macintosh network is easy: There's not much more to it than buying cables and plugging them in.

What is AppleTalk?

As I said, every Macintosh ever built has included networking support. The built-in networking features of the Macintosh don't compare with the capabilities of NetWare or even LANtastic, but they are enough to enable you to set up a basic network so that several users can share files and printers.

The Macintosh's built-in network feature is called *AppleTalk*. One of the advantages of having AppleTalk built in is that it has become an inarguable networking standard among Macintosh users. You don't have to worry about the differences between different network operating systems, because all Macintosh networking is based on AppleTalk.

Another advantage of AppleTalk is that access to the network is integrated with the rest of the operating system's user interface. You don't have to use arcane commands to set up your network configuration. Instead, you do it the Macintosh way: Point here, click there, drag this, drop that. You get the picture.

- ✔ AppleTalk has steadily improved over the years. In 1989, Apple introduced a major enhancement to AppleTalk called *AppleTalk Phase 2*, which allows more devices to be connected to the network and works more efficiently. With *System 7*, Apple introduced true peer-to-peer networking capabilities that are based on AppleTalk.

- ✔ AppleTalk lets you subdivide a network into *zones*, which are similar to workgroups in Windows for Workgroups. Each zone consists of the network users who regularly share information.

- ✔ Although basic support for networking is built into every Macintosh, you still have to purchase cables to connect the computers to one another. There are several types of cables to choose from. AppleTalk can be used with two different cabling schemes that connect to the Macintosh's printer port, or it can be used with faster Ethernet interface cards.

Who's winning in the AFP West?

AFP is not a division of the NFL, but an acronym for "AppleTalk Filing Protocol." It's the part of AppleTalk that governs how files are stored and accessed on the network. AFP is designed to allow files to be shared with computers that run DOS. Macintoshes can be integrated into any network operating system that recognizes AFP. NetWare's ability to support Macintoshes is built upon its support for AFP. Windows for Workgroups doesn't support AFP, so you can't use Macintoshes in a Windows for Workgroups network.

In case you're interested (and you shouldn't be), AFP is a presentation-layer protocol. See Chapter 20 if you don't have a clue as to what I'm talking about.

What is LocalTalk?

LocalTalk is Apple's cabling scheme for AppleTalk networks. To connect a Macintosh to a LocalTalk network, you plug a *LocalTalk connector* into the Macintosh's printer port. Then you attach the LocalTalk cable to the LocalTalk connector. Figure 22-1 shows a LocalTalk connector.

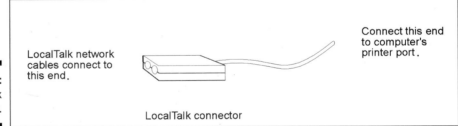

Figure 22-1: A LocalTalk connector.

LocalTalk network cables connect to this end.

Connect this end to computer's printer port.

LocalTalk connector

LocalTalk networks are configured in a bus arrangement, as shown in Figure 22-2. A LocalTalk connector is plugged into each computer's printer port, and the LocalTalk connectors are connected to one another with LocalTalk cables.

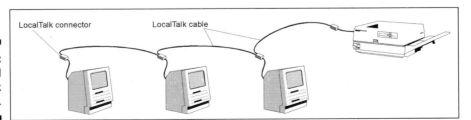

Figure 22-2: A small LocalTalk network.

LocalTalk connector LocalTalk cable

Notice that the laser printer is also connected to the network via a LocalTalk connector. That's a little different from the way printers are connected in a DOS-based peer-to-peer network. In a DOS-based network, a printer is usually attached to one of the network computer's printer ports. Then that computer acts as a printer server, providing print services for the entire network. In an AppleTalk network, printers operate as separate network nodes, so printer servers generally are not used.

- ✔ LocalTalk connectors are self-terminating, which means that separate terminators are not required on both ends of the cable segment.

- ✔ Each LocalTalk connector comes with a 2-meter-long LocalTalk cable (that's about 6½ feet). You can also purchase 10-meter cables if your computers aren't that close together.

- ✔ LocalTalk uses shielded twisted-pair cable. The shielding protects the cable from electrical interference, but limits the total length of cable used in a network segment to 300 feet.

- ✔ No more than 32 computers and printers can be connected to a single segment.

What is PhoneNET?

PhoneNET is an alternative wiring scheme for AppleTalk networks. It was originally developed by a company called Farallon Computing. PhoneNET cables and connectors are less expensive than their LocalTalk equivalents, and you can save even more money by buying cheaper knock-offs rather than genuine Farallon goods.

Because Macintosh users spent so much money on their computers, they're usually happy to cut costs on network cable. That's why PhoneNET is so popular.

As its name implies, PhoneNET uses phone cable rather than the shielded twisted-pair cable used by LocalTalk. PhoneNET can use standard modular phone cable and connectors that are available at just about any hardware store.

PhoneNET connectors look like LocalTalk connectors, except that they have two modular phone jacks rather than the LocalTalk jacks found in the LocalTalk connectors. You plug the PhoneNET connector's cable into the Mac's printer port, and then connect the connectors to one another by using modular phone cable.

- ✔ Unlike LocalTalk connectors, PhoneNET connectors are *not* self-terminating. After you connect all the computers with modular phone cable, two of the PhoneNET connectors will have an empty phone jack. You must plug a *terminating resistor* into each of these jacks for your network to operate. If you don't plug the empty jacks with terminators, air bubbles will be sucked into the network.

✔ The bus arrangement used for LocalTalk networks is also the most commonly used arrangement for PhoneNET networks. However, PhoneNET can also be set up in a star arrangement, where each computer is plugged into a central wiring hub.

✔ PhoneNET can often be used with the existing phone wiring in your building. Most phone wiring contains several unused cable pairs that can be used for the network. You'd better know what you're doing, though, before you start rerouting cable pairs in your phone system's wiring closet. Get help.

What about Ethernet?

LocalTalk and PhoneNET are widely used because they're inexpensive. They suffer from one major drawback, however: They're both unbearably slow. LocalTalk and PhoneNET both work through the Macintosh's serial printer ports, so they transmit data over the network at a paltry 230,400 bits per second. This transmission rate is acceptable for casual use of a network printer and occasionally copying a file to or from another computer, but it's not sufficient for serious networking.

Fortunately, AppleTalk also supports Ethernet network adapters and cables. With Ethernet, data is sent at 10 *million* bits per second. Much more suitable for real-life networking.

When you use Ethernet, you have access to all the cabling options described elsewhere in this book: 10base5 (yellow cable), 10base2 (thinnet), and 10baseT (twisted pair).

✔ An AppleTalk network that uses Ethernet is called an *EtherTalk* network.

✔ Ethernet interface cards for Macintoshes are more expensive than their PC counterparts, mostly because they aren't as widely used.

✔ When you opt for an Ethernet network, you have to contend with a device driver to support the network card. You use the Installer program to set up the driver.

✔ Apple has also developed a specialized interface for Ethernet cards called the Ethernet cabling system. When the Ethernet cabling system is used, the network cards themselves do not have coax or 10baseT connectors. Instead, they have a special type of connector called an Apple Attachment Unit Interface (AAUI). You must plug a device called a *transceiver* into the AAUI connector so that you can attach the computer to a coax or twisted-pair cable.

✔ You can use a router to connect a LocalTalk network to an Ethernet network. This arrangement is often used to connect a small group of Macintosh users to a larger network.

What You Need to Know to Use a Macintosh Network

Here are some of the most common questions that come up after you've installed the network cable.

How do I configure my Mac for networking?

Before you can access the network from your Mac, you must configure it for networking by activating AppleTalk and assigning your network name and password.

Activating AppleTalk

After all the cable is in place, you have to activate AppleTalk. Here's how:

1. Choose the Chooser desk accessory from the Apple menu.

2. Click the Active button.

3. Close the Chooser.

That's all there is to it.

Assigning your name and password

Next, you should assign an owner name, a password, and a name for your computer. This allows other network users to access your Mac. To do that:

1. Choose the Sharing Setup control panels from the Apple menu.

2. Type your name in the Owner Name field.

3. Type a password in the Owner Password field. Don't forget what the password is.

4. Type a descriptive name for your computer in the Macintosh Name field. This is the name that other network users will know your computer by.

5. Close Sharing Setup.

Piece of cake, eh?

How do I access a network printer?

Accessing a network printer with AppleTalk is no different than accessing a printer when you don't have a network. If more than one printer is available on the network, you use the Chooser to select the printer you want to use. Chooser displays all the available network printers; just pick the one you want to use.

✔ Be sure to enable Background Printing for the network printer. If you don't, your Mac will be tied up until the printer finishes your job—that could be a long time if someone else sent a 500-page report to the printer just before you. When Background Printing is enabled, your printer output is captured to a disk file, and then sent to the printer later while you continue with other work.

To enable Background Printing, choose the printer you want to use from the Chooser and click the Background Printing On button.

✔ Rescind that last order if a dedicated print server has been set up. In that case, print data is automatically spooled to the print server's disk, so your Mac doesn't have to wait for the printer to become available.

How do I share files with other users?

To share files on your Mac with other network users, you must set up a shared resource. You can share an entire disk, or you can share just individual folders. And you can restrict access to certain users if you want.

Activating file sharing

Before you can share files with other users, you must activate AppleTalk's file sharing feature. Here's how:

1. Choose the Sharing Setup control panel from the Apple Menu.
2. Click the Start button in the File Sharing section of the control panel.
3. Close Sharing Setup.

Sharing a folder or disk

To set up a folder or an entire disk so that other network users can access it, follow this procedure:

1. Choose the folder or disk you want to share.
2. Choose Sharing from the File menu.
3. Click the Share This Item and Its Contents box.
4. Close the window and click the Save button in the dialog box that appears.

You can reverse this procedure if you decide later that you don't want the folder or disk to be shared.

Restricting access to certain users

If you want, you can restrict access to your shared resources to certain users or groups. First, you must create a list of registered users:

1. Choose the Users & Groups control panel from the Apple menu.

2. Choose New User from the File menu.

3. Type the name of the user.

4. If you want to specify a password for the new user, double-click the user's icon and type the password.

If you want to grant access to a particular folder or disk to more than one user, you must create a group that contains each of those users. To create a group:

1. Choose the Users & Groups control panel from the Apple menu.

2. Choose New Group from the File menu.

3. Type a name for the group.

4. Drag the icon for each user you want in the group from the Users & Groups window to the New Group window.

Now that you've set up users and groups, here's how to restrict access for a folder or drive:

1. Choose the folder or disk you want to share.

2. Choose Sharing from the File menu.

3. Use the User/Group pop-up menu to choose an individual user or group for the folder or drive.

4. Uncheck the check boxes next to Everyone so that other users will have no access to the folder or disk

5. Close the window and click the Save button in the dialog box that appears.

Preventing guests from accessing your system

Even if you set up a list of registered users, anyone can access your Mac if you leave the Guest user enabled. To disable the Guest user, do this:

1. Choose the Users & Groups control panel from the Apple menu.

2. Double-click the Guest icon.

3. Uncheck the Allow Guests to Connect box.

4. Close the Guest window and click the Save button in the dialog box that appears. Then close the Users & Groups window.

How do I access other users' files?

To access files on another Macintosh, follow this procedure:

1. Choose the Chooser from the Apple menu.

2. Click the AppleShare icon from the Chooser window.

3. Click the name of the computer you want to access. (If your network has zones, you must first click the zone you want to access.)

4. Click the OK button.

5. A login screen appears. If you are a registered user on the computer, click the Registered User button and enter your user name and password. Otherwise, click the Guest button. Then click the OK button.

6. A list of shared folders and disks appears. Click the ones you want to access, and then click the OK button.

    A check box appears next to each item on this list. If you check this box, you'll be connected to the folder or disk automatically each time you start you computer.

What You Need to Know to Mix Macintoshes and PCs on a Network

Life would be too boring if Macs lived on one side of the tracks and PCs lived on the other. If your organization has a mix of both Macs and PCs, odds are you'll eventually want to network them together. There are two basic ways to do that: You can build an AppleTalk network and add a few PCs to it, or your can build a PC network and add a few Macs to it. Which route you take depends partly on which type of computer the network has more of and partly on which computers become networked first, but mostly on which type of computer you're more familiar with.

Can I connect DOS computers to AppleTalk?

If most of your computers are Macintoshes and you want to attach a few DOS-based PCs to your network, the easiest way to do it is to use PhoneNET PC, an AppleTalk-compatible program for DOS and Windows PCs made by Farallon, the makers of the PhoneNET wiring scheme described earlier. This same software is also available from Apple as AppleTalk Connection for DOS and Windows.

PhoneNET PC adds the basic functionality of the Chooser to a PC so that the PC user can access shared folders and printers. If you want Macintosh users to be able to access files on the PC, you need Timbuktu, a complete peer-to-peer networking system for PCs and Macintoshes. PhoneNET PC is a subset of Timbuktu.

It's easy to connect a PC to a Macintosh network if the Macs use Ethernet cards, because Ethernet cards are readily available for PCs. If your Mac network uses LocalTalk or PhoneNET, you must purchase a special LocalTalk interface board for the PC. Then you can attach the PC to the network by using LocalTalk or PhoneNET connectors.

✔ Even though you can connect PCs to Mac networks, you cannot freely exchange files between PCs and Macs unless you use application programs that are designed to do that. Programs such as Microsoft Word and PageMaker use the same file formats under Windows and the Macintosh, but most programs do not.

✔ The components you need to incorporate a PC into a Macintosh network are not cheap. In fact, a LocalTalk interface board, which operates at 230,400 bits per second, can cost as much as or more than a full-fledged Ethernet board that runs at full Ethernet speed. Such is the life of the Macintosh user.

Can I connect Macintoshes to a NetWare network?

If your PCs are networked with NetWare, you can easily add Macintoshes to the network. With NetWare, both PC and Macintosh users can access files and printers on the NetWare server. NetWare is not a peer-to-peer networking system, though, so it cannot be used to let a DOS user access files that reside on a Mac.

When you use a Macintosh in a NetWare 2.2 network, you access network resources the same as if the Mac were attached to an AppleTalk network, using the Chooser. With NetWare 3.11, a new desk accessory is installed on the Mac to give you access to other features of NetWare, such as print queues and access rights.

✔ Macintosh support is built into NetWare 2.2. For NetWare 3.11, Mac support is an extra you must purchase separately.

✔ NetWare has no trouble recording all 31 characters of a Macintosh filename that's stored on a NetWare server. But the name will be translated to an 11-character DOS filename if the file is accessed by a DOS user.

✔ NetWare volumes appear as drive icons on the Mac. When you open the icon, directories within the volume appear as folders.

Only a sadist would read this

One of the basic incompatibilities between Macintosh and DOS files is the way the two systems construct filenames. With DOS, each file is given a name of up to eight characters and an extension of up to three characters. So the maximum length for a DOS file name is 11 characters.

On a Mac, filenames can be up to 31 characters long, and there's no distinction between the name and extension.

These different file name formats present a problem when you try to share files between Macs and PCs. To translate a Mac file name to a DOS filename, the network removes spaces and periods, translates all letters to uppercase, converts special characters that aren't allowed in DOS filenames (like parentheses, question marks, and so on) to underscores, and drops all but the first 11 characters. The first eight are used for the filename, and the last three are the extension.

What if two Mac files with different names translate to the same shorter DOS filename? In that case, the last character of the filename for the second file is replaced with the digit 0. For the third file, the digit 1 is used, and so on.

Here are some examples:

Mac Filename	Translated DOS Filename
Letter to Bob	LETTERTO.BOB
Memo to Silvia	MEMOTOSI.LVI
Apr/May Sales	APR_MAYS.ALE
Apr/May Sales (Net)	APR_MAY0.ALE

As you can see, none of these translations produces a suitable DOS filename, especially when you consider the extensions. Most DOS users expect the file extension to identify the type of file — for example, .WK1 for a Lotus spreadsheet file or .DOC for a Microsoft Word document. The extensions that result from the Mac-to-DOS filename translation are usually gibberish. Bummer.

Chapter 23

Ten Programs That Make Network Life Easier

*A*s if the programs and utilities that come with the network operating system aren't enough, there are about a gazillion third-party utility programs you can buy to make your network life easier. This chapter lists several of the more useful ones.

You can purchase most of these programs at a software shop or through the mail, but many of them are shareware programs. That means you can pick up an evaluation copy of the program free (or nearly free), try it out, and buy the program if you like it.

Menu Programs

Many computer users aren't well versed in the subtleties of the DOS prompt. To help out these disadvantaged users, many network managers set up menu programs that display a list of the application programs that are available. The menu program runs automatically when the user logs in to the network, and sometimes the network is set up so that there's no way for the user to bail out of the menu program.

- If you use NetWare, you already have a menu program called MENU. It's not the easiest thing to use, but after you figure it out, it works. Anyway, the price is right.

- If you don't like the NetWare MENU command, or if you use a peer-to-peer network, you can pick from dozens of menu programs. My favorite is MarxMenu, because it sounds like it may be some sort of pinko-commie deal, but actually it's named after Mark, the guy who wrote it.

- If you don't want to invest your money in a menu program, you can invest your time in writing your own menus, using DOS batch files. This is certainly not the time or place to show you how to do that, though.

DOS Shell Programs

If you don't want to lock your users into a rigid menu system, you may want to consider setting them up with a DOS shell program instead. DOS shell programs are designed to replace DOS commands with an easy-to-use visual interface that lists files and directories and lets you choose commands from menus. Most DOS shell programs also let you set up menus of application programs.

DOS 5.0 and 6.0 come with a pretty good shell program called DOSSHELL. Better shells are available, of course, but DOSSHELL is more than adequate for most users. (DOSSHELL is available with MS-DOS 6.2, but you have to order the separate supplemental disks to get it. The shells for 5.0, 6.0, and 6.2 are identical, so you don't have to bother with the supplemental disks if you upgrade a 5.0 or 6.0 system to 6.2.)

Disk Utility Programs

As the network manager, you need a good suite of utility programs. Get a copy of PC Tools or The Norton Utilities. Or both.

DOS 6.2 comes with a pretty good disk utility program called ScanDisk. It checks the reliability of your disk drives and can correct the most common problems that occur. Both PC Tools and The Norton Utilities include similar programs with more sophisticated features, plus a load of other useful programs.

Backup Programs

Don't mess around with the DOS BACKUP command or even the DOS 6 MSBACKUP command. Do yourself a favor: Get a tape drive and a good backup program to support it. Read Chapter 14 if your backups are not under control.

Antivirus Programs

Don't forget to periodically scan your network for viruses. The MSAV command that comes with DOS 6 is good enough for light duty, but a grown-up antivirus program is better for networks. Get Central Point AntiVirus or Norton AntiVirus. If you're not innoculated against virus attack, read Chapter 14 to find out more.

Memory Management Programs

Memory management is often a problem on networks because the network drivers chew up valuable RAM on each workstation, sometimes leaving the hapless workstation users with less memory than they need to load their gargantuan spreadsheet files.

A memory management program often can reclaim that space. The best memory management programs try thousands of different ways to load your software into memory with hopes of finding the most optimum arrangement. DOS 6 comes with a memory manager named MEMMAKER that does just that. If it's not good enough for you, you can get third-party programs, such as QEMM-386 or 386MAX, that are even better.

Disk Compression Programs

You may have heard about DoubleSpace, the disk compression feature Microsoft introduced with MS-DOS 6.0 and improved with DOS 6.2. If you're using a peer-to-peer network and your file server has sufficient processing muscle (a fast 386 or better CPU), you should consider using DoubleSpace: It will most likely double the effective capacity of your network drive. It's one more thing to worry about, but it's pretty reliable, and the increased disk space is worth the hassle of learning how to use it.

If you just don't trust Microsoft, you can get several third-party disk compression programs that do the same thing DoubleSpace does. The best known is Stacker.

Remote Control Programs

As network manager, you sometimes need to know what's going on with another user's computer. In a small office, you do that by hopping on your skateboard and zipping over to your fellow user's office. In a large network, that's not always possible.

Thank an appropriate deity for the clever chap who first came up with the idea of writing a program that would tie your monitor and keyboard to another network user's monitor and keyboard, so that you can control the other user's computer and see what's on its monitor. These programs can save plenty of wear and tear on your skateboard. The best known example of this type of program is Carbon Copy.

Benchmark Programs

How do you know whether your network is operating efficiently? One way is to obtain a standardized benchmark program that tests the network's performance against some arbitrary standard. The people who first made up these programs must have been geologists, because they all seem to report performance in terms of *drystones, wetstones, netstones,* or *kidneystones.*

Benchmarks aren't that useful in and of themselves (who cares that your network clocks in at 2,300 RollingStones?), but they do come in handy when you're fiddling around with network parameters in an effort to speed up the network. In that case, you can run the benchmark once to establish a baseline, change a parameter, and run the benchmark again to evaluate the effect of the change.

Network Management Programs

The last category of utility programs I want to mention here is network management programs — programs that are designed specifically to help you manage a network. These programs help you keep track of the layout of your network, identify bottlenecks, or find faulty components. One of the best known collections of network management programs is the Frye Utilities.

Chapter 24

Ten Hot Network Buzzwords Guaranteed to Enliven a Cocktail Party

Tired of boring cocktail parties where everyone talks about the latest Oliver Stone movie or who's winning the late-night talk-show wars? Here are some conversation topics guaranteed to liven things up a bit or get you thrown out. Either way, they work. Try 'em.

Internet

What it means: *Internet* is a huge conglomeration of computer networks that are all linked together to form a mega-goliath-network. Internet is kind of like an information superhighway, except that all the road signs are written in an incomprehensible language. You need a copy of *Internet For Dummies* to figure it out.

Used in a sentence: Just send it to me over the Internet. You are on Internet, aren't you? You aren't? I thought *everyone* was on Internet these days!

Client/server

What it means: A computer system in which part of the work happens on a client computer and part of it happens on a server computer. To be a true client/server application, real work must be done on the server. Any server-based network can be loosely called client/server, but in a true client/server system, at least part of the real work — not just file access — is done on the server. For example, in a true client/server database, a database query is processed on the server computer, and just the results of the query are sent back to the client computer.

Used in a sentence: The client/server entrance is in the rear.

Enterprise Computing

What it means: The complete computing needs of a business enterprise. In the past, computing was too often focused on individual needs of small departments or workgroups. The result was a hodgepodge of incompatible systems: Marketing had a minicomputer, sales had a NetWare network, and accounting had an abacus. Enterprise computing views the computing needs of the organization as a whole. Very smart.

Used in a sentence: Our enterprise computing effort is sailing along at warp 9; I hear you guys are still stuck at one-quarter impulse. Fascinating.

Interoperability

What it means: Fitting round pegs into square holes. Literally, linking estranged networks together so that they work well together. This one is so hot that there's a whole trade show called Interop that's devoted to making different networks work together.

Used in a sentence: We've finally solved our interoperability problems—we fired the guy who bought the stuff that wasn't interoperable.

Fiber Optics

What it means: The fastest form of network cable, where signals are transmitted by light rather than by electricity. Fiber optics are typically used to form the backbone of large networks or to link networks in separate buildings, where the 500-meter limit of yellow cable just won't do. Fiber-optic cables hum along at a cool 100 Mbps (Megabits per second), 10 times faster than Pokey Little Ethernet.

Used in a sentence: What am I going to do now that I've linked three buildings on the campus, using a fiber-optic backbone? I'm going to Disneyland.

SNA

What it means: IBM's grand scheme of old to dominate the networking business. SNA is found wherever IBM mainframes are found. SNA stands for "Systems Network Architecture" and is pronounced *snaw* by mainframers.

Used in a sentence: Once we get the link between SNA and Ethernet worked out, our mainframe users will be able to access the advanced computing power of our PCs.

Groupware

What it means: Software that's designed to take advantage of network capabilities to facilitate collaborative work. For example, a word processor with groupware features lets several network users add comments or revisions to a document and keep track of who made what change and when.

Used in a sentence: Our productivity has shot up so much since we switched to groupware that we've decided to retire and move to Vail. I hear you're still using WordStar.

TCP/IP

What it means: TCP/IP is the protocol for Internet. It stands for "Transmission Control Protocol/Internet Protocol."

Used in a sentence: Don't worry, once you get TCP/IP up and running, you'll be on the Internet soon enough.

Frame Relay

What it means: Frame relay is a networking protocol that's used to link networks that are geographically separated. For example, frame relay might be used to connect a home office in Los Angeles to a branch office in San Francisco.

Used in a sentence: Too bad you guys still can't talk to your home office computers. Maybe you should look into frame relay — it works great for us.

Part V

References for
Real People

The 5th Wave   By Rich Tennant

"YEAH, I USED TO WORK ON REFRIGERATORS, WASHING MACHINES, STUFF LIKE THAT—HOW'D YOU GUESS?"

In this part...

This section summarizes the most commonly used commands for three popular network operating systems: NetWare, NetWare Lite, and LANtastic. Why? Because browsing through the commands that are available gives you a good idea of the capabilities of a network operating system. And if you decide to use one of these three systems, you'll be able to turn here for a quick refresher in case you forget the details of a command (nah, you'd never forget, would you?).

Chapter 25

NetWare Commands You'll Use

● ●

In This Chapter

▶ A summary of various NetWare commands

▶ The Sin Tax

▶ Examples

▶ A little BS about most of the commands

● ●

*I*n case you're a command-line junkie and want to get a feel for NetWare's commands, this chapter presents the ones you're most likely to want to use, along with a few you may not *want* to use but may *have* to, plus a few that are good to know about even if you never use them.

ATTACH

What it does: Connects you to another file server. Used only when your network has more than one server.

Syntax: **ATTACH** *server/user ID*

Example: **ATTACH SERVER2/BEAVER**

Who can use it: Anyone.

BS: If your account requires a password, you'll be prompted for it. ATTACH is often used in login scripts.

BINDFIX

What it does: Valiantly attempts to repair defects in the bindery, that all-important storehouse of information that's the lifeblood of a NetWare server.

Syntax: **BINDFIX**

Who can use it: Supervisors.

BS: Disable logins first. If BINDFIX doesn't work, run BINDREST to get back on your feet.

BROADCAST

What it does: Displays a message to all users who are logged in to a server.

Syntax: **BROADCAST** *message*

Example: **BROADCAST This network will self-destruct in five minutes!**

Who can use it: Console operators.

BS: BROADCAST is commonly used as a courtesy shortly before downing a server.

CAPTURE

What it does: Sets up network print spooling.

Syntax: **CAPTURE L=***port* **Q=***queue* **TI=***seconds*

Example: **CAPTURE L=2 Q=LASER TI=10**

Who can use it: Anyone.

BS: If you omit **L=***port*, LPT1 is captured. CAPTURE has a bunch of other options for customizing print jobs.

CHKDIR

What it does:	Displays information about a network directory.
Syntax:	**CHKDIR**
	CHKDIR *drive***:**
	CHKDIR *[server\]volume:directory*
Example:	**CHKDIR F:**
	CHKDIR WARD\SYS:PUBLIC
Who can use it:	Anyone.

CHKVOL

What it does:	Displays information about a server volume.
Syntax:	**CHKVOL**
	CHKVOL *drive***:**
	CHKVOL *[server\]volume:*
Examples:	**CHKVOL F:**
	CHKVOL WARD\SYS:
Who can use it:	Anyone.
BS:	Displays the size of the volume, the number of files on it, the disk space in use, the free disk space, and the number of directory entries available for new files.

CLAP ON

What it does:	Enables you to down the server by clapping your hands loudly once or twice.
Syntax:	**CLAP ON [1	2]**
Who can use it:	Console operators.
BS:	Yes.

CLEAR STATION

What it does:	Cleans up after a workstation that has crashed.
Syntax:	**CLEAR STATION** *n*
Who can use it:	Console operators.

CONFIG

What it does:	Displays information about your server's network configuration.
Syntax:	**CONFIG**
Who can use it:	Console operators.
BS:	The configuration info displayed by CONFIG includes the network drivers, the server's network address, network driver settings, and the server's disk configuration.

DISABLE LOGIN

What it does:	Prevents users from logging in to a file server.
Syntax:	**DISABLE LOGIN**
Who can use it:	Console operators.

BS: DISABLE LOGIN doesn't force anybody off the system, but it does prevent users who aren't logged in from logging in. It is usually used before a DOWN command. You can restore logins later by typing ENABLE LOGIN.

DISMOUNT

What it does: Takes a volume off the network so that you can perform maintenance tasks.

Syntax: **DISMOUNT** *volume*

Example: **DISMOUNT SYS2:**

Who can use it: Console operators.

BS: It would be polite to broadcast a message first (see the BROADCAST command.)

DOWN

What it does: Shuts down a file server.

Syntax: **DOWN**

Who can use it: Console operators.

BS: You should always use DOWN before turning off a server. It shuts down the server in an orderly fashion so that files that happen to be open won't be trashed in the process. It is polite to warn users with a BROADCAST command before downing a server.

DSPACE

What it does: Limits the amount of space a user can use.

Syntax: **DSPACE**

Who can use it: Supervisors.

BS: This is a menu-driven utility, so no command-line options are used.

ENABLE LOGIN

What it does:	Enables logins after a DISABLE LOGIN command has been used.
Syntax:	**ENABLE LOGIN**
Who can use it:	Console operators.
BS:	You don't have to use this command if you down a server and then restart it; logins are automatically enabled when the server starts.

ENDCAP

What it does:	Stops capturing printer output for network printing.
Syntax:	**ENDCAP [L=***port***]**
	ENDCAP ALL
	ENDCAP C=*port*
	ENDCAP CANCEL ALL
Example:	**ENDCAP L=1**
Who can use it:	Anyone.
BS:	If you type just ENDCAP with no options, print capture for LPT1 is stopped. ENDCAP ALL stops printer capture for all ports. ENDCAP C=port stops capture for the specified port and discards any output already captured; ENDCAP CANCEL ALL discards output for all ports.

ENGAGE

What it does:	Nothing, but it makes you feel like the Captain.
Syntax:	**ENGAGE**
Who can use it:	Picard.
BS:	Yes.

EXIT

What it does: After a server has been downed, returns to the DOS prompt.

Syntax: **EXIT**

Who can use it: Console operators.

BS: EXIT is sometimes used to restart a server with new parameters. First run DOWN, and then EXIT. This returns you to a DOS prompt, where you can run SERVER to restart the server with new parameters.

FCONSOLE

What it does: Displays information about the file server.

Syntax: **FCONSOLE**

Who can use it: Console operators.

BS: FCONSOLE provides a menu interface for some of the other NetWare console commands, such as BROADCAST and DOWN. These functions are only used by wimps, though. Real network geeks use FCONSOLE to peek at dirty cache buffers.

FILER

What it does: Creates and manages directories.

Syntax: **FILER**

Who can use it: Anyone.

BS: FILER is a menu-driven program with lots of options to let you look at directories and subdirectories and the files they contain. FILER also enables you to delete files, rename files, and copy or move files or entire subdirectories to another drive or directory.

For NetWare 4.0, the FILER command has been expanded to include the functions of the SALVAGE, PURGE, andVOLINFO commands.

FLAG

What it does:	Displays or sets file attributes.
Syntax:	**FLAG** *[directory/]filename [flags]*

Flags can be any of the following:

A   Archive needed

C   Copy inhibit (3.*x* only)

D   Delete inhibit (3.*x* only)

E   Execute only

H   Hidden

I   Indexed

P   Purge (3.*x* only)

RO   Read only

RW   Writable

R   Rename inhibit (3.*x* only)

S   Sharable

SY   System file

T   Transactional

Example:	**FLAG *.EXE SRO**
Who can use it:	Supervisors.
BS:	FLAG is often used after installing software to make program files shareable and read-only.

FLAGDIR

What it does:	Displays or changes directory attributes.
Syntax:	**FLAGDIR** *[directory] [flags]*

Flags can be any of the following:

D	Delete inhibit (3.*x* only)
H	Hidden
N	Normal
P	Private (2.*x* only)
P	Purge (3.*x* only)
R	Rename inhibit (3.*x* only)
SY	System

Example:	**FLAGDIR DOCS DR**
Who can use it:	Supervisors.

GRANT

What it does:	Grants rights to users for a file or directory.
Syntax:	**GRANT** *rights* **FOR** *path* **TO USER/GROUP** *name [/F* or */S]*
Example:	**GRANT S FOR SYS:DOCS TO USER BEAVER /S**
Who can use it:	Supervisors.
BS:	/F grants rights for files, /S for subdirectories. Rights can also be granted by the FILER command. After being granted, rights can be revoked by the REVOKE command.

LISTDIR

What it does:	Lists the directory structure of a volume.
Syntax:	**LISTDIR [/A]**
	LISTDIR [*server\\]volume:directory[/A]*
	LISTDIR *drive*: **[/A]**
Examples:	**LISTDIR WARD\SYS:**
	LISTDIR F: /A
Who can use it:	Anyone.
BS:	The /A switch displays additional information about the directories besides just the directory name.

LOAD (3.x oy)

What it does:	Loads an NLM (NetWare Loadable Module).
Syntax:	**LOAD** *name*
Who can use it:	Console operator.

LOGIN

What it does:	Logs you in to the network.
Syntax:	**LOGIN** *[user /ID]*
Example:	**LOGIN BEAVER**
Who can use it:	Anyone and everyone.
BS:	LOGIN prompts you for your password, and for your user ID if you don't include it as a commmand-line option. Before using LOGIN, you should switch to the network drive (typically F). Most of the time, the LOGIN command is added to your AUTOEXEC.BAT file.

LOGOUT

What it does:	Logs you off the network.
Syntax:	**LOGOUT**
Who can use it:	Anyone.

MAKEUSER

What it does:	Creates user accounts in batch mode by reading a script file that contains account definitions.
Syntax:	**MAKEUSER** *script file*
Who can use it:	Supervisors.
BS:	The script language used by MAKEUSER is complex, but can save you time if you have a lot of user accounts to define. USERDEF can help. If you have only a few accounts to create, you can probably do it faster by using SYSCON.

MAP

What it does:	Assigns drive letters to network drives.
Syntax:	**MAP** *[ROOT] drive:=vol:directory*
Example:	**MAP M:=SYS:DOCS**
Who can use it:	Anyone.
BS:	Drive can be a drive letter or a search drive letter (S1 through S16). If you include ROOT, NetWare treats the directory as the root directory of the mapped drive so that directories higher in the directory structure are inaccessible. MAP commands are usually included in the login script.

MEMORY

What it does: Displays the amount of memory available to the server.

Syntax: **MEMORY**

Who can use it: Console operators.

MENU

What it does: Displays a menu of program choices for insecure users.

Syntax: **MENU**

Who can use it: Anyone.

BS: MENU uses a menu definition file that contains a scripted description of the menu that should be displayed.

MODULES

What it does: Displays the various modules that are loaded in the server's memory.

Syntax: **MODULES**

Who can use it: Console operators.

MONITOR

What it does: Displays the NetWare console monitor screen.

Syntax: **MONITOR**

Who can use it: Console operators.

BS: MONITOR can be used to password-protect the console.

MOUNT

What it does:	Mounts server volumes so that they can be accessed by network users.
Syntax:	**MOUNT** *volume*
	MOUNT ALL
Who can use it:	Console operators.
BS:	MOUNT commands are usually kept in the AUTOEXEC.NCF file.

NCOPY

What it does:	Copies files from one location on a server to another location on the same server without sending the contents of the files over the network.
Syntax:	**NCOPY** *source target [options]*
Example:	**NCOPY M:MAY94*.* M:JUNE94*.***
Who can use it:	Anyone.
BS:	NCOPY works much like COPY, but is more efficient when both the source and destination are on the same server.

NDIR

What it does:	Displays directory listings for network drives, much like the DOS DIR command.
Syntax:	**NDIR** *path [/options]*
Example:	**NDIR SYS:*.EXE**
Who can use it:	Anyone.
BS:	NDIR has way too many options to list here. Sorry.

NETADMIN (4.0 only)

What it does: Manages the server.

Syntax: **NETADMIN**

Who can use it: Supervisors.

BS: NETADMIN is a menu-driven command, so no command-line options are used. NETADMIN combines the functions of the SYSCON, DSPACE, USERDEF, and SECURITY commands.

NPRINT

What it does: Prints a file on a network printer.

Syntax: **NPRINT** *file*

Example: **NPRINT CONFIG.SYS**

Who can use it: Anyone.

BS: NPRINT is the network equivalent of the DOS PRINT command.

PCONSOLE

What it does: Controls the network printer.

Syntax: **PCONSOLE**

Who can use it: Console operators.

BS: PCONSOLE is menu driven, so it's a complicated command even though it doesn't have elaborate command-line options.

PRINTCON

What it does: Configures printer jobs so that you don't have to type scads of options on CAPTURE and NPRINT commands.

Syntax: **PRINTCON**

Who can use it: Anyone.

BS: PRINTCON is menu-driven, so there aren't any command-line options. Sniff.

PRINTDEF

What it does: Defines special printer forms and print devices.

Syntax: **PRINTDEF**

Who can use it: Anyone.

BS: PRINTDEF is menu-driven, so there aren't any commmand-line options.

PSC

What it does: The command-line junkie's version of PCONSOLE.

Syntax: **PSC** *[options-ad-nauseum]*

Who can use it: Command-line junkies.

PURGE

What it does: Wipes files off the face of your disk.

Syntax: **PURGE**

Who can use it: Anyone.

BS: When you delete a file, the file isn't really deleted until you run PURGE.

RENDIR

What it does:	Renames a directory.
Syntax:	**RENDIR** *directory* **TO** *new name*
Example:	**RENDIR SYS:APPLES TO ORANGES**
Who can use it:	Anyone.
BS:	DOS should have had this command years ago.

REVOKE

What it does:	Removes rights granted by GRANT.
Syntax:	**REVOKE** *rights* **FOR** *path* **FROM USER/GROUP** *name [/F* or */S]*
Example:	**REVOKE S FOR SYS:DOCS FROM USER BEAVER /S**
Who can use it:	Supervisors.
BS:	This can also be done via the FILER command.

RIGHTS

What it does:	Views your rights for a directory.
Syntax:	**RIGHTS** *directory*
	RIGHTS *drive*
Example:	**RIGHTS SYS:ORANGES**
	RIGHTS L:
Who can use it:	Anyone.

SALVAGE

What it does: Recovers a deleted file.

Syntax: **SALVAGE**

Who can use it: Anyone.

BS: SALVAGE is a menu-driven program that prompts you through the process of recovering deleted files. It won't do you any good if you've purged your files with the PURGE command.

SECURE CONSOLE

What it does: Locks the file server up and throws away the key.

Syntax: **SECURE CONSOLE**

Who can use it: Console operator.

BS: SECURE CONSOLE is a good way to secure a file server. Among other things, it removes DOS from the server's memory.

SECURITY

What it does: Checks your system's security for possible leaks, like users without passwords.

Syntax: **SECURITY**

Who can use it: Paranoid supervisors.

SEND

What it does:	Sends a message to a specific user or users.
Syntax:	**SEND** *"message"* **TO** *user [,user...]*
Example:	**SEND "Pizza after work?" TO WALLY, BEAVER**
Who can use it:	Console operators.

SET

What it does:	Sets various server parameters.
Syntax:	**SET** *parameter=value*
Examples:	**SET MAXIMUM PACKET RECEIVE BUFFERS = 200**
	SET DIRECTORY CACHED BUFFER NONREFERENCED DELAY = 10
Who can use it:	Console operators.
BS:	There are loads and loads of parameters for this command. SET commands are usually included in the STARTUP.NCF file, so they're executed automatically whenever the server starts.

SET TIME

What it does:	Sets the date or time.
Syntax:	**SET** *[mm/dd/yy] [hh:mm:ss]*
Example:	**SET 05/16/94**
	SET 11:15:00
Who can use it:	Console operators.

SETPASS

What it does:	Lets you change your password.
Syntax:	**SETPASS** *[server]*
Who can use it:	Anyone.
BS:	SETPASS prompts you for your old password and then prompts you for a new password. The new password is not displayed as you type it, but you are asked to type the new password twice. That's a precaution — NetWare assumes that if you type the password the same way twice, you've typed it correctly.

SLIST

What it does:	Lists all the file servers on the network.
Syntax:	**SLIST**
Who can use it:	Anyone.

SYSCON

What it does:	SYSCON is the all-around console program for NetWare. You can do just about anything from it.
Syntax:	**SYSCON**
Who can use it:	Console operators. Users can access some of its functions.
BS:	Try it. You'll like it.

TRACK OFF

What it does: Stops displaying messages sent to or from a workstation or server.

Syntax: **TRACK OFF**

Who can use it: Console operators.

TRACK ON

What it does: Displays network messages sent to or from a workstation or server.

Syntax: **TRACK ON**

Who can use it: Console operators.

BS: TRACK ON has lots of other parameters. Check your NetWare manuals for more details.

UNLOAD (3.x only)

What it does: Unloads an NLM.

Syntax: **UNLOAD** *name*

Who can use it: Console operators.

USERDEF

What it does: Makes the MAKEUSER command easier to swallow.

Syntax: **USERDEF**

Who can use it: Supervisors who don't have time for MAKEUSER.

BS: USERDEF is a menu-driven version of MAKEDEF.

USERLIST

What it does:	Lists all the users who are currently logged in.
Syntax:	**USERLIST** *[/A]*
Who can use it:	Anyone.
BS:	/A causes USERLIST to include the address of each user.

VERSION

What it does:	Displays the version number for NetWare commands.
Syntax:	**VERSION** *[command]*
Example:	**VERSION**
	VERSION MAP
Who can use it:	Anyone.

VOLINFO

What it does:	Displays information about network volumes.
Syntax:	**VOLINFO**
Who can use it:	Anyone.
BS:	VOLINFO displays a list of all volumes on the default server along with the size of the volume and the amount of free space. The list is updated every five seconds.

VOLUMES

What it does:	Lists the currently available volumes.
Syntax:	**VOLUMES**
Who can use it:	Console operators.

VREPAIR

What it does:	Repairs damage to a network volume.
Syntax:	**LOAD VREPAIR**
Who can use it:	Console operators.

WHOAMI

What it does:	Tells you who you are. Sung by Jean Valjean in the first act of *Les Miserables*.
Syntax:	**WHOAMI**
Who can use it:	Anyone.
BS:	WHOAMI tells you your user ID, the address of the workstation you're logged into, and your directory rights. WHOAMI? 24601!

Chapter 26

NetWare Lite Commands You'll Use

NetWare Lite doesn't have nearly as many commands as full-blown NetWare, but it has enough to give you cramps. Here's the lowdown on the commands you'll use most.

CLIENT

What it does:	Loads the NetWare Lite client program so that your workstation can access the network.
Syntax:	**CLIENT**
Who can use it:	Anyone.
BS:	This command is usually added to the STARTNET.BAT file, so you don't have to run it separately.

DEDICATE

What it does:	Allows a network server to concentrate solely on network tasks.
Syntax:	**DEDICATE**

Who can use it: Administrators.

BS: A dedicated server runs more efficiently if you use DEDICATE, so you should always place this command at the end of the server's STARTNET.BAT file. DEDICATE will tie up the server so you can't use it for other work, but you can remove DEDICATE at any time simply by pressing any key on the keyboard.

NET

What it does: Provides menu-driven access to network functions.

Syntax: **NET**

Who can use it: Anyone who doesn't like command-line options.

NET ?

What it does: Displays help information about the NET command.

Syntax: **NET ?**

Who can use it: Anyone who is stuck.

NET BUD

What it does: Gives you a Bud (actually, a Lite).

Syntax: **NET BUD LITE**

Who can use it: Anyone over the legal age.

BS: Yes.

NET CAPTURE

What it does: Captures printer output and redirects it to the network.

Syntax: **NET CAPTURE** *port queue [options]*

Example: **NET CAPTURE LPT2 LASER W=5**

Who can use it: Anyone. Usually added to STARTNET.BAT.

BS: NET CAPTURE has lots of options to control printing. W=5 sets the time-out to five seconds so that programs that don't know about network printing will work.

NET HELP

What it does: Gives help on a specific command.

Syntax: **NET HELP** *command*

Example: **NET HELP CAPTURE**

Who can use it: Anyone who doesn't remember command-line switches so well.

NET INFO

What it does: Shows information about the network.

Syntax: **NET INFO**

Who can use it: Anyone who wants to know.

BS: NET INFO shows the name of the server, NetWare Lite version numbers, and your user name and machine address. It is the same as NET WHOAMI.

NET LOGIN

What it does:	Gets you in to the network.
Syntax:	**NET LOGIN** *[user ID]*
Example:	**NET LOGIN BEAVER**
Who can use it:	Anyone who isn't in yet.
BS:	If you omit your user ID, NetWare Lite prompts you for it.

NET LOGOUT

What it does:	Gets you out of the network.
Syntax:	**NET LOGOUT**
Who can use it:	Anyone.

NET MAP

What it does:	Assigns drive letters to network directories.
Syntax:	**NET MAP** *drive: directory server*
Example:	**NET MAP F: APPS WARD**
Who can use it:	Anyone.
BS:	Before you can access a network directory, the directory must be set up on the server by using the NET command.
	If you enter NET MAP without any options, NetWare Lite displays a list of all current drive mappings.

NET MAP DEL

What it does: Removes a drive mapping.

Syntax: **NET MAP DEL** *drive:*

Example: **NET MAP DEL F:**

Who can use it: Anyone.

NET NDLIST

What it does: Lists the network directories that are available.

Syntax: **NET NDLIST**

Who can use it: Anyone.

NET NPLIST

What it does: Lists the network printers that are available.

Syntax: **NET NPLIST**

Who can use it: Anyone.

NET PRINT

What it does: Prints a file on a network printer.

Syntax: **NET PRINT** *file*

Example: **NET PRINT CONFIG.SYS**

Who can use it: Anyone.

BS: NETPRINT is the network equivalent of the DOS PRINT command.

NET RECEIVE

What it does: Controls whether your workstation can receive messages from other users.

Syntax: **NET RECEIVE ON**

NET RECEIVE OFF

Who can use it: Anyone.

NET SAVE

What it does: Creates an NLLOGIN.BAT file that contains NET LOGIN, NET CAPTURE, NET MAP, and SET commands.

Syntax: **NET SAVE**

Who can use it: Anyone.

BS: Rather than create a batch file from scratch, you can experiment with NET commands until you get your network configured just the way you want, and then use NET SAVE to create a batch file that recreates your network setup. Very convenient.

NET SEND

What it does: Sends messages to other network users.

Syntax: **NET SEND** *"message text"* ALL

NET SEND *"message text"* user

Example: **NET SEND "The network dies in five" ALL**

Who can use it: Anyone.

NET SETPASS

What it does: Allows you to change your password.

Syntax: **NET SETPASS**

Who can use it: Anyone.

BS: NET SETPASS asks you to type your current password and then asks you to type the new password twice.

NET SLIST

What it does: Lists all available servers.

Syntax: **NET SLIST**

Who can use it: Anyone.

BS: NET SLIST only lists those servers that are currently on-line. Servers that are down aren't listed.

NET TIME

What it does: Synchronizes your computer's time with the server's time.

Syntax: **NET TIME** *server*

Example: **NET TIME WARD**

Who can use it: Anyone.

BS: Although the clocks in most computers are fairly accurate, it's a good idea to have your computer and the server computer synchronize their watches. It's also a good idea to check periodically to make sure your computer's clock is accurate.

NET ULIST

What it does: Lists users who are currently on the network.

Syntax: **NET ULIST**

Who can use it: Anyone.

NET USERLIST (1.1 only)

What it does: Lists users who are currently on the network.

Syntax: **NET USERLIST**

Who can use it: Anyone.

BS: This command does the same thing as NET ULIST. It was added to NetWare Lite 1.1 to be more compatible with full-fledged NetWare.

NET WHOAMI

What it does: Shows information about the network.

Syntax: **NET WHOAMI**

Who can use it: Anyone with an identity crisis.

BS: NET WHOAMI shows the name of the server, NetWare Lite version numbers, and your user name and machine address. It is the same as NET INFO.

NLCACHE

What it does: Caches disk I/O to improve performance.

Syntax: **NLCACHEX**

NLCACHEM

NLCACHEC

Who can use it: Anyone.

BS: The three NLCACHE commands use memory differently: NLCACHEX uses extended memory, NLCACHEM uses expanded memory, and NLCACHEC uses only conventional memory. All three commands have about 4 million parameters, which are best left set by NLCINST. See Chapter 13 for more information about disk caching.

NLCINST

What it does: Configures the NLCACHE program.

Syntax: **NLCINST**

Who can use it: Anyone.

BS: NLCINST asks you some questions about your computer and then constructs an NLCACHE command line to configure NLCACHE properly. It then inserts the command it composed into your AUTOEXEC.BAT, CONFIG.SYS, or STARTNET.BAT file.

NLSNIPES

What it does: Takes your mind off your problems.

Syntax: **NLSNIPES**

Who can use it: Anyone who doesn't have any real work to do.

BS: NLSNIPES is a game that comes with NetWare Lite. You can play against several network users if you want to waste everyone else's time too. Really, I'm not making this up.

SERVER

What it does: Loads the NetWare Lite server program so that the computer can act as a network server.

Syntax: **SERVER**

Who can use it: Anyone.

BS: This command is usually added to the STARTNET.BAT file, so you don't have to run it separately.

STARTNET

What it does: Starts the network. Very handy indeed.

Syntax: **STARTNET**

Who can use it: Anyone.

BS: STARTNET is a batch file that contains the commands necessary to start NetWare Lite on your computer. It usually includes a CLIENT command, a SERVER command (if your computer is a server), and a NET LOGIN command to log you in to the network.

Chapter 27
LANtastic Commands You'll Use

● ●

In This Chapter

▶ LANtastic commands you'll dread using

▶ The Sin Tax

▶ Examples

▶ What more could you ask?

● ●

*L*ANtastic isn't as complicated as NetWare, but it does have a covey of commands you need to use from time to time. Here they are. Not all of LANtastic's commands are here; just the ones you're likely to use.

AILANBIO

What it does: Loads the LAN BIOS program to make network services available on your computer.

Syntax: **AILANBIO** *[bevy of switches]*

Who can use it: Anyone.

BS: AILANBIO is required to use LANtastic, but it's placed in the STARTNET.BAT file automatically when you install LANtastic. You'll only worry about it when you want to fiddle with its switches, in which case you'll have to wade through the LANtastic manual. Bother.

ALONE

What it does: Allows a network server to concentrate solely on network tasks.

Syntax: **ALONE** *[PASSWORD=password]*

Example:	**ALONE PASSWORD=STOPPEN**
Who can use it:	Administrators.
BS:	A dedicated file server runs more efficiently if you use ALONE, so you should always place it at the end of the server's STARTNET.BAT file. Use the PASSWORD option if you don't want to lock out the server from folks who wander in off the street.

LANCACHE

What it does:	Speeds up disk access.
Syntax:	**LANCACHE** *[CACHE_SIZE=size] [NODELAYED_WRITES]*
Example:	**LANCACHE CACHE_SIZE=3072**
Who can use it:	Anyone.
BS:	If you don't use any switches, LANCACHE uses up to 2M of extended memory for its cache. If you have more memory than that, you may want to use the CACHE_SIZE switch to increase the size of the cache. Use NODELAYED_WRITES if you're paranoid.

LANPUP

What it does:	Allows you to control the network while you run other programs.
Syntax:	**LANPUP** *[LINE=line]*
Example:	**LANPUP LINE=3**
Who can use it:	DOS users (LANPUP doesn't work when Windows is active).
BS:	After you've run the LANPUP command, you can access the LANPUP program at any time by pressing Ctrl+Alt+L, even while another program is active. Then you can log in or out of servers, connect to network drives or printers, or send and receive e-mail.
	The LINE parameter lets you change the screen location where LANPUP pops up. For example, you can tell it to pop

up on line 15, near the bottom of the screen, or up at the top
on line 1.

NET

What it does:	Provides menu access to all the NET command's functions.
Syntax:	**NET**
Who can use it:	Anyone.
BS:	The NET command functions can be accessed through command line switches, which are treated as separate commands in the sections that follow.

NET ATTACH

What it does:	Enables you to automatically connect to every shared directory and drive on a file server.
Syntax:	**NET ATTACH** *[/VERBOSE]* *server*
Examples:	**NET ATTACH \\WARD**
Who can use it:	Anyone.
BS:	NET ATTACH saves you from typing separate NET USE commands if you want to connect to all of a server's shared drives and directories. When you use NET ATTACH, it picks the drive letters to assign to each network drive or directory; use the / VERBOSE switch so that you can see what drive letters it uses.

NET CHANGEPW

What it does:	Lets you change your password.
Syntax:	**NET CHANGEPW** *server old pw new pw*
Example:	**NET CHANGEPW \\WALLY SNERD*FACE WOMP*RAT**
Who can use it:	Anyone.

NET CHAT

What it does: Lets you talk with other network users.

Syntax: **NET CHAT**

Who can use it: Anyone who doesn't have real work to do.

BS: NET CHAT takes you directly to the NET program's CHAT menu. From there, you work the menus to talk with other users.

NET CLOCK

What it does: Tells your computer to synchronize watches with the server.

Syntax: **NET CLOCK ***server*

Example: **NET CLOCK \\\\WARD**

Who can use it: Anyone.

BS: It's a good idea to put a NET CLOCK command in your STARTNET.BAT file, right after the NET LOGIN command.

NET COPY

What it does: Copies a file on a server drive without sending the file over the network.

Syntax: **NET COPY** *from file to file*

Example: **NET COPY** *F:\\BBCAPR.WK1 F:\\BBCMAY.WK1*

Who can use it: Anyone.

BS: If you use the COPY command to copy a file from one disk location on the server to another, the file is sent over the network unnecessarily. NET COPY performs the copy at the server, avoiding unnecessary network traffic.

NET DETACH

What it does: Disconnects you from all disk resources on a particular server.

Syntax: **NET DETACH** *server*

Example: **NET DETACH \\WARD**

Who can use it: Anyone.

BS: NET DETACH is the same as using a NET UNUSE command for each disk on the server.

NET DIR

What it does: Displays information about files on a network server.

Syntax: **NET DIR** *[/ALL] filename*

Example: **NET DIR F:*.DOC**

NET DIR /ALL M:

Who can use it: Anyone.

BS: NET DIR displays a bit more information than the DOS DIR command, but doesn't include all the DOS DIR command's bells and whistles. This one's not too useful unless you use LANtastic's indirect file feature.

NET DISABLEA

What it does: Disables your account so that it cannot be used to access the server.

Syntax: **NET DISABLEA** *server password*

Example: **NET DISABLEA \\KNIGHT TROUTHE**

Who can use it: Anyone who wants to kiss the network goodbye.

BS: To reenable an account, you must log in as the network administrator and use the NET_MGR program to reset the user's number of concurrent logins to 1 or more.

NET ECHO

What it does:	Works like the DOS ECHO command, but lets you include special LANtastic strings.
Syntax:	**NET ECHO** *text to echo*
Example:	**NET ECHO HELLO !"USER"**
Who can use it:	Anyone crazy enough to want to write batch files that display LANtastic strings.

NET FLUSH

What it does:	Flushes all network buffers.
Syntax:	**NET FLUSH**
Who can use it:	System managers.
BS:	Insert your own joke here.

Don't read this if you're strung out

LANtastic contains a bunch of "strings" that contain information about the network. You can use these like DOS environment variables or in NET ECHO commands. As if you're interested, here's the list of LANtastic strings you can use:

String	Purpose
!"DATE"	The current date.
!"DAY"	The day of the week.
!"DIRECTORY"	The current drive and directory.
!"ETEXT=n"	The error message for error number *n*.
!"FILE=file"	The first line of the specified file.
!"INSTALLED"	A goofy string that tells you whether NETBIOS, REDIR, SERVER, and LANPUP are installed.
!"LOGIN=server"	TRUE if you are logged in to the server, FALSE if you are not.
!"NODEID"	The 12-digit node number for your computer.
!"MACHINEID"	The name of your machine.
!"PROGRAM"	The full DOS path for the NET program; for example, "C:\LANTASTI\NET.EXE."
!"TIME"	The current time.
!"USER"	The default user name for the workstation.
!"USERID"	The current user ID.

NET LOGIN

What it does:	Logs you in to a server.
Syntax:	**NET LOGIN** *[/WAIT or /DEFERRED]* *server [user] [password]*
Example:	**NET LOGIN \\WARD BEAVER**
Who can use it:	Anyone.
BS:	If you use NET LOGIN in a batch file, don't include your password directly on the command. Let LANtastic prompt you for it instead. /WAIT tells NET LOGIN to twiddle its fingers until the server becomes available. /DEFERRED tells NET LOGIN to try again later if the server isn't available now.

NET LOGOUT

What it does:	Logs you out of a server.
Syntax:	**NET LOGOUT** *server*
Example:	**NET LOGOUT \\WARD**
Who can use it:	Anyone.
BS:	Cancels any NET USE commands for the server.

NET LPT COMBINE

What it does:	Lets you redirect output from batch file commands to a network printer and treat all the redirected output as one print job.
Syntax:	**NET LPT COMBINE**
Who can use it:	Computer geeks who write batch files that use redirection to print command output.

NET LPT FLUSH

What it does: If you use LPT COMBINE, LPT FLUSH forces a batch file's redirected printer output to be closed and a new job to begin.

Syntax: **NET LPT FLUSH**

Who can use it: The same computer geeks who use NET LPT COMBINE.

NET LPT NOTIFY

What it does: Tells LANtastic to inform you when your print jobs have finished printing.

Syntax: **NET LPT** */ENABLE* **NOTIFY**

NET LPT /DISABLE NOTIFY

Who can use it: Anyone.

BS: If you want to be notified when your print jobs finish, add a NET LPT /ENABLE NOTIFY command to your STARTNET.BAT file.

NET LPT SEPARATE

What it does: Rescinds the NET LPT COMBINE command.

Syntax: **NET LPT SEPARATE**

Who can use it: Anyone who shows remorse for using NET LPT COMBINE.

NET LPT TIMEOUT

What it does: Sets the amount of time LANtastic waits before deciding that a print job is complete.

Syntax: **NET LPT TIMEOUT** *seconds*

Example: **NET LPT TIMEOUT 10**

Who can use it:	Anyone.
BS:	This command is usually used when you have a program that prints very sloooowly.

NET MAIL

What it does:	Sends an e-mail message to another user.
Syntax:	**NET MAIL** *filename \\server user [*"*comment*"*]*
Example:	**NET MAIL GETTHIS.TXT \\WARD BEAVER "Read it & weep"**
Who can use it:	Anyone.
BS:	To use NET MAIL, you must first compose your message as a text file, using an editor like the DOS EDIT command. If you use the NET command's menu-driven mail functions, you can compose your message and send it by using NET's built-in mail editor.

NET MASSAGE

What it does:	Helps you relax.
Syntax:	**NET MASSAGE** *[NECK] [SHOULDERS] [BACK]*
Example:	**NET MASSAGE NECK BACK**
Who can use it:	Anyone who needs to unwind.
BS:	Yes.

NET MESSAGE

What it does:	Lets you block out annoying messages sent to you by other users.
Syntax:	**NET MESSAGE** *DISABLE*
	NET MESSAGE ENABLE [BEEP or **POP]**

Who can use it:	Anyone.
BS:	When you enable messages, BEEP tells LANtastic to beep when someone sends you a message; POP tells LANtastic to display the message immediately. If POP is off, you have to use NET RECEIVE to display the message.

NET PAUSE

What it does:	Works like the DOS PAUSE command but lets you specify a time for the pause and display a message.
Syntax:	**NET PAUSE** *[/NEWLINE] "message" [time]*
Example:	**NET PAUSE "Wait a minute..." 60**
Who can use it:	Sadistic computer geeks who like to write batch files that make their users wait.

NET POSTBOX

What it does:	Checks your mail.
Syntax:	**NET POSTBOX** *[\\server]*
Example:	**NET POSTBOX \\WARD**
Who can use it:	Anyone.
BS:	Add this to STARTNET.BAT. If you have several servers but only one is used for mail, specify the server on the NET POSTBOX command.

NET PRINT

What it does:	Prints a file on a network printer.
Syntax:	**NET PRINT** *[/BINARY] filename printer "comment" [copies]*
Example:	**NET PRINT *.TXT LPT2**
	NET PRINT REPORT.PRT \\WARD\@LASER "Status report" 3

Who can use it: Anyone.

BS: The file to be printed must be a printable file — either a text file or a print file prepared by an application program. If the file contains graphics, you should specify /BINARY.

NET QUEUE HALT

What it does: Stops the print queue before it prints 5,000 copies of the wrong report.

Syntax: **NET QUEUE HALT** *server [printer or ALL]*

Example: **NET QUEUE HALT \\WARD LPT1**

Who can use it: Anyone with the Q privilege, which allows the user to play with the print queue.

BS: To restart the queue, use NET QUEUE START. When you do, the current job restarts from the beginning.

NET QUEUE PAUSE

What it does: Temporarily halts the print queue.

Syntax: **NET QUEUE PAUSE** *server [printer or ALL]*

Example: **NET QUEUE PAUSE \\WARD LPT1**

Who can use it: Anyone with the Q privilege, which alows the user to play with the print queue.

BS: The difference between NET QUEUE PAUSE and NET QUEUE HALT is that PAUSE doesn't force the current print job to restart from the beginning. When you start the queue again with NET QUEUE START, the current job picks up where it left off.

NET QUEUE RESTART

What it does:	Restarts the current print job at the beginning.
Syntax:	**NET QUEUE RESTART** *server [printer or ALL]*
Example:	**NET QUEUE RESTART \\WARD LPT1**
Who can use it:	Anyone with the Q privilege, which allows the user to play with the print queue.

NET QUEUE SINGLE

What it does:	Prints the next job in the queue and then stops.
Syntax:	**NET QUEUE SINGLE** *server [printer or ALL]*
Example:	**NET QUEUE SINGLE \\WARD LPT1**
Who can use it:	Anyone with the Q privilege, which alows the user to play with the print queue.

NET QUEUE START

What it does:	Starts a queue.
Syntax:	**NET QUEUE START** *server [printer or ALL]*
Example:	**NET QUEUE START \\WARD LPT1**
Who can use it:	Anyone with the Q privilege, which allows the user to play with the print queue.
BS:	NET QUEUE START is used when despooling is disabled with the NET_MGR program's server start-up parameters or when you've used a NET QUEUE HALT, PAUSE, or STOP command.

NET QUEUE STATUS

What it does:	Tells you what a printer is up to.
Syntax:	**NET QUEUE STATUS** *server [printer* or *ALL]*
Example:	**NET QUEUE STATUS \\WARD ALL**
Who can use it:	Anyone.

NET QUEUE STOP

What it does:	Stops a queue.
Syntax:	**NET QUEUE STOP** *server [printer* or *ALL]*
Example:	**NET QUEUE STOP \\WARD LPT1**
Who can use it:	Anyone with the Q privilege.
BS:	Use NET QUEUE START to start a printer after you've stopped it with NET QUEUE STOP.

NET RECEIVE

What it does:	Displays messages sent to you.
Syntax:	**NET RECEIVE** *[line] [delay]*
Example:	**NET RECEIVE 5 20**
Who can use it:	Anyone.
BS:	The line option tells NET RECEIVE where on the screen to display the message, and the delay option says how long to leave the message there.

NET SEND

What it does:	Annoys other users by interrupting them with a message.
Syntax:	**NET SEND** *machine "message"* [*server user*]
Example:	**NET SEND * "Made you look!" \\WARD BEAVER**
	NET SEND * "Made you ALL look!"
Who can use it:	Anyone.
BS:	Use an asterisk for the machine option to send the message to all computers. Use \\server user to send the message to a specific user.

NET SHOW

What it does:	Shows all your network attachments.
Syntax:	**NET SHOW** [*/BATCH*]
Example:	**NET SHOW /BATCH >NET.BAT**
Who can use it:	Anyone.
BS:	/BATCH is really cool because it shows your network configuration in the form of NET commands that can be used to recreate the configuration. Redirect this output to a file and *voilà*! Instant batch file!

NET SHUTDOWN

What it does:	Schedules a server shutdown.
Syntax:	**NET SHUTDOWN** *server* [*minutes*] *"message"*
	NET SHUTDOWN CANCEL
Example:	**NET SHUTDOWN \\WARD 5 "The server will self-destruct in 5 minutes"**

Who can use it: Anyone with the S (System Manager) privilege.

BS: If you beam aboard an enemy ship, wander onto the bridge, and hear the computer counting backwards slowly, BEAM OFF IMMEDIATELY! Or type **NET SHUTDOWN CANCEL** to cancel the scheduled shutdown.

NET SLOGINS

What it does: Enables or disables logins to a server.

Syntax: **NET SLOGINS** *ENABLE* *server*

NET SLOGINS *DISABLE* *server*

Example: **NET SLOGINS DISABLE \\WARD**

Who can use it: Anyone with the S privilege.

BS: Use this when you need to work on the server.

NET TERMINATE

What it does: Blows a user off the network.

Syntax: **NET TERMINATE** *server user [machine] [minutes]*

Example: **NET TERMINATE \\WARD BEAVER**

NET TERMINATE \\WARD *

Who can use it: Anyone with the S privilege.

BS: Use * as the user ID to blow off all users on the server. If a user is logged in to a server from more than one machine, use the machine option to tell which one you want blown off. If you're in a good mood, use the minutes option to give the user time to get his or her affairs in order. Then the user sees a message such as `We give you two of your earth minutes.`

NET UNUSE

What it does: Cancels a network drive or printer connection.

Syntax: **NET UNUSE** *drive* or *printer*

Example   **NET UNUSE L:**

    NET UNUSE LPT1

Who can use it: Anyone.

NET USE

What it does: Sets up network drive and printer connections.

Syntax: **NET USE** *drive:* *[/DEFERRED]* *server**resource*

    NET USE *printer:* *[/DEFERRED]* *server**resource*

Example: **NET USE F: \\WARD\C-DRIVE**

    NET USE LPT2: \\WARD\@LASER

Who can use it: Anyone.

BS: /DEFERRED tells NET USE not to panic if the server is off-line; the connection will be established whenever the server comes on-line. NET USE commands are usually placed in the STARTNET.BAT file.

NET USER

What it does: Sets the user ID and password for automatic logins.

Syntax: **NET USER** *[/DISABLE]* *user* *[password]*

Example: **NET USER WALLY**

Who can use it: Anyone.

BS: This command lets you connect to a server without first using a NET LOGIN command. If you add this command to a batch file and include your password right there in the batch file where everyone can see, your dog will die.

NET_MGR

What it does: Starts the NET_MGR program, which has lots of menu options for managing a server.

Syntax: **NET_MGR**

Who can use it: The network administrator.

NET_MGR BACKUP

What it does: Backs up the server's control directory to a file.

Syntax: **NET_MGR BACKUP** *control directory backup file*

Example: **NET_MGR BACKUP LANTASTI.NET LANTASTI.BAK**

Who can use it: The network administrator.

NET_MGR CREATE

What it does: Creates an individual or wild-card user account.

Syntax: **NET_MGR CREATE** *INDIVIDUAL name*

                NET_MGR CREATE *WILDCARD name*

Example: **NET_MGR CREATE INDIVIDUAL WALLY**

Who can use it: The network administrator.

BS: The account will be created with default options. To change the options, use NET_MGR SET.

NET_MGR DELETE

What it does:	Deletes an individual or wild-card user account.
Syntax:	**NET_MGR DELETE** *INDIVIDUAL name*
	NET_MGR DELETE *WILDCARD name*
Example:	**NET_MGR DELETE INDIVIDUAL WALLY**
Who can use it:	The network administrator.

NET_MGR RESTORE

What it does:	Restores a previously backed-up network control directory.
Syntax:	**NET_MGR RESTORE** *backup file control directory*
Example:	**NET_MGR RESTORE LANTASTI.BAK LANTASTI.NET**
Who can use it:	Network administrators caught in a jam.

NET_MGR SET

What it does:	Changes the attributes of an individual or wild-card user account.
Syntax:	**NET_MGR SET** *INDIVIDUAL name [attrib=value]*
	NET_MGR SET *WILDCARD name [attrib=value]*
Example:	**NET_MGR SET INDIVIDUAL WALLY LOGINS=5**
Who can use it:	Network administrators.
BS:	Up to four account attributes can be changed in a single NET_MGR command. The account attributes are:
USERNAME	Account name.
PASSWORD	Password.
LOGINS	Number of concurrent logins (0-255).

PRIVILEGES	Account privileges (AQMUSOD).
ACCT_EXP	Date the account expires.
PW_EXP	Date the password expires.

NET_MGR SHOW

What it does:	Shows the status of an individual or wild-card account.
Syntax:	**NET_MGR SHOW** *INDIVIDUAL name*
	NET_MGR SHOW *WILDCARD name*
Example:	**NET_MGR SHOW INDIVIDUAL WALLY**
Who can use it:	Network administrators.

REDIR

What it does:	Loads LANtastic's REDIR program so that your workstation can access the network.
Syntax:	**REDIR** *[LOGINS=n] [SIZE=size]*
Example:	**REDIR LOGINS=5 SIZE=2048**
Who can use it:	Anyone.
BS:	This command is usually added to the STARTNET.BAT file, so you don't have to run it separately. LOGINS sets the limit for how many file servers you can access. Size sets the size of the network buffers.

SERVER

What it does:	Loads LANtastic's server program so that the computer can act as a network server.
Syntax:	**SERVER** *[tons o' parameters]*

Who can use it: Anyone.

BS: This command is usually added to the STARTNET.BAT file, so you don't have to run it separately. The parameters correspond to the server start-up parameters available from NET_MGR.

STARTNET

What it does: Starts the network.

Syntax: **STARTNET**

Who can use it: Anyone.

BS: STARTNET is a batch file that contains the commands necessary to start LANtastic on your computer.

The 5th Wave   By Rich Tennant

"NO, THEY'RE NOT REALLY A GANG, JUST A PARTICULARLY AGGRESSIVE LAN."

Glossary

10base2 The type of coax cable most often used for Ethernet networks. AKA *thinnet*, *cheapernet*. The maximum length of a single segment is 185 meters (600 feet).

10base5 The original Ethernet coax cable, now used mostly used as the backbone for larger networks. AKA *yellow cable*, *thick cable*. The maximum length of a single segment is 500 meters (1,640 feet).

10baseT Twisted-pair cable, commonly used for Ethernet networks. AKA *UTP*, *twisted pair*, or *twisted sister*. The maximum length of a single segment is 100 meters (330 feet). Of the three Ethernet cable types, this one is the easiest to work with.

802.2 The forgotten IEEE standard. The more glamorous 802.3 standard relies upon 802.2 for moral support.

802.3 The IEEE standard known in the vernacular as "Ethernet."

80286 processor *Computo-habilis*, an ancient ancestor to today's modern 386 and 486 computers; still used by far too many people.

80386 processor The first 32-bit microprocessor chip used in personal computers, now replaced by the 486 chip. 386 computers are slower than their 486 counterparts, but they get the job done.

80486 processor The most popular CPU chip for personal computers today. The Pentium is newer and better but still too expensive.

8088 processor The microprocessor chip around which IBM's original PC was designed, marking the transition from the bronze age to the iron age.

AAUI *Apple Attachment Unit Interface*, a type of connector used in some Apple Ethernet networks.

access rights A list of rights that tell you what you can and cannot do with network files or directories.

account You can't get into the network without one of these. The network knows who you are and what rights you have on the network by virtue of your account.

acronym An abbreviation made up of the first letters of a series of words.

adapter card An electronic card that can be plugged into one of your computer's adapter slots to give it some new and fabulous capability, like displaying 16 million colors, talking to other computers over the phone, or accessing a network.

address book In an e-mail system, a list of users with whom you regularly correspond.

administrator The big network cheese who is responsible for setting things up and keeping them running. Pray that it's not you.

AFP *Apple Filing Protocol*, a protocol for filing used by Apple. (That helps a lot, doesn't it?)

AILANBIO.EXE The LANtastic program that implements NETBIOS.

allocation unit DOS allocates space to files one allocation unit at a time; the allocation unit is typically 2,048 or 4,096 bytes, depending on the size of the disk. AKA *cluster*. NetWare uses a more efficient allocation scheme, as does DoubleSpace.

antivirus program A program that sniffs out viruses on your network and sends them into exile.

AppleTalk Apple's networking system for Macintoshes.

application layer The highest layer of the OSI reference model, which governs how software communicates with the network.

archive bit A flag that's kept for each file to indicate whether the file has been modified since it was last backed up.

ARCnet A slow but steady network topology developed originally by Datapoint. ARCnet uses a token-passing scheme similar to Token Ring.

Artisoft The company that makes LANtastic.

attributes Characteristics that are assigned to files. DOS alone provides four attributes: system, hidden, read-only, and archive. Networks generally expand the list of file attributes.

AUI *Attachment Unit Interface*, the big connector found on many network cards and 10baseT hubs that's used to attach yellow cable via a transceiver.

AUTOEXEC.BAT A batch file that DOS executes automatically every time you start your computer.

AUTOEXEC.NCF A batch file that NetWare executes automatically every time you load the server software.

backbone A trunk cable used to tie sections of a network together. The backbone is often 10base5 or fiber-optic cable.

backup A copy of your important files made for safekeeping, in case something happens to the original files; something you'd better do every day.

banner A fancy page that's printed between each print job so that you can easily separate jobs from one another.

batch file In DOS, a file that contains one or more commands that are executed together as a set. You create the batch file by using a text editor (like the DOS EDIT command) and run the file by typing its name at the command prompt.

benchmark A repeatable test you use to judge the performance of your network. The best benchmarks are the ones that closely duplicate the type of work you routinely do on your network.

bindery The big database where user accounts and other related info are stored on a NetWare server.

BNC connector A three-piece connector that's used with 10base2 cable.

bottleneck The slowest link in your network, which causes work to get jammed up. The first step in improving network performance is identifying the bottlenecks.

bridge Not the popular card game, but a device that lets you link two networks together. Bridges are smart enough to know which computers are on which side of the bridge, so they only allow those messages that need to get to the other side to cross the bridge. This improves performance on both sides of the bridge.

Btrieve An indexed file access method commonly used on NetWare networks.

buffer An area of memory that's used to hold data enroute to somewhere else. For example, a disk buffer holds data as it travels between your computer and the disk drive.

BUFFERS A line in CONFIG.SYS that sets up buffers used for disk I/O. If a disk cache is used, BUFFERS should specify a low number, like 2 or 3.

bus A type of network topology in which network nodes are strung out along a single run of cable called a *segment*. 10base2 and LocalTalk networks use a bus topology. *Bus* also refers to the row of expansion slots within your computer.

cache A sophisticated form of buffering in which a large amount of memory is set aside to hold data so that it can be accessed quickly.

CAPTURE The NetWare command used to redirect printer output to a network printer. CAPTURE is usually run in a batch file or login script.

cc:Mail A popular electronic mail program.

CD-ROM A high-capacity disk that uses optical technology to store data in a form that can be read but not written over.

Certified NetWare Engineer Someone who has studied hard and passed the official exam offered by Novell. AKA *CNE*.

Certified Network Dummy Someone who knows nothing about networks but nevertheless gets the honor of installing one. AKA *CND*.

CGA A crude type of graphics display used on early IBM computers. CGA stands for *Crayon Graphics Adapter*.

chat What you do on the network when you talk "live" with another network user.

Chaucer A dead English dude.

cheapernet See *10base2*.

CHKDSK A DOS command that checks the record-keeping structures of a DOS disk for errors.

click What you do in Windows to get things done.

client A computer that has access to the network but doesn't share any of its own resources with the network. See *server*.

CLIENT.EXE The NetWare Lite program you load to access the network as a client workstation.

client/server A vague term meaning roughly that the work load is split between a client and server computer.

Clouseau The most dangerous man in all of France. Some people say he only plays the fool.

cluster See *allocation unit.*

coaxial cable A type of cable that contains two conductors. The center conductor is surrounded by a layer of insulation, which is then wrapped by a braided-metal conductor and an outer layer of insulation.

COM1 The first serial port on a computer.

CompuServe An on-line information network you can access to talk with other users about issues such as NetWare, LANtastic, politics, and the weather.

computer name A unique name assigned to each computer on a network.

concentrator In Ethernet, a multiport hub used mostly with 10baseT cabling. The hub typically has 8 or 12 ports, plus a BNC connector for 10base2 and an AUI port for a 10base5 transceiver.

CONFIG.SYS A file on every DOS computer that contains configuration information. CONFIG.SYS is processed every time you start your computer.

console In NetWare, the file server's keyboard and monitor. Console commands can be entered only at the server console.

console operator In NetWare, a user working at the file server's console.

Control Panel In Windows, an application that lets you configure various aspects of Windows' operation.

conventional memory The first 640K of memory on a DOS-based computer.

CPU The *central processing unit*, or brains, of the computer.

crimp tool A special tool used to attach connectors to cables. No network manager should be without one.

CSMA/CD An acronym for *Carrier Sense Multiple Access with Collision Detection.* The traffic management technique used by Ethernet.

daisy chain A way of connecting computer components in which the first component is connected to the second, which is connected to the third, and so on. In 10baseT Ethernet, concentrators can be daisy chained together.

DAT *Digital audiotape*, a type of tape often used for network backup.

data link layer The second layer of the OSI model, responsible for transmitting bits of data over the network cable.

dedicated server A computer used exclusively as a network server.

delayed write A disk-caching technique in which data written to disk is placed in cache memory and actually written to disk later.

differential backup A type of backup in which only the files that have changed since the last full backup are backed up.

digitized sound A file containing a sound that can be played if the computer is equipped with a sound card. See *Clouseau*.

DIP switch A bank of switches used to configure an adapter card. See *jumper block*.

directory hash A popular breakfast food enjoyed by NetWare managers.

disk A device that stores information magnetically on a disk. A *hard disk* is permanently sealed in an enclosure and has a capacity usually measured in hundreds of megabytes. A *floppy disk* is removable and can have a capacity of 360K, 720K, 1.2MB, 1.44MB, or 2.88MB.

DMA channel A direct pipeline for I/O that's faster than normal I/O. Network cards use DMA for fast network access.

DOS *Disk Operating System*, the most popular operating system for IBM and IBM-compatible computers.

DOS shell program A program that makes DOS easier to use by replacing the barren command prompt with a friendly menu-driven interface.

dot-matrix printer A printer that works by striking an inked ribbon with a series of pins to form letters. Once the mainstay printer for PCs, dot-matrix printers are giving way to laser printers. High- speed matrix printers still have their place on the network, though, and matrix printers have the advantage of being able to print multipart forms.

DoubleSpace A new feature of DOS 6.0 and 6.2 that compresses data so that it requires less disk space. This increases the effective capacity of the disk, often by a factor of 2:1 or more.

dumb terminal Back in the heyday of mainframe computers, a monitor and keyboard attached to the central mainframe. All of the computing work occurred at the mainframe; the terminal only displayed the results and sent input typed at the keyboard back to the mainframe.

e-mail An application that lets you exchange notes with other network users.

Eddie Haskel The kid who's always sneaking around, poking his nose into other people's business, and generally causing trouble. Every network has one.

editor A program for creating and changing text files. DOS 5.0 and later versions come with a basic editor called EDIT. Other editors are avaiable, but EDIT is good enough for most network needs.

EDLIN A primitive editor that came with DOS 1.0 and was not improved upon until DOS 5.0. EDLIN has a distinct mainframe feel to it, which is why network geeks like it.

EGA The color monitor that was standard with IBM AT computers, based on 80286 processors. Now obsolete, but plenty of them are still in use.

EISA bus *Extended Industry Standard Architecture.* An improved I/O bus that is compatible with the standard ISA bus but provides advanced features. Computers with an EISA bus are often used as file servers. See *ISA bus* and *Micro Channel bus.*

ENDCAP The NetWare command you use to stop network printer redirection.

enterprise computing A trendy term that refers to a view of an organization's complete computing needs, rather than just a single department's or group's needs.

ESDI An older style of disk drive that's not often used nowadays.

Ethernet The World's Most Popular Network Standard.

EtherTalk What you call Ethernet when you use it on a Macintosh.

ETLA *Extended Three- Letter Acronym.* An acronym with four letters. See *TLA.*

expanded memory An ancient technique for blasting past the 640K limit. Unlike extended memory, expanded memory can be used with 8088 computers.

extended memory Memory beyond the first 640K. Available only on 80286 or better computers. Most computers today have extended memory.

fake network See *zero-slot network.*

Farallon The company that popularized PhoneNET as a cheaper and more flexible alternative to LocalTalk, Apple's cabling scheme for networking Macintoshes.

FAT The *file allocation table*, a record-keeping structure DOS uses to keep track of the location of every file on a disk.

FDDI *Fiber Distributed Data Inferface*, a 100-Mbps network standard used with fiber-optic backbone. When FDDI is used, FDDI FDDI/Ethernet bridges are used to connect Ethernet segments to the backbone.

ferrule The outer metal tube that you crimp on to attach a BNC connector to the cable.

fiber-optic cable A blazingly-fast network cable that transmits data using light rather than electricity. Fiber optic cable is often used as the backbone in large networks, especially where great distances are involved.

file server A network computer containing disk drives that are available to network users.

full backup A backup of all the files on a disk, whether or not the files have been modified since the last backup. See *differential backup*.

fulminic acid An unstable acid (CNOH) that forms explosive salts of some metals, especially mercury. Used to punish users who write their passwords on Post-it Notes stuck on their monitors.

gateway A device that connects dissimilar networks. Gateways are often used to connect Ethernet networks to mainframe computers.

GB Gigabyte, roughly a billion bytes of disk storage (1024MB to be precise). See *K*, *MB*, and *TB*.

generation backup A backup strategy in which several sets of backup disks or tapes are retained, sometimes called grandfather-father-son.

generation gap What happens when you skip one of your backups.

glass house The room where the mainframe computer is kept. Symbolic of the mainframe mentality, which stresses bureaucracy, inflexibility, and heavy iron.

group account A grouping of user accounts that share common access rights.

groupware A relatively new category of application programs that are designed with networks in mind to allow and even promote collaborative work.

guru Anyone who knows more about computers than you do.

hub See *concentrator*.

I/O port address Every I/O device in a computer — including network interface cards — must be assigned a unique address. The port address is configured by using DIP switches, jumper blocks, or a software configuration routine.

IACI International Association of the Computer Impaired.

IDE The most common type of disk interface in use today, popular because of its low cost and flexibility. *IDE* stands for *Integrated Drive Electronics*.

IEEE *Institute of Electrical and Electronic Engineers*. Where they send computer geeks who've had a few too many parity errors.

incremental backup A type of backup in which only the files that have changed since the last backup are backed up. Unlike a differential backup, an incremental backup resets each file's archive bit as it backs it up. See *archive bit, differential backup*, and *full backup*.

Internet A humongous network of networks that spans the globe and gives you access to just about anything you could ever hope for, provided you can figure out how to work it.

interoperability Providing a level playing field for incompatible networks to work together, kind of like NAFTA.

IPX The transport protocol used by NetWare.

IPX.COM The program file that implements IPX.

IRQ *Interrupt ReQuest*. Network interface cards must be configured for the proper IRQ in order to work. The IRQ is configured by using a DIP switch, jumper block, or a software configuration routine.

ISA bus The most popular type of expansion bus for accomodating adapter cards. *ISA* stands for *Industry Standard Architecture*. See *EISA bus* and *Micro Channel bus*.

ISO *International Standards Organization*, whom we can thank for OSI.

jumper block A device used to configure an adapter card. To change the setting of a jumper block, you remove the jumper from one set of pins and replace it on another.

K Kilobytes, roughly one thousand bytes (1024 to be precise). See *GB, MB*, and *TB*.

LAN *Local-area network*; what this book is all about.

LAN Manager Microsoft's big network operating system.

LAN Server IBM's version of LAN Manager.

LANcache The disk caching program that comes with LANtastic.

LANtastic The most popular peer-to-peer network operating system.

LapLink A program that links computers via serial or printer ports, used mostly to transfer files to and from laptop or notebook computers.

laser printer A high-quality printer that uses lasers and photon torpedoes to produce beautiful output. See *dot-matrix printer*.

LASTDRIVE A line in CONFIG.SYS that tells DOS how many drive letters to set aside for itself. NetWare uses this setting to determine which drive letter to map to the server's login directory.

lemon-pudding layer A layer near the middle of the OSI reference model that provides flavor and moisture to an otherwise dry and tasteless fruitcake.

LLC sublayer The *logical link sublayer* of layer 2 of the OSI model. The LLC is addressed by the IEEE 802.2 standard.

local bus A relatively new type of expansion bus that is tied directly to the CPU, so it operates at the same clock speed as the CPU. See *VESA* and *PCI*.

local resources Disk drives, printers, and other devices that are attached directly to a workstation rather than accessed via the network.

local-area network See *LAN*.

LocalTalk Apple's scheme for cabling Macintosh networks by using the Mac's printer ports. PhoneNET is a cabling scheme that's compatible with LocalTalk but less expensive.

login The process of identifying oneself to the network (or a specific network server) and gaining access to network resources.

LOGIN The NetWare command used to log in to a NetWare network.

LOGIN directory In NetWare, a network directory that's mapped to the workstation before the user has logged in. The LOGIN directory contains commands and programs that are accessible to every computer on the network, whether or not a user has logged in. Chief among these commands is the LOGIN command.

login script A file of NetWare commands that is executed when a user logs in.

login-name In Windows for Workgroups, the name that identifies a user uniquely to the network. Same as *username* or *user ID*.

logon Same as *login*.

logout The process of leaving the network. When you log out, any network drives or printers you were connected to become unavailable to you.

LOGOUT In NetWare, the commmand you use to log out.

LPT1 The first printer port on a PC. If a computer has a local printer, it will more than likely be attached to this port. That's why it's a good idea to set up printer redirections using LPT2 and LPT3.

MAC sublayer The *media access control* sublayer of layer 2 of the OSI model. The MAC is addressed by the IEEE 802.3 standard.

Macintosh A cute little computer that draws great pictures and comes with built-in networking.

mail server The server computer on which e-mail messages are stored. This same computer also may be used as a file and print server, or it may be dedicated as a mail server.

mainframe A huge computer housed in a glass house on raised floors. The cable that connects the disk drives to the CPU weighs more than most PCs.

mapping Assigning unused drive letters to network drives or unused printer ports to network printers. See *redirection*.

MB Megabytes, or roughly one million bytes (1,024K to be precise). See *GB*, *K*, and *TB*.

MEM The DOS command that displays information about memory.

MEMMAKER The DOS 6.0 and 6.2 command that optimizes your memory use.

memory The electronic storage where your computer stores data that's being manipulated and programs that are running.

menu program A program that makes a network user's life easier by hiding the DOS prompt behind a list of choices the user can choose by pressing a number or letter.

metaphor A literary construction suitable for Shakespeare and Steinbeck but a bit overused by computer writers.

Micro Channel bus The bus standard used in certain IBM PS/2 computers.

Microsoft Mail A popular e-mail program from a big company in Redmond, WA.

modem A device that converts signals the computer understands into signals that can be accurately transmitted over the phone to another modem, which converts the signals back into their original form. Computers use modems to talk to each other. *Modem* is a combination of *mo*dulator-*dem*odulator.

monochrome Monitors that display only one color, usually green or amber against a dark background. Monochrome monitors are often used on dedicated server computers, where flashy color displays would be wasted on an empty closet.

mouse The obligatory way to use Windows. When you grab it and move it around, the cursor moves on the screen. After you get the hand-eye coordination down, using it is a snap. *Hint:* Don't pick it up and talk into it like Scotty did in *Star Trek 4.* Very embarrassing, especially if you've travelled millions of miles to get here.

Mr. McFeeley The nerdy-looking mailman on Mr. Rogers' Neighborhood. He'd make a great computer geek. Speedy delivery!

MSAV The DOS 6.0 and 6.2 command that scans your computer for virus infection. OK for local computer use, but a more powerful program is best for the network.

MSBACKUP The DOS 6.0 and 6.2 command for backing up data to floppy disks. Because it doesn't support tape drives, it's not suitable for network backups.

MSD Microsoft Diagnostics, a program that comes with DOS 6.0 and 6.2 and Windows 3.1. MSD gathers and displays useful information about your computer's configuration.

NE2000 The standard by which network interface cards are judged. If your card is NE2000 compatible, you can use it with just about any network.

NET The catch-all network command center for both LANtastic and NetWare Lite.

NETBIOS *Network basic input output system*, a high-level networking standard developed by IBM and used by most peer-to-peer networks. It can be used with NetWare as well.

NET LOGIN The LANtastic and NetWare Lite commmand to log in to the network.

NET LOGOUT The LANtastic and NetWare Lite commmand to log out of the network.

NetWare The chief priest of network operating systems, the proud child of Novell, Inc.

NetWare 2.2 NetWare's "Good" version, designed for 80286-based processors and that is still widely used on smaller networks.

NetWare 3.11 NetWare's "Better" version, designed with 80386 processors in mind. The best choice for most new networks.

NetWare 4.0 NetWare's latest and "Best" version, filled with all sorts of bells and whistles for larger networks, but a bit much for the novice to take on.

NetWare Directory Services The cool new feature of NetWare 4.0 whereby the resources of the servers are pooled together to form a single entity.

NetWare Lite The peer-to-peer version of NetWare, comparable to LANtastic but not as powerful.

NetWare Loadable Module A program that's loaded at the file server, a.k.a. *NLM*. NLMs extend the functionality of NetWare by providing additional services. Btrieve runs as an NLM, as do various backup, antivirus, and other utilities.

network What this book is about. For more information, see Chapters 1 through 27.

network administrator Hope that it is someone other than you.

network drive A drive that resides somewhere out in the network rather than on your own computer.

network interface card An adapter card that lets the computer attach to a network cable. AKA *NIC*.

network layer One of the layers somewhere near the middle of the OSI reference model. It addresses the interconnection of networks.

Network Operating System An operating system for networks, such as NetWare or LANtastic. AKA *NOS*.

network resource A disk drive, printer, or other device that's located in a server computer and shared with other users, in contrast with a *local resource*, which is located in a user's computer.

NIC See *Network Interface Card*.

NLCACHE The disk caching program that comes with NetWare Lite.

NLM See *NetWare Loadable Module*.

node A device on the network, typically a computer or printer.

Norton Utilities A big box chock-full of useful utilities, all for one affordable price. Get it.

NOS See *Network Operating System*.

Novell The folks you can thank or blame for NetWare, depending on your mood.

off-line Not available on the network.

on-line Available on the network.

operator A user who has control over operational aspects of the network, but doesn't necessarily have the power to grant or revoke access rights, create user accounts, and so on.

OSI The agency Lee Majors worked for in *The Six Million Dollar Man*. Also, the *Open System Interconnection* reference model, a seven-layer `fruitcake` framework upon which networking standards are hung.

packets Data is sent over the network in manageable chunks called *packets*, or *frames*. The size and makeup of a packet is determined by the protocol being used.

parallel port A port normally used to connect printers to DOS-based computers, sometimes called a *printer port*. Parallel ports send data over eight "parallel" wires, one byte at a time. See *serial port*.

partition A division of a single disk drive into several smaller units that are treated by the operating system as if they were separate drives.

password The only thing protecting your files from an impostor masquerading as you. Keep your password secret, and you will have a long and happy life.

patch cable A short cable used to connect a computer to a wall outlet, or one running from a patch panel to a hub.

PC Tools A grab bag of useful utility programs all for one low, affordable price. It includes an excellent backup and antivirus program. Get it.

PCI *Peripheral Component Interconnect*, one of two competing standards for local bus. See *VESA*.

PCONSOLE The NetWare command you use to manage network printing.

peer-to-peer network A network in which any computer can be a server if it wants to be. Kind of like the network version of the Great American Dream. LANtastic, NetWare Lite, and Windows for Workgroups are examples of peer-to-peer networks.

PhoneNET An alternative cabling scheme for Macintosh networks, cheaper than Apple's LocalTalk cables.

physical layer The lowest layer of the OSI reference model (whatever that is). It is the only part of the network you can touch.

pocket protector A status symbol among computer geeks.

port A connector on the back of your computer you can use to connect a device such as a printer, modem, mouse, and so on.

presentation layer The sixth layer of the OSI reference model, which handles data conversions, compression, decompression, and other menial tasks.

print job A report, letter, memo, or other document that has been sent to a network printer but hasn't printed yet. Print jobs wait patiently in the queue until a printer agrees to print them.

Print Manager In Windows, the program that handles print spooling.

print queue The line that print jobs wait in until a printer becomes available.

print server A computer that handles network printing.

PRN The DOS code name for the first parallel port. A.k.a. LPT1.

protocol The rules of the network game. Protocols define standardized formats for data packets, techniques for detecting and correcting errors, and so on.

punch-down block A gadget for quickly connecting a bunch of wires, used in telephone and network wiring closets.

QIC *Quarter inch cartridge*, the most popular and least-expensive form of tape backup. See *DAT*.

queue A list of items waiting to be processed. The term usually refers to the list of print jobs waiting to be printed, but networks have lots of other types of queues as well.

RAID *Redundant Array of Inexpensive Disks*, a bunch of disk drives strung together and treated as if they were one drive. The data is spread out over several drives, and one of the drives keeps checking information so that if any one of the drives fails, the data can be reconstructed.

RAM *Random access memory*, your computer's memory chips.

real network A full-featured network that requires skill and expertise to install. NetWare is the best-known example.

REDIR.EXE The program in LANtastic that enables your computer to join the network.

redirection One of the basic concepts of networking, in which a device such as a disk drive or printer appears to be a local device but actually resides on the network. The networking software on your computer intercepts I/O requests for the device and redirects them to the network.

repeater A device that strengthens a signal so that it can travel on. Repeaters are used to lengthen the cable distance between two nodes. A *multiport repeater* is the same as a *hub* or *concentrator*.

resource A disk drive, disk directory, printer, modem, CD-ROM, or other device that can be shared on the network.

ring A type of network topology in which computers are connected to one another in a way that forms a complete circle. Imagine the Waltons standing around the Thanksgiving table holding hands and you have the idea of a ring topology.

RJ-45 The kind of plug used by 10baseT networks. It looks kind of like a modular phone plug, but it's bigger.

router A device that works like a bridge but can handle different protocols. For example, a router can link Ethernet to LocalTalk or a mainframe.

ScanDisk A new DOS 6.2 command that examines your hard disk for physical defects.

scheduling software Software that schedules meetings of network users. Works only if all network users keep their calendars up-to-date.

SCSI *Small computer systems interface*, a connection used mostly for disk drives but also suitable for CD-ROM, tape drives, and just about anything else. Also winner of the Acronym Computer Geeks Love to Pronounce Most award.

segment A single-run cable, which may connect more than two computers, with a terminator on each end.

serial port A port normally used to connect a modem or mouse to a DOS-based computer, sometimes called a *communications port*. See *parallel port*.

server A computer that is on the network and shares resources with other network users. The server may be dedicated, which means that it's sole purpose in life is to provide service for network users, or it may be used as a client as well. See *client*.

session layer A layer somewhere near the middle of the beloved OSI reference model that deals with sessions between network nodes.

SFT *System Fault Tolerance*, a set of networking features designed to protect the network from faults, such as stepping on the line (known as a "foot fault").

shared resource A resource such as a disk or printer that is made available to other network users.

shielded twisted pair Twisted-pair cable with shielding, used mostly for Token Ring networks. AKA *STP*. See *twisted pair*.

SMARTDRV A disk caching program that comes with DOS versions 5 and 6 and Windows 3.1.

smiley A face made from various keyboard characters; often used in e-mail messages to convey emotion **:)**

SNA *Systems Network Architecture*, a networking standard developed by IBM that dates from the mid-Mainframerasic, approximately 65 million years ago. Used by fine IBM mainframe and AS/400 minicomputers everywhere.

sneakernet The cheapest form of network, in which users exchange files by copying them to a disk and walking them between computers.

SNMP *Simple Network Mangement Protocol*, a standard for exchanging network management information between network devices that is anything but simple.

ST-506 An old type of disk drive interface that is obsolete but still found on far too many computers.

star A type of network topology in which each node is connected to a central wiring hub. This gives the network a star-like appearance.

STARTNET.BAT The batch file used by LANtastic and NetWare Lite to start the network.

superserver A server computer that seems more like a mainframe than a PC.

SUPERVISOR The top-dog account in NetWare. Log in as SUPERVISOR and you can do just about anything.

switch A mechanical or electronic device that can be used in lieu of a network to share a printer among a small number of users.

SYS The volume name of the system volume on most NetWare servers.

System 7 The latest and greatest operating system for Macintoshes.

system fault tolerance See *SFT*.

tape drive The best way to back up a network server. Tape drives have become so inexpensive that even small networks should have one.

task For a technically accurate description, enroll in a computer science graduate course. For a layperson's understanding of what a task is, picture the guy who used to spin plates on the Ed Sullivan show. Each plate is a task. The poor guy had to frantically move from plate to plate to keep them all spinning. Computers work the same way. Each program task is like one of those spinning plates; the computer must service each one periodically to keep it going.

TB Terrazzo bytes, imported from Italy. Approximately one trillion bytes (1024 GB to be precise). See *GB*, *K*, and *MB*.

TCP/IP *Transmission Control Protocol/Internet Protocol*, the protocol used by Internet.

terminator The little plug you have to use at each end of a segment of thin coax cable (10baseT) or PhoneNET cable.

thinnet See *10base2*.

three-letter acronym See *TLA*.

time sharing A technique used on mainframe computers to allow several users to access the computer at the same time.

time-out How long the print server will wait while receiving print output before deciding that the print job has finished.

TLA A three-letter acronym, such as FAT (file allocation table), DUM (dirty upper memory), and HPY (hidden private yodel).

token The thing that gets passed around the network in a Token Ring topology. See *Token Ring*.

Token Ring A network that is cabled in a ring topology in which a special packet called a *token* is passed from computer to computer. A computer must wait until it receives the token before sending data over the network.

topology The shape of the network; how its computers and cables are arranged. See *bus*, *star*, and *ring*.

transceiver A doohicky that connects a Network Interface Card (NIC) to a network cable. A transceiver is always required to connect a computer to the network, but 10base2 and 10baseT NICs have built-in transceivers. Transceivers are used mostly with yellow cable.

transport layer One of those layers somewhere near the middle of the OSI reference model that addresses the way data is escorted around the network.

trojan horse A program that looks interesting but turns out to be something nasty, like a hard-disk reformatter.

twisted pair A type of cable that consists of one or more pairs of wires that are twisted in a certain way to improve the cable's electrical characteristics. See *unshielded twisted pair* and *shielded twisted pair*.

uninterruptible power supply See *UPS*.

unshielded twisted pair Twisted-pair cable that doesn't have a heavy metal shield around it. Used for 10baseT networks. AKA UTP. See *twisted pair*.

upper memory The portion of memory jammed in between 640K and 1MB. It's set apart for use by device adapters like disk controllers and video cards. Because much of it is unused in most computers, DOS 5 and 6 can reclaim it for other uses.

UPS *Uninterruptible power supply*, a gizmo that switches to battery power whenever the power cuts out. The *Enterprise* didn't have one of these; that's why Spock always had to manually switch to auxiliary power.

users' group A local association of computer users, sometimes with a particular interest, such as networking.

user ID The name by which you are known to the network.

UTP *Unshielded twisted pair*. See *10baseT*.

Value Added Processes See *VAP*.

vampire tap A whirlygig that lets you tap into a 10base5 cable to attach a transceiver.

VAP Value added processes, Programs that run at the server computer with NetWare 2.2.

VESA A local bus design created by the *Video Electronics Standards Association.* See *local bus, PCI.*

VGA *Video Graphics Array*, the current standard in video monitors. Most VGA adapters these days are actually *super VGA* adapters, which are compatible with VGA adapters but have extra bells and whistles.

Vines A network operating system made by Banyan, comparable to *NetWare* or *LAN Manager.*

virus An evil computer program that slips into your computer undetected, tries to spread itself to other computers, and may eventually do something bad like trash your hard disk.

volume name In NetWare, each disk volume has a name. Most NetWare servers have a volume named SYS.

Windows An "operating environment" that makes DOS computers easier to use, courtesy of Microsoft.

Windows for Workgroups The peer-to-peer version of Windows.

wiring closet Large networks need a place where cables can congregate. A closet is ideal.

workstation See *client.*

yellow cable See *10base5.*

zero-slot network A network built without the use of special network cards, using the computers' existing serial or parallel ports. Cheap, but slow.

Index

• *N* •

Notes

Notes

Notes

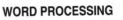

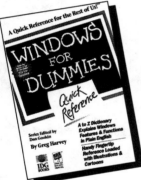

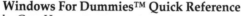

Order Form

Order Center: (800) 762-2974 (8 a.m.-5 p.m., PST, weekdays) or (415) 312-0650

For Fastest Service: Photocopy This Order Form and FAX it to : (415) 358-1260

Quantity	ISBN	Title	Price	Total

Shipping & Handling Charges

Subtotal	U.S.	Canada & International	International Air Mail
Up to $20.00	Add $3.00	Add $4.00	Add $10.00
$20.01-40.00	$4.00	$5.00	$20.00
$40.01-60.00	$5.00	$6.00	$25.00
$60.01-80.00	$6.00	$8.00	$35.00
Over $80.00	$7.00	$10.00	$50.00

In U.S. and Canada, shipping is UPS ground or equivalent.
For Rush shipping call (800) 762-2974.

Subtotal _____

CA residents add applicable sales tax _____

IN residents add 5% sales tax _____

Canadian residents add 7% GST tax _____

Shipping _____

TOTAL _____

Ship to:

Name _____

Company _____

Address _____

City/State/Zip _____

Daytime Phone _____

Payment: ❑ Check to IDG Books (US Funds Only)   ❑ Visa   ❑ MasterCard   ❑ American Express

Card # _____ Exp. _____ Signature _____

Please send this order form to: IDG Books, 155 Bovet Road, Suite 310, San Mateo, CA 94402.
Allow up to 3 weeks for delivery. Thank you!

BOBFD

IDG BOOKS WORLDWIDE REGISTRATION CARD

RETURN THIS REGISTRATION CARD FOR FREE CATALOG

Title of this book: Networking For Dummies

My overall rating of this book: ☐ Very good [1] ☐ Good [2] ☐ Satisfactory [3] ☐ Fair [4] ☐ Poor [5]

How I first heard about this book:

☐ Found in bookstore; name: [6] _____

☐ Advertisement: [8] _____

☐ Word of mouth; heard about book from friend, co-worker, etc.: [10] _____

☐ Book review: [7] _____

☐ Catalog: [9] _____

☐ Other: [11] _____

What I liked most about this book:

_____
_____
_____

What I would change, add, delete, etc., in future editions of this book:

_____
_____
_____

Other comments:

_____
_____

Number of computer books I purchase in a year: ☐ 1 [12] ☐ 2-5 [13] ☐ 6-10 [14] ☐ More than 10 [15]

I would characterize my computer skills as: ☐ Beginner [16] ☐ Intermediate [17] ☐ Advanced [18] ☐ Professional [19]

I use ☐ DOS [20] ☐ Windows [21] ☐ OS/2 [22] ☐ Unix [23] ☐ Macintosh [24] ☐ Other: [25]_____
(please specify)

I would be interested in new books on the following subjects:
(please check all that apply, and use the spaces provided to identify specific software)

☐ Word processing: [26] _____

☐ Data bases: [28] _____

☐ File Utilities: [30] _____

☐ Networking: [32] _____

☐ Other: [34] _____

☐ Spreadsheets: [27] _____

☐ Desktop publishing: [29] _____

☐ Money management: [31] _____

☐ Programming languages: [33] _____

I use a PC at (please check all that apply): ☐ home [35] ☐ work [36] ☐ school [37] ☐ other: [38] _____

The disks I prefer to use are ☐ 5.25 [39] ☐ 3.5 [40] ☐ other: [41]_____

I have a CD ROM: ☐ yes [42] ☐ no [43]

I plan to buy or upgrade computer hardware this year: ☐ yes [44] ☐ no [45]

I plan to buy or upgrade computer software this year: ☐ yes [46] ☐ no [47]

Name: _____ **Business title:** [48] _____ **Type of Business:** [49] _____

Address (☐ home [50] ☐ work [51]/Company name: _____)

Street/Suite# _____

City [52]/**State** [53]/**Zipcode** [54]: _____ **Country** [55] _____

☐ **I liked this book!** You may quote me by name in future IDG Books Worldwide promotional materials.

My daytime phone number is _____

IDG BOOKS

THE WORLD OF COMPUTER KNOWLEDGE

❑ # YES!

Please keep me informed about IDG's World of Computer Knowledge.
Send me the latest IDG Books catalog.

COMPUTER
BOOK SERIES
FROM IDG